Contents

Part A Getting into AutoCAD   1
  1 What is AutoCAD?   3
  2 The MSDOS and Windows operating systems   8
  3 Hardware requirements   11
  4 Getting into the AutoCAD program   15
  5 Beginning an AutoCAD drawing   21
  6 Introductory exercise   24

Part B 2D draughting on AutoCAD   81
  Lesson 1 Basic techniques   83
  Lesson 2 Draughting aids and set-up   107
  Lesson 3 Editing techniques   123
  Summary exercises: Lessons 1–3   140
  Lesson 4 Dimensioning and units   144
  Lesson 5 Text and style   155
  Lesson 6 Further draughting   164
  Lesson 7 2D solid work, PLINE and SKETCH   184
  Summary exercises: Lessons 4–7   190
  Lesson 8 Isometric drawing   192
  Lesson 9 Polyline editing (PEDIT command)   196
  Lesson 10 Blocks and attributes   209

Part C 3D modelling on AutoCAD   217
  Lesson 11 Simple 3D techniques   219
  Lesson 12 3DFACE, XYZ lines and 3D point filters   224
  Lesson 13 UCS and WCS   231
  Lesson 14 Continued 3DFACE and invisible edges   238
  Lesson 15 3D display techniques   247
  Lesson 16 Perspective display techniques   257
  Lesson 17 3D surface modelling—MESH commands   270
  Lesson 18 3D polylines   283
  Lesson 19 3DMESH and mesh editing   293
  Lesson 20 An introduction to 3D solid modelling   298

Part D Summary 3D exercise: Helicopter   307
        Appendix A   The AutoCAD program file structure   321
        Appendix B   Menus, windows, toolbars and dialog boxes   322
        Appendix C   Standard text fonts and character mappings   334

Index   338

Succeeding with AutoCAD®

Succeeding with AutoCAD®

A full course in 2D drafting and 3D modelling

BARRY HAWKES

McGraw-Hill Book Company

London · New York · St Louis · San Francisco · Auckland
Bogotá · Caracas · Lisbon · Madrid · Mexico
Milan · Montreal · New Delhi · Panama · Paris · San Juan
São Paulo · Singapore · Sydney · Tokyo · Toronto

Published by
McGRAW-HILL Book Company Europe
Shoppenhangers Road, Maidenhead, Berkshire, SL6 2QL, England
Tel 01628 23432; Fax 01628 770224

British Library Cataloguing in Publication Data
Hawkes, Barry
  Succeeding with AutoCAD
  I. Title
  620.004202855369

  ISBN 0-07-709071-3

Library of Congress Cataloging-in-Publication Data
Hawkes, Barry.
   Succeeding with AutoCAD : a full course in 2D drafting and 3D
modelling / Barry Hawkes.
     p.   cm.
   Includes index.
   ISBN 0-07-709071-3
   1. Computer graphics.   2. AutoCAD (Computer file)   I. Title.
T385.H36   1995
620′.0042′02855369–dc20

                                                                95-9897
                                                                CIP

12345 CL 98765

Typset by TecSet Ltd, Wallington, Surrey
Printed and bound in Great Britain at Clays Ltd, St Ives plc
Printed on permanent paper in compliance with ISO Standard 9706

Part A

Getting into AutoCAD

1

What is AutoCAD?

AutoCAD is a general purpose computer-aided drawing and design (CAD) program which runs on a wide range of low-cost microcomputers. It is an advanced, comprehensive package, written in a high-level language called 'C'. Marketed by Autodesk Ltd, it was first launched in 1982 and has since become the world's most popular CAD system.

Reasons for AutoCAD's success

Advanced CAD at a low price

The advantages of CAD over traditional drawing methods have been increasingly appreciated in recent years. CAD provides drawings which are neater and far more accurate than those created on a drawing board, and at faster rates of production. The computer graphics routines available with CAD provide special draughting techniques, such as zooming and 3D manipulation, which were previously unheard of. CAD also avoids the time-wasting and errors which can result from repetition of drawing work. Once a CAD drawing, or part-drawing, is completed, it may be stored in the computer memory for future use. This is particularly useful when drawing a range of components with a similar shape. The computer memory is also ideal for compiling libraries of symbols, standard components, and geometric shapes. Further repetition of tasks may be avoided by linking CAD data directly with other computer systems, such as scheduling databases, bills of materials, desktop publishers, manufacturing systems, and analytical systems such as stresswork and finite element analysis.

However, the sophisticated technology required for professional CAD work has hitherto only been available in expensive packages requiring large, costly computer systems to run on. AutoCAD has effectively revolutionized the development of CAD by bringing the benefits of a high-performance, low-cost CAD facility within the reach of desktop microcomputer users.

Wide range of specialisms

Many of the costlier CAD packages specialize in particular areas of design and draughting, whereas AutoCAD is used by designers of every discipline. Applications include:

- Architecture
- Drawings for electronic, chemical, civil, mechanical, automative and aerospace engineering
- Schematics
- Flow charts
- Surveying and cartography
- Factory and office layout
- Technical illustration
- Graphic artwork
- Musical scores

Continuous development

Since AutoCAD was first made available in 1982, the AutoCAD program has been continuously developed, with regular major updates. Thus AutoCAD has kept pace with advancements in CAD technology and increased in sophistication without any corresponding increase in relative cost or restriction in availability.

Ease of use and varied selection procedures

The AutoCAD program is structured with straightforward, logical commands which may be actioned by a variety of selection procedures, ranging from basic keyboard techniques to menu and Windows selection routines via the computer screen or electronic tablets.

2D and 3D facilities

As will be explained later, there is a basic difference between a CAD system which can accommodate data of only 'flat' 2D shapes and those which can also display representations of 3D shapes with 'depth'.

Later versions of AutoCAD have progressively increased the extent to which 3D shapes may be created, visualized and manipulated, without altering the basic procedures for creating drawings in which only 2D geometry is required. AutoCAD's 3D capabilities improved radically with the issue of Release 10, which has full 3D wireframe construction and surface modelling facilities of a sophistication usually associated with far costlier systems. Further releases have extended these capabilities, with 3D solid modelling becoming available on the standard AutoCAD package from Release 13 onwards.

The 'open' nature of AutoCAD

The underlying philosophy of the AutoCAD program is that it may be customized to suit the particular needs of the user. For example, the full AutoCAD package incorporates a high-level programming language called AutoLISP which enables the user to create automatic draughting routines for specialist shapes and extend the standard AutoCAD drawing facilities as required.

It is also possible to convert AutoCAD drawings into a systematically structured format called a Data Interchange (DXF) File, which may be observed and analysed. DXF files may be used to link AutoCAD data to other software packages and vice versa. Autodesk's DXF format has now gained international acceptance as a standard for communicating graphics data, and therefore many other software manufacturers provide facilities for a DXF interface with AutoCAD. The AutoCAD package also supports IGES, another international standard of graphics communication.

Since AutoCAD became available on multi-tasking platforms such as Microsoft Windows and Windows NT, data such as wordprocessed text, spreadsheet analysis and graphics may be easily imported and exported between AutoCAD and other software via a common 'Clipboard' facility which is available to all the different software packages being run on the computer system. For example, AutoCAD drawing data could be placed onto the Clipboard and would then be directly available to a user of, say, the wordprocessing package Word for Windows which also has access to the Clipboard. The Word user could take the AutoCAD data from the Clipboard and 'paste' it onto a Word file, thus achieving a combination of drawing and text. Similarly, a Word text file could be pasted onto an AutoCAD drawing.

Using the Windows environment, you can also use other software packages simultaneously with AutoCAD via a Dynamic Data Exchange (DDE) capability. This can use a 'hot link' which automatically updates data in all linked applications when any changes are made in any one of the applications. For example, you could alter drawing coordinate data listed on a spreadsheet such as Microsoft Excel, and see the linked AutoCAD drawing correspondingly change shape on the same screen display.

Autodesk openly encourage AutoCAD users to customize their own screen menus and tablet menus so that they may make the most efficient use of their own standards libraries and satisfy their specific draughting requirements. Such customization facilities are easily accessible to the system. Also, many independent companies sell 'ready-made' menus and standards libraries (often directed at specialist markets) for exclusive use on AutoCAD.

Compatibility of AutoCAD

AutoCAD is available for use on a wide range of popular CAD computer equipment and operating systems. At the time of publication, the computer systems on which you can run the most recent versions of AutoCAD include:

- IBM XT/AT and PS/2 microcomputers (and the complete range of compatible computers) using MSDOS, Microsft Windows, Windows NT, PCDOS or OS/2 operating systems
- Apollo DN3000 and DN4000 computers, using the AEGIS operating system
- Apple Macintosh II computer
- DEC VAXstation 2000/3000 II/RCGPX computer, using the VMS operating system
- Sun Microsystems computers (Sun-3/Sun-4/Sun 386i), using the UNIX operating system.

AutoCAD files can be used interchangeably on any of the above computers and operating systems. Modern AutoCAD drawing files may be transferred between any of the operating systems listed, without translation. Thus you can transfer and share AutoCAD files in a network containing computers of different types without conversions of any kind.

AutoCAD also supports many makes and models of other CAD hardware, such as plotters, printer/plotters and digitizers.

The AutoCAD program

AutoCAD is supplied to the purchaser in the form of a package, the most important contents of which are an extensive reference manual and the AutoCAD program itself. The AutoCAD program is made up of a number of *program files* stored on either *floppy disks* or *compact disc* (CD-ROM). The number of disks supplied depends on their storage density and whether you have the full AutoCAD package.

There are several different types of file which make up the complete program. In the MSDOS and Windows operating systems, the type of file is classified by three characters called an *extension* at the end of the filename. For example, one of the main program files is called:

ACAD.EXE

This is an 'executable program file' and thus has the extension EXE. Other examples include:

ACAD0.OVL   (an 'overlay' program file)
ACAD.MNU   (a 'menu' file)

More information about the full AutoCAD package is given in Appendix A.

Installing the AutoCAD program

Residing in your computer there is a *hard disk* which has much more memory storage capacity than the floppy disks provided with the AutoCAD package. The storage memory of the hard disk may be segmented into *directories*.

When you install the AutoCAD program onto your computer system, these program files must be copied from the floppy disks or compact disc provided onto the hard disk of the computer. In the MSDOS operating system they are normally put into a directory of the hard disk called ACAD. In the Windows operating system, this directory is normally called ACADWIN.

AutoCAD drawing files

These are computer files which contain drawing data and are created each time you produce a drawing on AutoCAD. Drawing files used as standards will normally be stored on the hard disk of the computer. Individual drawing files should either be saved directly to floppy disk for the personal use of the draughtsperson, or saved to a specific drawing storage directory on the hard disk, to be subsequently copied to floppy disk. The latter approach gives faster response time and better drawing file security.

A drawing file may be called anything you wish up to eight characters in length (not including the extension). When you produce your drawing, AutoCAD creates the drawing file and adds the extension DWG to the filename you have chosen. For security purposes, it also creates an identical backup drawing file, with the extension BAK after the same filename. For example, if you call your drawing NEWDESIN, AutoCAD creates two files called NEWDESIN.DWG and NEWDESIN.BAK and saves them on a specified disk.

2

The MSDOS and Windows operating systems

An operating system is a computer software package that performs all the 'housekeeping chores' of the computer system. It is entirely independent of CAD packages like AutoCAD and could also be used to manage many other application programs, such as word processors, databases, spreadsheets, manufacturing packages and stress analysis packages, all of which may be contained on the hard disk along with AutoCAD. Typical operating system tasks include: copying files between disks, saving files to disk, creating and accessing directories on the hard disk, obtaining lists of files, and executing programs like AutoCAD.

As we have said, AutoCAD may be run on several different operating systems, but at present it is most commonly run on microcomputers using either the MSDOS system or the Windows system (both of which are produced and marketed by the Microsoft Corporation). MSDOS is the base system upon which Windows has more recently been developed, so if you are using Windows then this will be running 'on top' of the base MSDOS system, with facilities to exit from Windows to MSDOS and vice versa. (The last statement is not the case if you are using Windows NT—a more sophisticated version of Windows particularly aimed at networked business systems. This runs on its own operating platform, independent of MSDOS.) The philosophy of Windows is that of performing operating system tasks via a graphical user interface (GUI) with strong emphasis on screen menus and 'icon' pictures accessed via a pointing device such as a 'mouse'. This is in contrast to MSDOS, which adopts the more conventional approach of entering text commands from the keyboard. The Windows system is gaining in popularity over MSDOS as the more modern environment in which to use AutoCAD, and Windows is becoming the favoured system in marketing by Autodesk.

Getting into the operating system

In most cases you automatically 'boot-up' to the operating system when you switch on your computer. In the case of Windows, a screen menu of rectangular areas called *windows* is then displayed. Inside each window is a collection of small graphical symbols called *icons*. It is assumed here that the display will include an AutoCAD icon picture which may be selected by the mouse to access the AutoCAD software package.

In some cases, you may be taken to MSDOS before you access Windows, in which case a typical screen prompt might be:

> `C:\>`

This would indicate that you are logged-on to the main directory of Drive C (the most common name for the hard disk drive). In this case you could usually access Windows via the keyboard by typing:

> `WIN`

followed by pressing the RETURN key.

If you are using AutoCAD on MSDOS (commonly known as 'DOS') you may be taken straight into the base operating system, or your computer may be customized to display a text menu of the software packages available. It is assumed here that any such menu would include an AUTOCAD option, and a facility to go into MSDOS.

Typical examples of MSDOS command routines are shown below (all are assumed to be typed in at the keyboard and followed with a RETURN):

> `A:`
'Log-on' to Drive A, i.e. make Drive A current

> `COPY A: BOLT.DWG`
Copy the file BOLT.DWG from Drive A to the current drive

> `COPY *.BAK B:`
Copy all files with the extension .BAK from the current drive to Drive B

> `DIR *.DWG`
Get a list of all files with extension .DWG, i.e. all AutoCAD drawing files on the current drive and directory

> `DEL HOUSE.BAK`
Delete the file HOUSE.BAK from the current drive and directory

> `CD ACAD`
Change to the ACAD directory

> `CD\`
Change to the main 'root' directory

Note that, in the Windows environment, the above commands will also be used by the system to perform the tasks described, but will be automatically actioned once the user has selected the appropriate icons and screen menu options. These are all initially available by selecting the File Manager icon from the Main group window.

AutoCAD commands

All AutoCAD operations are initiated by selecting standard *commands*. These all have logical names. For example, the command for drawing a line on the screen is LINE; to erase that line from the screen, you would use the command ERASE; and so on. When you select a command, you are then usually offered a number of *options* to choose from.

The most basic way of selecting AutoCAD commands and options is to type them in at the keyboard. In each case the selection is completed by pressing the RETURN key (sometimes called the ENTER key) on the keyboard. For example, if you wanted to draw an ellipse on the screen, you could do this by typing the following command at the keyboard:

ELLIPSE (then press the RETURN key)

An alternative method of selecting AutoCAD commands and their options is via a *menu*. This is a selection of commands/options, displayed for you to choose from. Having made your choice, you select it by pointing to it with a pointing device. In most cases the pointing device is either a *mouse*, or a *puck*. These devices are described in subsequent sections.

Menus may be displayed either as *screen menus*, or on an *electronic digitizing tablet*. All types of menu are described in Appendix B.

If you are using AutoCAD on the Windows operating system you can also use screen *toolbars* and *palettes*. These are special windows containing icons which represent popular commands and options. The required commands/options may be actioned by selecting the appropriate icon with a pointing device. Toolbars are further described in Appendix B.

3

Hardware requirements

AutoCAD is a computer program which makes up the *software* of the CAD system. It needs *hardware* equipment to run. A typical computer system might include the following hardware:

A commercial computer with a high resolution graphic screen—sometimes referred to as a VDU (visual display unit)

Some systems incorporate a separate screen for text, but this is not essential as AutoCAD has a 'flip screen' facility which alternates between graphics display and text display, depending on the nature of the command entered. The Windows version of AutoCAD also has re-sizable text display which may be observed in conjunction with the graphics display. To run the later releases of AutoCAD on IBM/MSDOS/Windows format, it is recommended that the computer be of 486 DX 33 (preferably 486 DX2 66) or Pentium capacity, and have between 16 and 24 Mbyte RAM (random access memory), for Windows systems, or between 12 and 16 Mbyte RAM for MSDOS systems. Computers of 386 and 486 SX capacity can only support later releases of AutoCAD if they are fitted with an additional *mathematical co-processor*.

The computer must be supplied with a *keyboard*, and be fitted with at least two *data communications ports*, one of which should be for *serial communication* (called an RS-232C port) and the other for *parallel communication*. Serial and parallel communication are two different methods of transporting data between the computer and external devices, and have different types of cable connection (at the computer end, these cable connections are called *ports*). Most makes of printer/plotter, and some makes of plotter, use parallel communication. Serial communication is often used for plotters and digitizers.

The computer will normally be required to support MSDOS, Windows, Windows NT, OS/2, or UNIX operating systems, although some other alternatives have previously been mentioned.

A hard disk drive and at least one floppy disk drive

A compact disc (CD-ROM) drive is also useful for recent releases. These drives will normally be fitted to the computer internally. The hard disk drive should preferably be of 200 Mbyte storage capacity or more, and will contain the AutoCAD program (once installed), the operating system, and any other software packages you use outside AutoCAD. In the MSDOS system the hard disk drive is usually called Drive C. The floppy disk drive and/or CD-ROM drive is used for storing drawing/backup files, and for copying the AutoCAD program from floppy disks to hard disk when it is being installed. Most modern systems use high density $3\frac{1}{2}''$ floppy disks, although earlier releases of AutoCAD may be suitably run on computers using $5\frac{1}{4}''$ floppy disks (high or low density). In the MSDOS and Windows systems, single floppy disk drives are usually called Drive A. If your computer is fitted with twin floppy disk drives, these are usually called Drive A and Drive B.

A mouse pointing device

This is used for specifying point locations on the screen and selecting commands from screen menus (and icons in the Windows system). As you move a mouse around any horizontal surface, a pair of cursor cross-hairs correspondingly move on the screen. The movement of the cursor is, in fact, relative to the movement of a roller-ball beneath the mouse. Thus, although the movement of the screen cursor is relative to the movement of the mouse on its surface, the position of the cursor on the screen is not directly related to the position of the mouse on its surface. For example, if you picked up the mouse and moved it to a new position, the ball would not roll during that period and thus the screen cursor would remain where it was until the mouse started moving on its surface again. When the intersection of the cross-hairs reaches the point location you require, you press the PICK button on the mouse (this operation is called PICKing). A mouse normally has two buttons—the second one is used for RETURNing (i.e. it fulfils the same function as the RETURN key on the keyboard). In AutoCAD it is pressed mainly when you complete a command. Some mice have multiple buttons. In such cases the extra buttons are used for quick selections of frequently-used commands. Most models of computer now include a mouse as a standard item.

A plotter

This is used for producing a *hard copy* of your AutoCAD computer drawing on paper or plastic film. Traditionally, *pen plotters* have been used. These commonly employ the principle of a moving pen over a stationary plotter surface. Other pen pointers, particularly the larger ones (up to A0 size), are vertically-standing and incorporate a rotating drum to which the paper/film is attached. Consequently, the pen and paper move simultaneously while plotting. Most pen plotters have up to eight pens or more. Using a multi-pen plotter, you can specify different parts of your computer drawing to be plotted in different colours.

A more modern approach is to use a *raster* device which creates plots from successive horizontal sweeps of a writing head. Common types include electrostatic plotters, inkjet plotters and laser printer/plotters. These operate more efficiently and produce superior line quality to pen plotters, and have the ability to produce colour plots of shaded and rendered 3D images.

AutoCAD supports a wide range of plotters, including all the different types mentioned above.

A digitizing tablet (or digitizer)

As with a mouse, a digitizer is used both for screen pointing and menu selection. However, whereas a mouse may be operated on any surface, the digitizer can only be operated by moving a device called a puck (or sometimes an electronic pen) over an electronic tablet surface.

The tablet has an area set aside for screen pointing. When you move the puck across the tablet in this area, the screen cursor cross-hairs correspondingly move (as with the mouse). Unlike the principle of the mouse, however, the position of the puck on the tablet may be directly related to the position of the cursor on the screen. For example, if you picked up the puck and moved it to a new position on the tablet, the screen cursor would correspondingly move to the same relative position on the screen. Thus a digitizer can be calibrated to trace an existing paper drawing (placed on the tablet) to any required scale, so that it may be converted to a CAD drawing. Such an application would not be possible using a mouse.

As with the mouse, a puck incorporates a PICK button for selecting the screen cursor position, and a RETURN button for completing commands. Most pucks have four buttons and some have more, the additional buttons being used for quick selection of frequently-used commands.

Other areas of the tablet are set aside for menu selection. The AutoCAD package includes a standard tablet overlay template, showing the screen pointing area and the menu areas. This is described in subsequent chapters. Typical menu items are: AutoCAD commands, standard component shapes for automatic inclusion on a CAD drawing, and frequently-used keyboard characters. Each menu item is shown (either in written form or as a simple picture) on a small square in the menu area of the tablet. To choose a menu item on the tablet, you move the puck to touch the allotted square for the required menu item, then press the PICK button. Digitizer menus generally provide speedier selection procedures than the other alternatives (i.e. selection by keyboard or selection by screen menus). Also, the inclusion of keyboard characters in the tablet menu means that, by using a digitizer, you very rarely need to use the keyboard while you are in AutoCAD.

If you wish, you may also use the puck to make selections from screen menus. (It is not possible to use a mouse to select from a tablet menu.)

4

Getting into the AutoCAD program

This chapter assumes that AutoCAD has been installed in its own directory (commonly called ACAD using MSDOS or ACADWIN using Windows) on the hard disk of your computer and has been configured so that it will work on all the devices you are using.

The most basic way of getting into the AutoCAD program on systems using MSDOS or Windows is as follows:

1. Switch on your computer. This 'boots-up' the operating system. If you intend to save your AutoCAD drawings directly to floppy disk, place a formatted floppy disk into an appropriate drive (this will usually be Drive A).
2. (a) If you are using the MSDOS operating system and your computer boots to a customized text menu, select the AutoCAD option by keyboard.
   (b) If you are using MSDOS and your computer boots to the base MSDOS system at the root directory of the hard disk, you will usually have to enter the name of a *batch file* which contains a number of MSDOS commands for setting up and entering AutoCAD. The name of the batch file depends on your release of AutoCAD and whether the file is customized. Common names include: ACAD, ACADR12 and ACADR13. Enter the name of your batch file at the keyboard, followed by a RETURN.
   (c) If you are using the Windows operating system and your computer boots directly to the Windows display, you will initially see the Windows Program Manager which includes the Main group window. Move your pointing device to the top title called Window and PICK to reveal a 'pull-down' menu. PICK AutoCAD from this menu. This will display the AutoCAD group window containing the AutoCAD icon. Move your pointing device to the AutoCAD icon and PICK twice. (In some cases the computer will be set up to show all other group windows in tiled format along with the Main group window as soon as you enter the Windows system (Fig. A4.1).

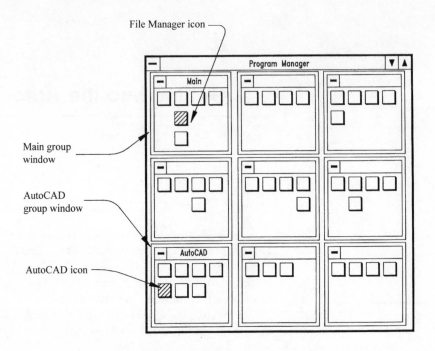

Figure A4.1.   The
Microsoft Windows
operating system
(Program Manager and
tiled group windows).

This will include the AutoCAD group window, from which the AutoCAD icon may be selected directly.)

(d) If you are using Windows and your computer boots to MSDOS first, you will usually be able to enter the Windows display by entering the name of the batch file WIN at the keyboard (followed by RETURN). You may then proceed to enter AutoCAD as described in (c).

Note: If you are using AutoCAD on an operating system other than MSDOS or Windows, the procedures will be similar to those described above, but will vary between different systems and set-ups. In this case you should consult your AutoCAD dealer or instructor.

The AutoCAD drawing screen display

The appropriate procedure for your system will thus get you into the AutoCAD program, and later releases of AutoCAD will then take you straight to the AutoCAD drawing screen display.

The traditional display is shown in Fig. A4.2. You will see this display if you are using the MSDOS operating system. (Earlier releases show an AutoCAD menu at this stage. In this case, you should select the Begin a New Drawing option, and then enter the drawing name shown in the subsequent 'Beginning an AutoCAD Drawing' section.)

Initially, there are five areas of interest on the display:

● The *drawing area* at the centre of the screen.
● The *command/prompt area* at the bottom edge of the screen. This always displays a 'prompt' message to which AutoCAD expects you to respond

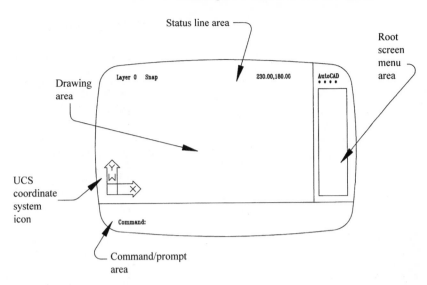

Status line area

Root
screen
menu
area

Drawing
area

Layer 0   Snap   230.00,180.00   AutoCAD

UCS
coordinate
system
icon

Command:

Figure A4.2. The
traditional AutoCAD
screen display.

Command/prompt
area

by entering an appropriate command or option. At present, the prompt
Command: is displayed, indicating that AutoCAD is waiting for you
to enter a command.
- The *root screen menu area* at the right-hand edge of the screen. This may
  be used to select commands and options by PICKing with a pointing
  device. It is one of the screen selection menus discussed in Appendix B.
- The *status line area* at the top edge of the screen. This gives information
  about the current state of the drawing being produced, including: the
  current 'layer' being drawn on (layers are discussed in Lesson 3 in Part
  B; this display shows that we are currently on layer 0, to which all new
  drawings are initially set); any special drawing modes in effect (only
  'Snap' is displayed at present); and the X, Y coordinates of the most
  recent point selected (initially set at 0.0000, 0.0000) relative to the current
  User Coordinate System (see below).
- The *coordinate system icon* at lower left of screen. This is available from
  Release 10 onwards and helps you to keep track of the current User
  Coordinate System (UCS) in operation. More information about the
  UCS and its relationships with the World Coordinate System (WCS) is
  given later in this chapter and in Lesson 13.

The AutoCAD Windows drawing screen display

If you are using AutoCAD Windows or Windows NT, you will see a display
similar to that shown in Fig. A4.3. As with the traditional MSDOS display,
the Windows version contains a drawing area, a command/prompt area, a
status line area and the coordinate system icon.
   However this display has a number of other features which are specific to
the Windows environment. These include:

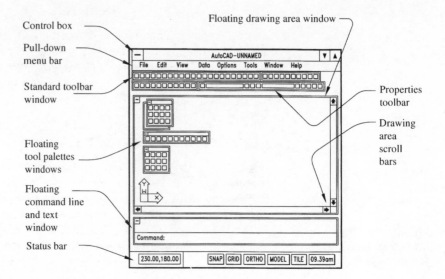

Control box

Pull-down
menu bar

Standard toolbar
window

Floating
tool palettes
windows

Floating
command line
and text
window

Status bar

Floating drawing area window

Properties
toolbar

Drawing
area
scroll
bars

Figure A4.3. The
AutoCAD Windows and
Windows NT screen
display.

- Floating *toolbars* and *palettes*. These are special windows which contain icons representing the more frequently used AutoCAD commands. A required command may be actioned by PICKing the appropriate icon with a pointing device. Being 'Microsoft-type windows' they may be moved to any part of the screen, be temporarily switched off whenever required, and are resizable.

    From Release 13 onwards, you may see multiple tool palettes on the same screen display, and observe *flyout palettes* of icons for selecting options of the command you have picked from the main palette. Also, the palettes are user definable, enabling you to choose the commands you wish to be included, and edit the icons.

    Toolbars and palettes are further discussed in Appendix B.

- Floating *command window*. This is available from Release 13 onwards. It serves the same function as the Command/Prompt area of the MSDOS screen display but, being a window, may be moved to any part of the screen and is resizable. When 'stretched' vertically, it displays the AutoCAD text screen, which may thus be viewed in conjunction with the drawing area. It also contains vertical *scroll bars* to scroll the contents of the text screen upwards or downwards.

    Further information about this, and other windows, is supplied in Appendix B.

- Floating *drawing area window*. This also has the standard Windows properties of being movable and resizable. In addition, it contains vertical and horizontal scroll bars which enable you to shift the display of a drawing in any direction. This effect may be used as an alternative to the PAN command (described in Lesson 1, Part B).

- Horizontal *menu bar*. This contains titles which are broad classifications of AutoCAD command types. If any of these titles are PICKed with a pointing device, a pop-up menu of the associated commands will appear on the screen. The required command can then be PICKed.

A horizontal menu bar is also available in the MSDOS version of AutoCAD. This gives pull-down menus but is not initially displayed when you first enter the AutoCAD drawing screen (see Appendix B).

Assumptions for command selection

It has been previously stated (and this will be enlarged upon in subsequent lessons) that AutoCAD drawing routines are actioned via commands which may be entered in a number of different ways, including screen menus and dialog boxes, toolbars and tablet menus. However, for the remainder of Part A, it will be assumed that you are using the most basic method of entering AutoCAD commands, i.e. by simply typing them in at the keyboard. (The last statement applies whether you are using MSDOS, Windows or any other operating system.) You are advised to keep to this approach for at least part of the initial exercise since it will make you more familiar with important AutoCAD command names than the other selection methods are likely to at this stage.

The exercises in Part A also assume that your screen pointing device is either a mouse or a puck with two buttons (PICK and RETURN; see page 12).

If you really want to use the menus or toolbars now, refer to Appendix B, browse through the options, and apply these to the instructions given in the drawing exercises of Part A. This approach will cause some variation from the user input and computer responses described, but should not give disastrous problems.

Note: When you enter the name of any command or option by keyboard, this must always be immediately followed by RETURN. That is not the case when you PICK commands or options from menus or toolbars with a pointing device. The RETURN facility on the latter approach is reserved for completing sequences of actions during the execution of commands (such as completing your selection of a number of objects you might wish to ERASE when using that command).

If you do decide to use menus and/or toolbars at an early stage and have Release 13 onwards (earlier versions vary slightly), you may find the following useful as a rough guide:

- Basic draw commands, such as LINE, CIRCLE, ARC, may be actioned via the Draw menu (MSDOS) or the Draw toolbar (Windows).
- Modifying commands, such as ERASE, MOVE, ROTATE, STRETCH, may be actioned via the Modify menu (MSDOS) or the Modify toolbar (Windows).
- Construction commands, such as COPY, MIRROR, FILLET, may be actioned via the Construct menu (MSDOS) or the Modify toolbar (Windows).

- Display commands, such as ZOOM, may be actioned via the View menu (MSDOS) or the Standard toolbar (Windows).
- Drawing aids commands, such as GRID and SNAP, may be actioned via the Options menu (MSDOS and Windows) or the status bar (Windows).
- Assistance techniques, such as OBJECT SNAPPING and POINT FILTERS, may be actioned via the Assist menu (MSDOS) or the Standard toolbar (Windows).
- File commands, such as SAVE, OPEN and END, may be actioned via the File menu (MSDOS and Windows).

5

Beginning an AutoCAD drawing

In later releases of AutoCAD (Release 12 onwards) you begin a new drawing after bringing up the AutoCAD screen display of Figs A4.2 or A4.3, and selecting the NEW command. There are a number of methods of performing this selection, but at this stage it is suggested that you type it in at the keyboard, by entering:

NEW   (RETURN)

Under default settings (see Appendix B) AutoCAD then displays the Create New Drawing dialog box, shown in Fig. A5.1.

Respond by moving your pointing device to the empty box area to the right of the New Drawing Name title and PICK (i.e. press the PICK button of your pointing device).

The next step assumes you are going to store your drawing work directly onto a floppy disk placed in Drive A. In later exercises this may not be the most efficient approach for your system—you should consult your AutoCAD dealer or instructor regarding the ideal option in subsequent sections.

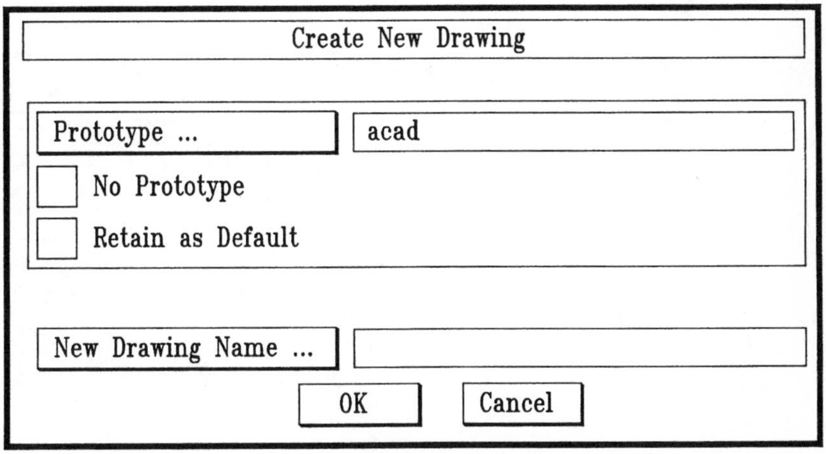

```
┌─────────────────────────────────────────────────────────┐
│              Create New Drawing                          │
│  ┌────────────────────┐  ┌──────────────────────────┐   │
│  │  Prototype ...     │  │  acad                    │   │
│  └────────────────────┘  └──────────────────────────┘   │
│  ☐  No Prototype                                         │
│  ☐  Retain as Default                                    │
│                                                          │
│  ┌────────────────────┐  ┌──────────────────────────┐   │
│  │  New Drawing Name ...│ │                          │   │
│  └────────────────────┘  └──────────────────────────┘   │
│              ┌──────┐    ┌──────────┐                   │
│              │  OK  │    │  Cancel  │                   │
│              └──────┘    └──────────┘                   │
└─────────────────────────────────────────────────────────┘
```

Figure A5.1. The Create New Drawing dialog box.

However, our assumption is fine for the basic routines in Part A, so proceed as follows.

Enter the following drawing name via the keyboard:

A:CAN

Now move your pointing device to the 'OK' box and PICK.

This completes the NEW command, and we have thus instructed AutoCAD to create a new drawing file called CAN on the floppy disk (assumed to be in Drive A).

Opening existing drawings

Before we start doing any drawing work, it would be useful to be aware of another basic AutoCAD filing facility—that of viewing and retrieving existing drawings stored on disk.

This is done via the OPEN command (Release 12 onwards).

As with the NEW command, it is suggested at this stage that you select OPEN via the keyboard by typing:

OPEN   (RETURN)

Under default settings, AutoCAD then displays a dialog box. Figure A5.2 shows the Windows version of this dialog box (the MSDOS version is similar). The data in Fig. A5.2 indicates that you are about to open an existing drawing called GARDEN which is currently residing in the ACADWIN directory of Drive C. Via the Preview box, you may also see a preview display of the drawing about to be opened.

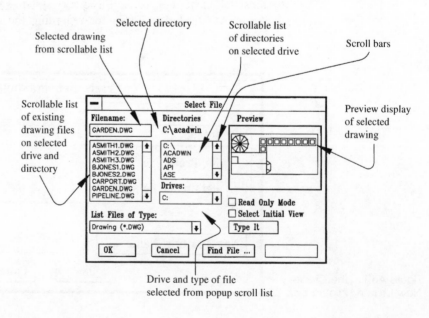

Figure A5.2.   Opening an existing drawing.

Note: The following is a practice exercise only. We will not actually be opening an existing drawing at this point, so *do not PICK the OK box at any stage of the 'Open Drawing' exercise*.

To select a drive from which to open a drawing you may move your pointing device to the arrow in the Drives box and PICK. This displays a 'pop-up' list of disk drives from which you may PICK the drive you require. (For the purpose of this exercise, the most suitable selection is probably the C drive.) The Directories box then displays all the directories which exist in the selected drive. If this is a lengthy list you may repeatedly PICK one of the arrows in the scroll bar to scroll this list upwards or downwards. Look for a directory where you think some drawing files are stored. Having found the directory you require you may point to its name and PICK it. The selected directory name will then appear above the Directories box, and all the drawing files which are stored in this directory will appear in the large filename box on the left-hand side of the dialog display. You may scroll this list upwards or downwards using the scroll bar arrows as done previously for the directories list. Choose any drawing name from the list, point to it, and PICK. The selected drawing name then appears in its own box above the Filename box.

Note: We do not actually want to open the selected drawing at this stage, so point to the Cancel box and PICK. This terminates the command procedure.

If you *had* picked the OK box, the selected drawing would have appeared on the screen.

The OPEN command can be used as follows. You may need to end your current session on AutoCAD at any stage before completing the drawing work in Part A. You can do so via the END command, which will take you out of AutoCAD, while also saving your partially-completed drawing to the drive/directory specified in the NEW command. On any subsequent AutoCAD session, your drawing may then be retrieved, exactly as it was when you ENDed it, via the OPEN command procedure.

6

Introductory exercise

In this chapter we continue with our drawing called CAN.

Note: Figure A6.1 is a hybrid diagram showing the alternative positions of status area and command text prompts for traditional MSDOS platforms and later releases of AutoCAD Windows. Similar hybrid diagrams will be used in most of the remaining figures in Part A. (Text prompt positions assumed to be as later Windows format.)

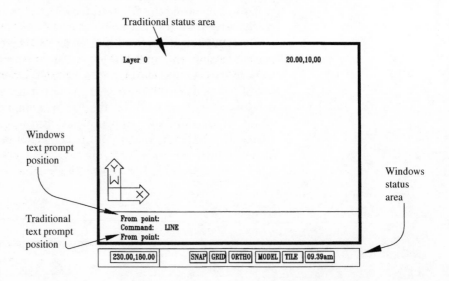

Figure A6.1. Hybrid diagram showing alternative status areas and text prompt positions.

Initial settings

Throughout our drawing work, we will need to make various settings to control the draughting environment. Initially we need to make just one setting. This is to ensure that Blip marks will appear on the screen when we draw. Blip marks are discussed in a later section and are controlled via a system variable called BLIPMODE.

If you have AutoCAD Release 12 onwards, type:

BLIPMODE   (RETURN)

then type:

ON   (RETURN)

(With earlier versions of AutoCAD, you would need to type: SETVAR (RETURN) before actioning the previous routine.)

'Rough' drawing techniques

Press the CTRL key and the B key simultaneously. This is an example of a 'toggle-switch' device, which, in this case, switches off the Snap facility. Note that the word 'Snap' has now disappeared from the screen status area. (In AutoCAD Windows, this may also be achieved by PICKing SNAP from the status bar with your pointing device.) Snap will be switched on again and used later in this chapter.

We will now draw some lines and circles on the screen. Type LINE at the keyboard (then RETURN). AutoCAD then displays the prompt:

From point:

Respond by moving your pointing device. As you do so, you will see two cursor cross-hairs moving on the screen in conjunction with the pointing device. At any point, say somewhere to the lower left of the screen, press the PICK button of your pointing device. This specifies the start point of your line.

AutoCAD then displays the prompt:

To point:

Respond by moving the cross-hairs to another point on the screen (say somewhere to upper right). As you do so, you will see a 'rubber band' line emerging (Fig. A6.2a). PICK again. This specifies the endpoint of your line.

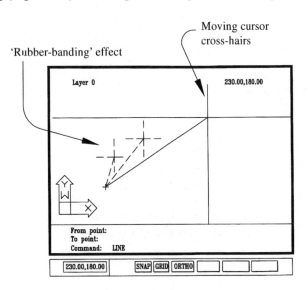

Figure A6.2. (a) Emerging rubber band line with moving cursor cross-hairs;   (a)

Press the RETURN button of your pointing device. This completes the
LINE command and you should now have a line displayed on the screen
(Fig. A6.2b).

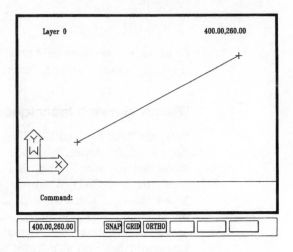

Figure A6.2.
(b) completed line.   (b)

AutoCAD then awaits your next command by redisplaying the
COMMAND: prompt.

Now we will draw a circle on the screen. Type CIRCLE at the keyboard
(then RETURN). AutoCAD then displays the prompt:

3P/2P/TTR/<Centre point>:

This represents a number of alternative *option* procedures for drawing
circles. Any prompt display inside '<>' type brackets represents the current
default option setting. AutoCAD assumes that you wish to use this option
unless you specify another one. At present the current default setting is
'Centre point', so AutoCAD is expecting you to specify the centre point
of your circle. This is the option we require, so move the cross-hairs to a
convenient circle centre position (say towards the middle of the screen) and
press the PICK button of your pointing device.

AutoCAD then displays the prompt:

Diameter/<Radius>:

This means that you can specify the size of your circle either by its diameter or by its radius, but at present AutoCAD assumes you are about to
enter a radius value.

Move the cross-hairs away from the specified centre point. As you do so,
you will see the dynamic display of a circle being 'dragged' to an increasing
radius (Fig. A6.3a). When the circle has reached a suitable size, PICK this
radius value. This completes the CIRCLE command, AutoCAD redisplays
the Command: prompt, and you should now have a line and a circle
displayed on your screen (Fig. A6.3b).

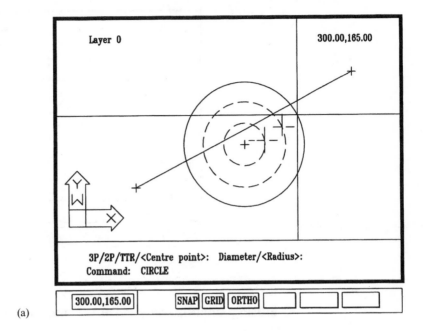

(a)

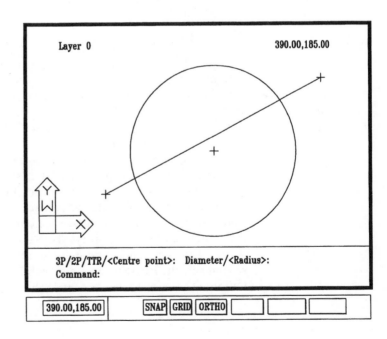

Figure A6.3.   (a) Circle being 'dragged' to size with moving cursor; (b) completed circle.

(b)

Now draw another line and another circle to achieve a display similar to that shown in Fig. A6.4.

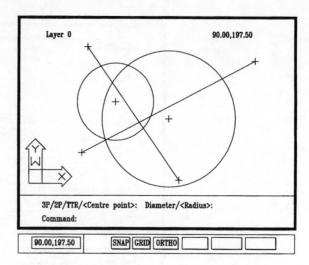

Figure A6.4.   Erasing
entities (plus REDRAW and
OOPS).

Erasing entities (plus REDRAW and OOPS)

We will now erase two of our drawing objects or *entities*.

Type ERASE at the keyboard (then RETURN). AutoCAD then displays
the prompt:

        Select objects:

Respond to this by moving your pointing device. As you do so, you will
see that the cross-hairs have been replaced with a small square (called a
pickbox). This is displayed whenever AutoCAD is expecting you to select an
entity already drawn and EDIT it in some way. Move the pickbox until it
touches one of your lines at any point, then PICK (i.e. press the PICK
button). The selected line will be *highlighted* (i.e. it will have the appearance
of being partially erased, as in Fig. A6.5a.

AutoCAD then redisplays the Select objects: prompt, ready
for you to select another entity to be erased. Move the pickbox until it
touches one of your circles anywhere on its circumference, then PICK.
Both the selected line and the selected circle should now be partially erased,
and AutoCAD again redisplays the Select objects: prompt (Fig.
A6.5b). Let us assume we do not wish to erase any more entities at present,
so complete the ERASE command with RETURN (i.e. press the RETURN
button). The selected line and circle should now be completely erased (Fig.
A6.5c).

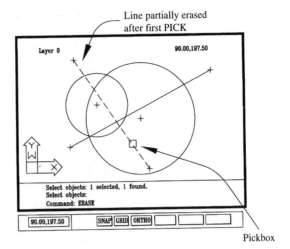

(a)

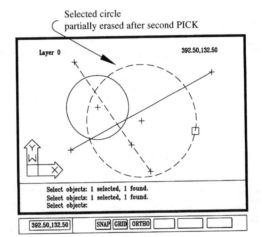

(b)

Figure A6.5.   (a) Selecting
line for erasing with
pickbox; (b) selection of
circle for erasing with
pickbox; (c) selected line
and circle completely
erased after RETURN;

(c)

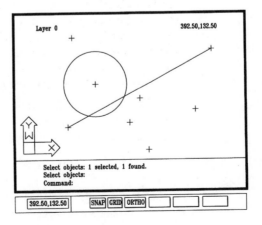

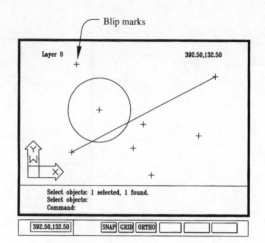

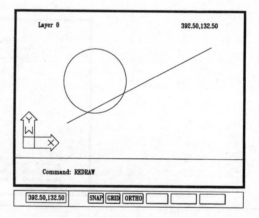

Figure A6.5.   (d) blip marks on screen; (e) blip marks removed with REDRAW command.

Note that, although the selected entities have been erased, there remain some untidy marks on the screen (Fig. A6.5d). These are called 'blip marks' and can be very useful in monitoring the positions of points previously PICKed. However, they are not required in this exercise and the screen may be 'cleaned up', as shown in Fig. A6.5e, by typing the command:

REDRAW   (RETURN)

Let us suppose we have had second thoughts about erasing the selected circle and wish to retrieve it.

You can achieve this by typing the command:

OOPS   (RETURN)

The OOPS command always retrieves the last entity erased, so the erased circle now reappears (Fig. A6.6).

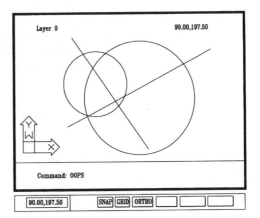

Figure A6.6.   Erased line and circle retrieved after OOPS command.

The drawing we have produced is very primitive, since positions and sizes have not been specified accurately. In order to start again and do some accurate drawing we will now erase all we have drawn so far.

Select the ERASE command as previously. When AutoCAD displays the `Select objects:` prompt, respond by typing: W (RETURN).

AutoCAD is then expecting you to select objects to be edited by placing a rectangular box called a *window* (no direct connection with Microsoft-type windows) around them, and displays the prompt:

`First corner:`

Respond by moving the cross-hairs just beyond the lower left extent of the complete drawing and PICK (Fig. A6.7a).

AutoCAD then displays the prompt:

`Other corner:`

Respond by moving the cross-hairs towards the upper right of the screen. As you do so, you will see the rectangular window dynamically emerging.

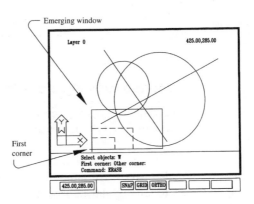

Figure A6.7.   (a) Emerging window after first corner has been PICKed;   (a)

Continue enlarging the window until it encloses all the entities of your drawing (Fig. A6.7b), then PICK. All entities should now be highlighted (Fig. A6.7c). Complete the ERASE command with RETURN.

This gives you a clear screen (Fig. A6.7d).

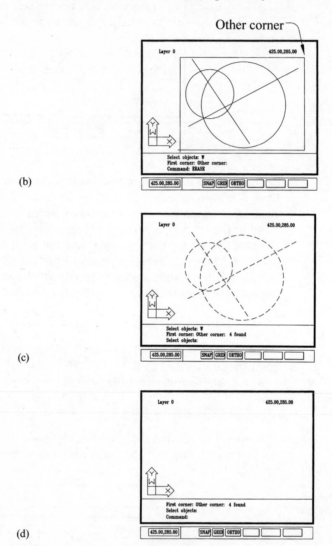

Figure A6.7.   (b) full window; (c) selected objects highlighted after PICKing other corner; (d) all entities erased after RETURN.

Accurate drawing via numeric input

One way of drawing accurately is via *numeric keyboard input*, during which you may specify values using:

1. Absolute Cartesian coordinates
2. Relative Cartesian coordinates
3. Relative polar coordinates

If you specify values in absolute Cartesian coordinate form, all distances are assumed to be measured from the same zero datum origin of two invisible axes, similar to the X and Y axes of a graph. This principle is illustrated in Fig. A6.8. There is also an invisible 'Z axis' which is used in 3-dimensional (3D) drawing, but at present we will assume we are working in two dimensions (2D) only (i.e. in the same way that you would draw on a flat sheet of paper).

We will draw a line and circle using absolute Cartesian coordinates. Select the LINE command as previously. Respond to the `From point:` prompt by typing:

$$60,42.5 \quad \text{(RETURN)}$$

Respond to the `To point:` prompt by typing:

$$200,150 \quad \text{(RETURN)}$$

Complete the command with another RETURN.

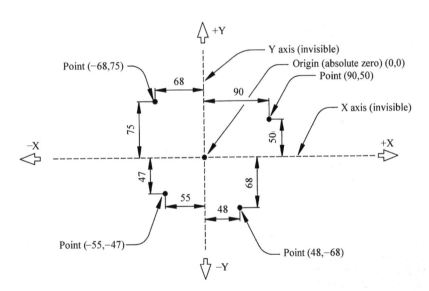

Figure A6.8.   Principle of absolute Cartesian coordinates.

As shown in Fig. A6.9, this gives you an accurate line whose points are both specified via horizontal and vertical (i.e. X, Y) coordinates from the same zero datum. In this case, the line starts at 60 units horizontally rightwards (i.e. positive X direction) and 42.5 units vertically upwards (i.e. positive Y direction) from zero datum; it finishes at 200 units (positive X) and 150 units (positive Y) from the same zero datum.

(If your system is not at default settings you may not see the desired display in Fig. A6.8. In this case you may need to reset your limits and do some zooming before continuing with the exercise. Limits and zoom are explained on pages 45–49.)

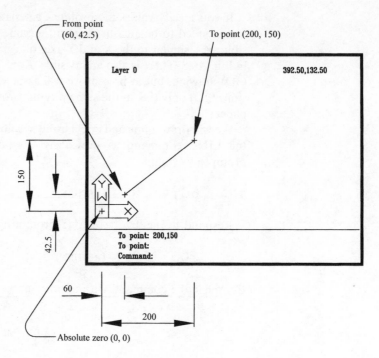

Figure A6.9. Accurate line using absolute Cartesian coordinates.

Select the circle command as previously. Respond to the `3P/2P/TTR/<Centre point>:` prompt by typing the centre point specification:

      `110,52.75`   (RETURN)

Respond to the `Diameter/<Radius>:` prompt by typing the radius value:

      `39.5`   (RETURN)

As shown in Fig. A6.10, your accurate line should now be accompanied by an accurate circle whose centre point is 110 units (positive X), 52.75 units (positive Y) from zero datum and which has a radius of 39.5 units.

Now use absolute Cartesian coordinates to drawn an accurate line from point (0.5, 180) to point (415.8, 0) and an accurate circle at centre point (365, 145) with a radius of 76.5 units. Thus achieve the display shown in Fig. A6.11. Then ERASE all your entities as previously, to return to a clear screen.

If you specify values in relative Cartesian coordinate form, X, Y distances are assumed to be measured from the previous point specified.

Radius 39.5   Centre point (110, 52.75)

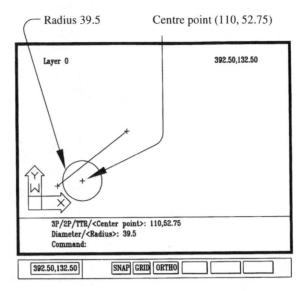

Figure A6.10. Accurate
circle drawn via Cartesian
coordinates and numeric
keyboard input.

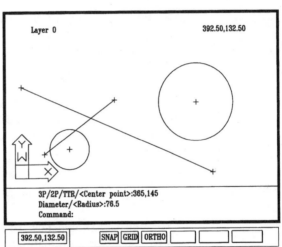

Figure A6.11. Accurate
circle and line drawn using
Cartesian coordinates.

For example, we may redraw our first accurate line using relative Cartesian coordinates as follows.

Select LINE, then specify the first point as previously, i.e. type the absolute Cartesian coordinates:

60,42.5   (RETURN)

Respond to the To point: prompt by typing:

@140,107.5   (RETURN)

By typing '@' before the Cartesian coordinates, you have told AutoCAD that you wish the specified X, Y distances 140 and 107.5 to be measured

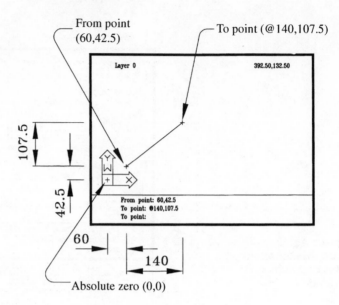

Figure A6.12.   Accurate
line using relative
Cartesian coordinates.

from the start point of the line instead of from the zero datum (Fig. A6.12).

Now, in response to the To point: prompt, type:

@-20,-60   (RETURN)

You will see that you have drawn another line joined to the end of the first one. The endpoint of the second line is positioned at an X, Y point of –20, –60 from the endpoint of the first line.

Note that the To point: prompt has reappeared, and respond by typing:

@0,-40   (RETURN)

Your display should now be as Fig. A6.13. In addition to introducing relative Cartesian coordinates, the current exercise also reveals that a 'chain' of joined lines may be drawn under a single LINE command by repeatedly specifying a new point (instead of a RETURN) in response to the To point: prompt. This may also be done using absolute Cartesian coordinates, but is more logically achieved via relative Cartesian coordinates, relative polar coordinates, or PICKing positions with a pointing device.

Now use relative Cartesian coordinates to complete a square of side 40 units joined to the existing lines, as shown in Fig. A6.14.

The LINE command is finally completed by typing RETURN in response to the To point: prompt. When you have completed this exercise, erase all the entities as previously and thus return to a clear screen.

Relative polar coordinates specify the position of a point in terms of its angle of inclination and radial distance from the previous point specified.

For example, you could draw a line using relative polar coordinates as follows.

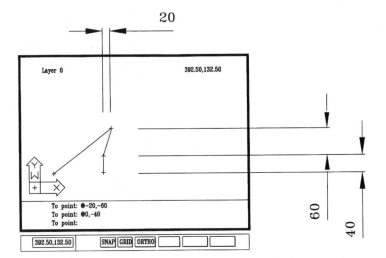

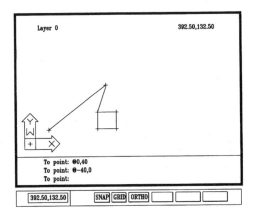

Figure A6.13.   Chain of lines using relative Cartesian coordinates.

Figure A6.14. Completing a square.

Use the previous procedures to select the LINE command and specify a start point at absolute Cartesian coordinates (80, 60).

Respond to the To point: prompt by typing:

@97.5<60   (RETURN)

This draws a line of radial length 5 units from the start point and at an angular inclination of 60 degrees (measured anticlockwise from a '3 o'clock' datum) (Fig. A6.15).

Now successively respond to the repeated To point: prompts by typing the following:

@50<225   (RETURN)
@60<90   (RETURN)
@60<180   (RETURN)
@60<270   (RETURN)
@60<0   (RETURN)
RETURN

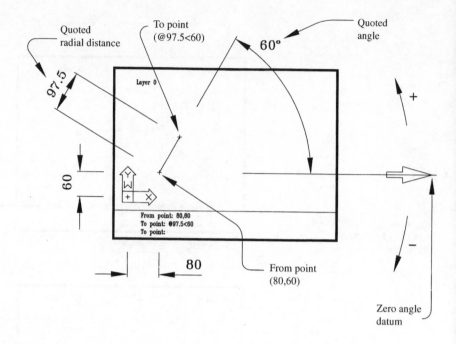

Figure A6.15.   Accurate
line drawn using relative
polar coordinates.

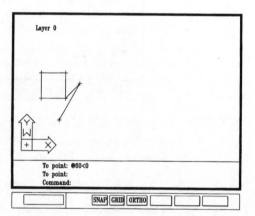

Figure A6.16.   Chain of
lines drawn using relative
polar coordinates.

Your display should now appear as shown in Fig. A6.16.

Note that the last four lines drawn have created a square of side 60 units.

Complete the exercise by drawing the equilateral triangle of side 110 units shown in Fig. A6.17. (Each point of an equilateral triangle has an inclusive angle of 60 degrees.)

Then erase all the entities as previously, giving you a clear screen once more.

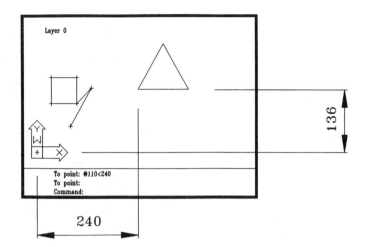

Figure A6.17. Triangle
drawn using relative polar
coordinates.

Accurate drawing via object snapping (OSNAP)

Entities can be drawn accurately via a pointing device if you employ certain
techniques. Two common facilities here are the SNAP command and the
coordinate display. These are used later in this chapter.

Another method of achieving accurate detail with a pointing device is the
object snapping technique, which enables you to 'snap' the drawing cursor
accurately onto existing features of a drawing. Object snapping can be done
via the OSNAP command, but here we will be invoking the technique during the operation of other commands.

Draw two lines intersecting each other and a circle by any method you
wish, to obtain a display similar to that shown in Fig. A6.18.

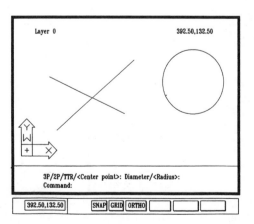

Figure A6.18.

Select the LINE command. In response to the `From point:` prompt, type:

>   END   (RETURN)

AutoCAD responds to this by displaying the prompt:

>   Of:

If you move your pointing device you will see that the moving screen cursor now has a rectangular box (called a 'target sight') around the intersection of the cross-hairs. Move the cursor until an end of one of the lines you have already drawn lies somewhere inside the target sight box (Fig. A6.19a). Then PICK. You will see that the cursor 'snaps on' exactly to the endpoint of the selected line, and AutoCAD displays the prompt:

>   To point:

Respond to this prompt by again typing:

>   END   (RETURN)

As before, AutoCAD responds by displaying the prompt:

>   Of:

Noting that the target sight box is redisplayed, move the cursor until an end of the other line you drew lies somewhere inside the target sight box (Fig. A6.19b). Then PICK. You will see that a new line has been 'snapped on' exactly between the ends of the two original lines. Complete the LINE command with RETURN (Fig. A6.19c). If you move your pointing device now, you will see that the target sight box is no longer displayed.

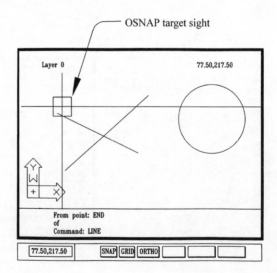

Figure A6.19.   (a) Object snapping (endpoint);

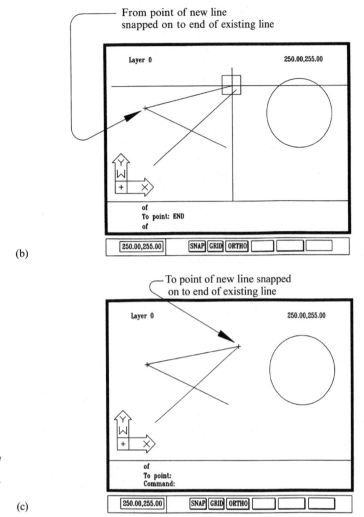

Figure A6.19.   (b) new line snapped on; (c) completed line via object snapping (endpoint routine).

We will now snap a line from the intersection of the first two lines drawn and the centre of the circle. The interaction between AutoCAD and yourself should be as follows:

AutoCAD screen prompt	*Your response*
Command:	Type LINE (RETURN)
From point:	Type INT (RETURN)
Of:	Move cursor until the intersection of the original lines lies

	somewhere inside the target sight box (see Fig. A6.20a). Then PICK.
To point:	Type CEN (RETURN)
Of:	Move cursor until part of the circumference of the circle lies somewhere inside the target box (see Fig. A6.20b). Then PICK.
To point:	RETURN

Intersections of lines inside OSNAP target sight

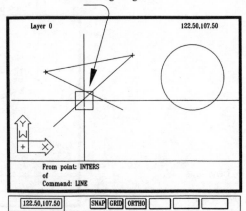

(a)

Circumference of circle inside OSNAP target sight

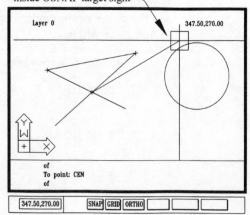

Figure A6.20.   (a) Object snapping (intersection routine); (b) object snapping (centre routine);   (b)

Your display should now be similar to that shown in Fig. A6.20c.

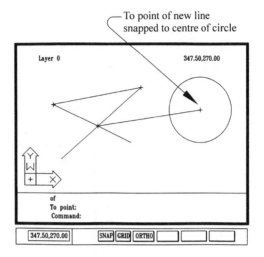

Figure A6.20.   (c) new line
completed.   (c)

We will now snap a new circle onto an end of one of the original lines. The
interaction between AutoCAD and yourself should be as follows:

AutoCAD screen prompt	Your response
Command:	Type CIRCLE (RETURN)
3P/2P/TTR/<Centre point>:	Type END (RETURN)
Of:	Move cursor until the required line end point lies somewhere inside the target sight box (see Fig. A6.21a). Then PICK.

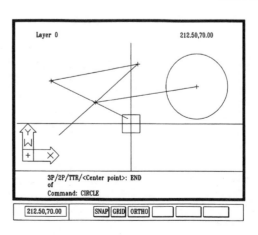

Figure A6.21.   (a) Object
snapping (circle to end of
line);   (a)

`Diameter/<Radius>:`

Move cursor until
you drag to a circle
radius similar to that
shown in Fig.
A6.21b. Then PICK.

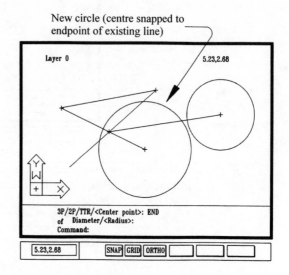

New circle (centre snapped to
endpoint of existing line)

Layer 0   5.23,2.68

3P/2P/TTR/<Center point>: END
of Diameter/<Radius>:
Command:

5.23,2.68   SNAP GRID ORTHO

Figure A6.21.   (b)
completed circle.   (b)

Our last object-snapping exercise here will be to draw a line which is
tangential to our two circles. The interaction between AutoCAD and yourself should be as follows:

AutoCAD screen prompt	*Your response*
`Command:`	Type LINE (RETURN)
`From point:`	Type TAN (RETURN)
`To:`	Move cursor approximately to the position shown in Fig. A6.22a, with part of the circle circumference lying somewhere inside the target sight box. Then PICK.

To point:	Type TAN (RETURN)
To:	Move cursor approximately to the position shown in Fig. A6.22b, with part of the circumference of the other circle lying somewhere inside the target sight box. Then PICK.
To point:	RETURN

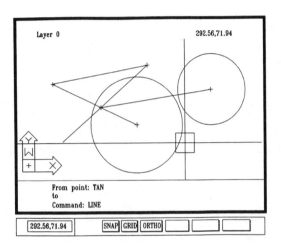

(a)

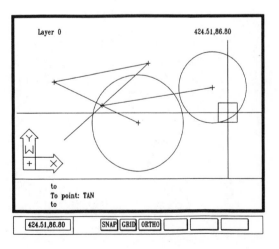

Figure A6.22.   (a) Object snapping (line tangential to two circles). Take target sight to first circle; (b) take target sight to second circle;

Your display should now be similar to that shown in Fig. A6.22c.

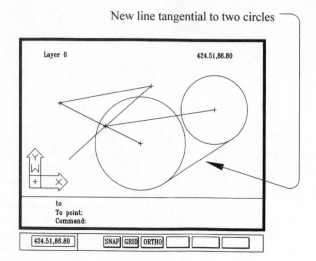

New line tangential to two circles

Figure A6.22. (c)
completed line.   (c)

Display techniques

Now we will experiment with some screen display techniques.
    Type the command:

    LIMITS   (RETURN)

The limits of an AutoCAD drawing may be thought of as the 'size of the drawing sheet' on which you are working. For example, when you first begin a new AutoCAD drawing, its standard limit settings extend from a lower left-hand corner of 0, 0 to an upper right-hand corner of 420, 297. In this case AutoCAD responds to the command, with the prompt:

    ON/OFF/<Lower left corner> <0,0>:

In response to this, press RETURN to retain the current lower left-hand corner setting (i.e. 0, 0 in this case). AutoCAD then responds by displaying the prompt:

    Upper right corner <420,297>:

Respond by typing in larger values than the current one, for example:

    1000,1000   (RETURN)

Your AutoCAD drawing limits would then be set to 0, 0 (lower left corner) and 1000, 1000 (upper right corner).

Type the command:

ZOOM   (RETURN)

AutoCAD then responds by displaying the prompt:

All/Centre/Dynamic/Extents/Left/
Previous/Window/<Scale(X)>:

Respond to this prompt by typing:

A   (RETURN)

By typing A you have asked AutoCAD to display ALL of the drawing on the screen, as far as the limits you have set for your 'drawing sheet'. You should thus now have a display similar to that shown in Fig. 6.23. This operation may be likened to that of you, the viewer, moving further away from a paper drawing until you can see the complete sheet. The individual objects on the drawing would thus appear smaller than previously to you (although their actual sizes have not changed).

Select the ZOOM command again. This may either be achieved by typing: ZOOM (RETURN) again, or you may employ this useful AutoCAD facility: *the most recent AutoCAD command may always be retrieved by entering a* RETURN *in response to the* Command: *prompt.* The RETURN may be entered either via the keyboard or via the appropriate button of a pointing device.

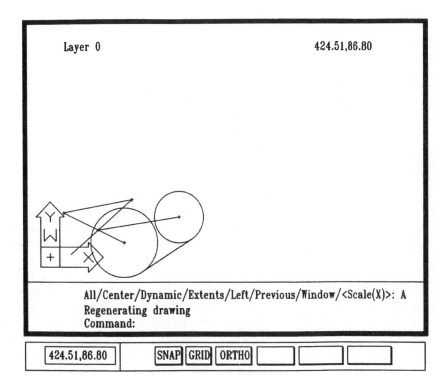

Figure A6.23. ZOOM ALL display.

Whichever procedure you adopt for reselecting the ZOOM command, AutoCAD will respond by repeating the prompt:

```
All/Centre/Dynamic/Extents/Left/
Previous/Window/<Scale(X)>:
```

This time, respond by typing:

P   (RETURN)

This tells AutoCAD that you wish to retrieve the previous view you had displayed. AutoCAD thus responds by replacing the ALL view with the one shown in Fig. A6.22c. The ZOOM command is then complete.

Reselect the ZOOM command again (e.g. by pressing RETURN). As before, AutoCAD responds by displaying the screen prompt:

```
All/Centre/Dynamic/Extents/Left/
Previous/Window/<Scale(X)>:
```

This time, respond by typing:

W   (RETURN)

This tells AutoCAD that you wish to 'zoom in' to a small area of the drawing which will be specified by a window. We have already used the Window option in conjunction with the ERASE command. In fact, the Window option is available within many different AutoCAD commands and, once selected, always results in the same routine. Thus AutoCAD will respond to your selection of the Window option by displaying the prompt:

First corner:

Respond to this by moving your pointing device until the screen cursor is approximately at the position shown in Fig. A6.24a. Then PICK.

AutoCAD then responds by displaying the prompt:

Other corner:

Respond to this by moving your pointing device until the screen cursor is approximately at the position shown in Fig. A6.24b. Then PICK.

This completes the ZOOM command and your resulting display should be similar to that shown in Fig. A6.24c. Note that the area enclosed by the window operation now completely fills the screen. This effect may be likened to viewing the windowed area through a rectangular-shaped magnifying glass. The objects observed thus appear larger to you, the viewer (although their actual sizes have not changed).

Now complete the zooming exercise by selecting the ZOOM command once more, and then selecting the Previous option. Thus retrieve the view shown in Fig. A6.22c.

Before we embark on our next stage in the use of AutoCAD, create a blank screen via ERASE WINDOW as we have done on previous occasions.

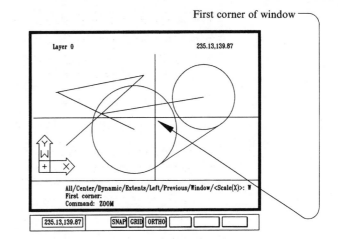

Figure A6.24. (a) ZOOM
WINDOW (first corner); (b)
ZOOM WINDOW (other
corner); (c) zoomed view.

Setting up your drawing (SNAP and GRID)

We will now make some settings which will help us to draw more accurately and efficiently.

Type the following command:

GRID   (RETURN)

AutoCAD then responds by displaying the prompt:

Grid spacing(X) or ON/OFF/SNAP/
Aspect<0>:

Respond to this by typing:

10   (RETURN)

Note that an array of equally-spaced dots covers the screen (Fig. A6.25). This completes the GRID command.

Now type the following command:

SNAP   (RETURN)

AutoCAD then responds by displaying the prompt:

Snap spacing or ON/OFF/Rotate/Style<10>:

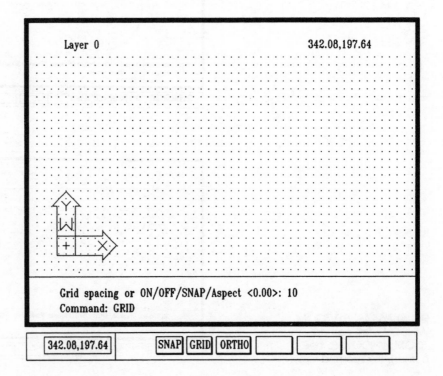

Figure A6.25.   GRID displayed.

Respond to this by typing:

    5   (RETURN)

This tells AutoCAD that you wish Snap to be switched back on again with a regular spacing of 5 units. Note that the word 'Snap' has reappeared in the status line at the top of the screen.

Now move your pointing device and observe the corresponding movement of the screen cursor, You will note that the cursor cannot take up any position, but is forced to 'jump' at intervals of 5 units spacing (i.e. the value set for SNAP). This has the effect that the cursor moves only to the grid dots (set at a value of 10 units spacing) and to the mid-positions between the grid dot spacings.

Note that the two numerical values displayed towards the right of the top screen status line. It was stated earlier that these keep track of the current X, Y position of the screen cursor (relative to the zero datum set by the current UCS). During the previous routines, you may have noticed these continually changing value as the screen cursor moved. Note that, with the Snap value set to 5, these X, Y values display only multiples of 5 as the screen cursor 'jumps' to its successive snap spacings (Fig. A6.26).

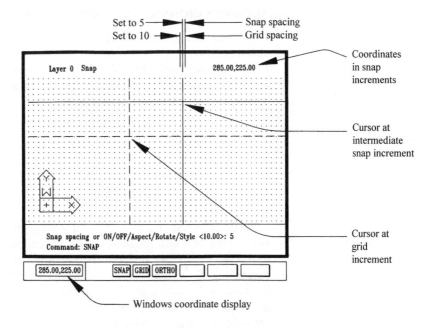

Figure A6.26. Cursor movement restricted to Snap increments.

Setting the thickness

At this point we need to set a THICKNESS value whose use will become apparent when we start working in three dimensions (3D). This will be achieved by accessing the THICKNESS system variable as follows.

Type the command:

SETVAR   (RETURN)

AutoCAD then responds by displaying the prompt:

Variable name or ?:

Respond to this by typing:

THICKNESS   (RETURN)

AutoCAD responds by displaying the prompt:

New value for THICKNESS <0.00.0.00>:

Respond to this by typing:

120   (RETURN)

Similarly, make the following system variable settings in order to achieve efficient 3D displays in later work. Access system variable WORLDVIEW and enter a value of 0. Access system variable UCSICON, select ORIGIN option. (You may bypass SETVAR from Release 12 onwards.)

Accurate drawing via coordinate display

We will now start on the main drawing exercise, i.e. that of drawing a simple watering-can.

This will be drawn accurately, but on this occasion the accuracy will be achieved via a screen-pointing technique as an alternative to the numeric keyboard routines described earlier.

Type the command:

LINE   (RETURN)

As on previous occasions, AutoCAD responds by displaying the prompt:

From point:

Respond to this by moving your screen-pointing device. As you do so, look at the two continually-changing numbers displayed in the horizontal screen status line. As we have already indicated, these are continually monitoring the X, Y position of the screen cursor by displaying its changing position in absolute Cartesian coordinates from the current UCS. This type of coordinate display is known as *dynamic XY*. As we shall soon see, there are other types of coordinate display.

We will start our line at the X, Y position 200, 70. Therefore, move your cursor until the figures:

200,70

are displayed at the status line (Fig. A6.27a), then PICK.

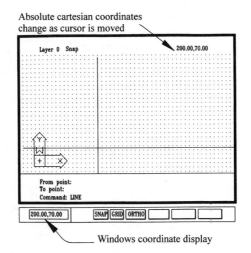

Figure A6.27. (a) Move cursor to the required 'From point' position of the line using dynamic XY coordinate display;

(a)

As on previous occasions, AutoCAD responds by displaying the prompt:

> To point:

Now press the CTRL key and the D key at the same time (or in the later Windows releases, PICK the coordinates box in the bottom status area). Then move your pointing device, noting the effect on the coordinate display. Keep repeating the process until the coordinates are in the form shown below:

> 22.46<65

This indicates that the coordinates of the cursor position are now displayed in dynamic polar form *relative to the 'From point' of the line being drawn* (Fig. A6.27b). Thus, in the example quoted, the cursor would be at a radial distance of 22.46 units from the 'From point' and displaced through an angle of 65 degrees (measured anticlockwise from a rightward '3 o'clock' horizontal datum through the 'From point').

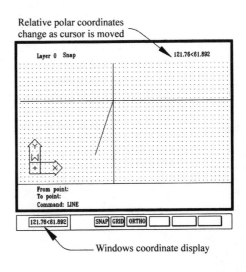

Figure A6.27. (b) dynamic polar coordinate display (after 'Ctrl D' operation);

(b)

Absolute Cartesian coordinates
change as cursor is moved

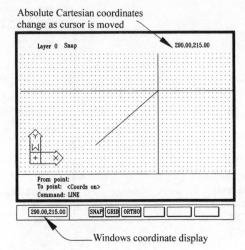

(c)

Windows coordinate display

Absolute Cartesian coordinates
stay constant as cursor is moved

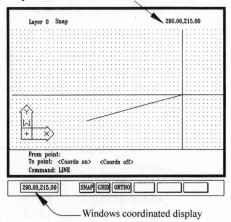

(d)

Windows coordinated display

Relative polar coordinates
change as cursor is moved

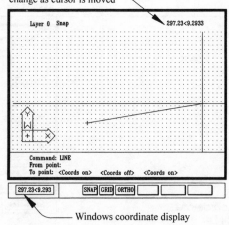

Figure A6.27.   (c)
dynamic XY coordinate
display (after 'Ctrl D'
operation); (d) static XY
coordinate display (after
second 'Ctrl D' operation);
(e) retrieved dynamic
polar coordinate display
(after third 'Ctrl D'
operation).

(e)

Windows coordinate display

Before we complete our line, we can experiment further with the coordinate display. Press the CTRL key and the D key at the same time, or PICK the Windows coordinate box again, and then move your pointing device. You will see that the message <Coords on> is displayed at the bottom of the screen, and that the coordinate display has reverted to dynamic XY (i.e. absolute Cartesian) form (Fig. A6.27c). Now perform the CTRL-D operation again and move your pointing device. You will see that the message <Coords off> has been added to the lower screen display and that the coordinate display is no longer dynamic, but has been 'frozen' at the absolute XY value which was the current one when CTRL-D was actioned. This is called *static XY* format (Fig. A6.27d). Perform the CTRL-D operation once more and move your pointing device. You will see that another <Coords on> message has been added to the lower screen display and that the coordinate display has now returned to dynamic polar format. This sequence of changing coordinate display format is illustrated in Fig. A6.27e and is called a 'circular toggle' principle.

With the coordinate display now back in dynamic polar format, move your pointing device rightwards until you see the following coordinate display:

> 120<0

then PICK.

As on previous occasions, AutoCAD responds by repeating the prompt:

> To point:

Respond to this by moving your pointing device upwards until you see the following coordinate display.

> 160<90

then PICK.

Continue this routine until you have drawn a rectangle, 120 wide by 160 units high. If you are still unsure of the procedure, the interaction sequence between AutoCAD and yourself for drawing the complete rectangle (less our brief excursion into the CTRL-D routine) is shown below:

AutoCAD screen prompt	*Your response*
Command:	Type LINE (RETURN)
From point:	Move pointing device until you see the coordinate display:
	200,70
	Then PICK.

To point: Move pointing device until
                             you see the coordinate
                             display:

                                   120<0

                             Then PICK.

To point: Move pointing device until
                             you see the coordinate
                             display:

                                   160<90

                             Then PICK.

To point: Move pointing device until
                             you see the coordinate
                             display:

                                  120<180

                             Then PICK.

To point: Move pointing device until
                             you see the coordinate
                             display:

                                  160<270

                             Then PICK.

To point: RETURN

You should now have the required rectangle displayed, as shown in Fig. A6.28.

Fillet radii

We can complete this view by putting *fillet radii* in the right-hand corners. To do this we will use the FILLET command in two stages:

1. To set a radius value for the fillets
2. To PICK the entities forming the corners to be filleted

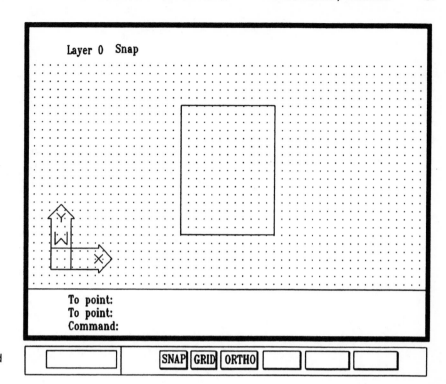

Layer 0   Snap

To point:
To point:
Command:

SNAP GRID ORTHO

Figure A6.28.   Completed
rectangle.

The sequence of interaction between AutoCAD and yourself for putting
fillets on the corners is as follows:

AutoCAD screen prompt	*Your response*
Command:	Type FILLET (RETURN)
Polyline/Radius/ <Select two objects>:	Type R (RETURN)
Enter fillet radius <0.0000>:	Type 40 (RETURN)
Command:	RETURN (to retrieve the FILLET command).
Polyline/Radius/ <Select two objects>:	Move pointing device until the pickbox touches baseline near bottom right corner (see Fig. A6.29a). Then PICK.

Move pointing device until the pickbox touches rightward edge near bottom right corner (see Fig. A6.29a). Then PICK (see Fig. A6.29b).

Command:

RETURN (to retrieve the FILLET command).

Polyline/Radius
<Select two objects>:

Move pointing device until the pickbox touches rightward edge near top right corner (Fig. A6.29c). Then PICK.

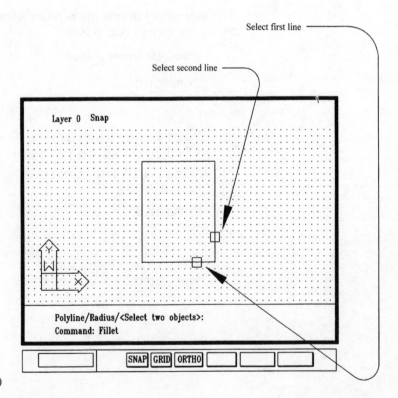

Figure A6.29. (a) Procedure for FILLET command;   (a)

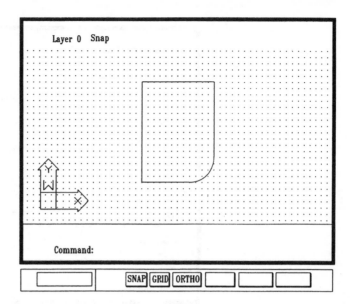

Figure A6.29.
(b) completed fillet;

Move pointing
device until the
pickbox touches
top edge near top
right corner (Fig.
A6.29c). Then
PICK (see Fig.
A6.29d).

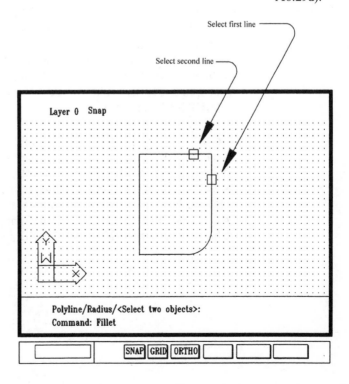

Figure A6.29.
(c) procedure for second
fillet;

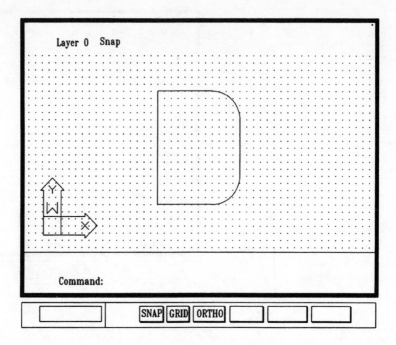

Figure A6.29. (d) second
fillet completed.

3D display

So far, we have been working in a 'flat' two-dimensional (2D) world. For example, the shape we have on the screen now has been considered as if it were made of flat sheet with no thickness. However, everything has some thickness and every shape may be viewed in a three-dimensional (3D) world with depth. (In fact, you will recall that, in the section 'Setting the thickness' (see page 51) we told AutoCAD we wanted our shape to have a THICKNESS of 120.)

The thickness of our shape is not yet apparent because we are looking at it 'from above' as a plan or 'bird's-eye' view. To continue with the bird analogy, you can consider that you, the viewer (in your feathered form), are hovering at a 'height' which is directly above the WCS (world coordinate system). The WCS is the absolute zero point of AutoCAD and lies in the 'ground level' plane which contains both the X axis and the Y axis. In the real world, the 'ground' is a plane lying parallel to the computer screen which is the flat world used for 2D drawings.

The 'height' of the 3D world is in fact the Z axis, which is only used for 3D work and is perpendicular to the screen (*outwards* from the screen is the *positive* Z direction; *inwards* to the screen is the *negative* Z direction). The X, Y and Z axes are thus mutually perpendicular in a three-dimensional world. The 3D principle of AutoCAD is illustrated in Fig. A6.30.

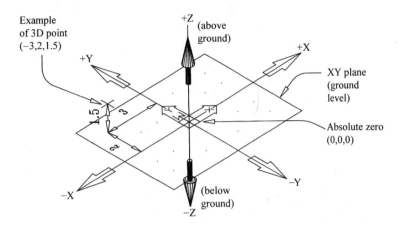

Figure A6.30.

To obtain a 3D view of our shape, and observe its thickness, type the command:

    VPOINT   (RETURN)

AutoCAD then responds with the screen prompt:

    Rotate/<View point> <0,0,1>:

Respond to this by typing:

    -1,-1,1   (RETURN)

You should now have a 3D display of your shape, as shown in Fig. A6.31. (Note that the UCS icon is also shown in 3D.) The VPOINT value −1, −1, 1 represents a displacement of the viewer position in distance ratios along the X, Y and Z axes respectively. Thus it is as if you, the 'observing bird', have flown westerly (say 1 metre distance), and southerly (1 metre) from the WCS zero datum, while retaining a 'height' above ground level of 1 metre. Looking back at the shape from your new viewing point, you can now see the object in its true 3D form instead of as a plan view. *Note*: The actual X, Y, Z displacement values are not important—it is only their *ratios* which affect the 3D view displayed. For example, the same effect would have been achieved by typing −10, −10, 10; −35, −35, 35; −540, −540, 540, etc. (Fig. A6.32).

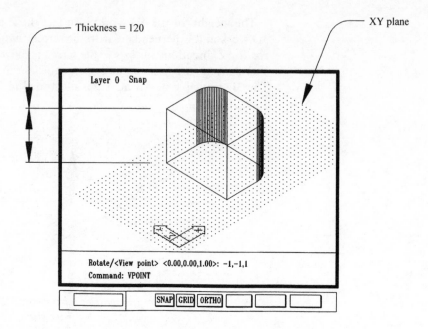

Figure A6.31.   3D display.

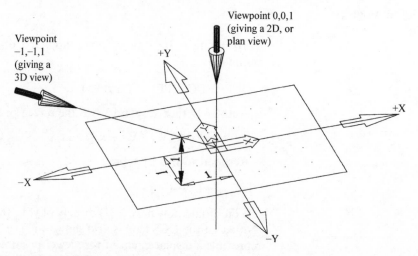

Figure A6.32.   Viewpoint principle.

Saving your work

Before we continue with our drawing, it would be advisable to save what we have done so far. This safeguards our work against 'accidents', such as power-cuts, in which we could lose our drawing data.

Type the command:

SAVE   (RETURN)

In the later releases, AutoCAD then responds by displaying the Save Drawing dialog box. Respond by PICKing the File box and entering the filename:

A:CAN

Then PICK the OK box.

AutoCAD then saves the current drawing under the filename CAN.DWG on the floppy disk in Drive A (it also creates a backup file called CAN.BAK on the same floppy disk).

You should perform a SAVE operation at regular intervals throughout the creation of your drawing (particularly after you have done a complex routine). Then, even if you do lose your current computer drawing, you will have retained most of your drawing data on disk (up to the time when you last selected the SAVE command). This will progressively overwrite and update the files CAN.DWG and CAN.BAK now residing on the floppy disk in Drive A according to the current state of the drawing.

In subsequent parts of this exercise, it is assumed that you will be regularly selecting the SAVE command as instructed.

The User Coordinate System

We have already stated that the WCS is AutoCAD's absolute zero datum, and its position is fixed. However, another coordinate system is available from Version 10 onwards. This is called the User Coordinate System (UCS). Unlike the WCS, the UCS may be repositioned at any time, and its X, Y, Z axis framework may be rotated in 3D to any direction required (although the three axes retain the same perpendicular directions relative to each other). All coordinate values for drawing entities (and object thicknesses) are understood by AutoCAD to be relative to the current UCS, whatever its current position and orientation.

At present our current UCS is the same as the WCS. (This is why a 'W' is displayed on the UCS icon.)

We will now reposition and rotate our UCS as follows. Type the command:

UCS   (RETURN)

AutoCAD then responds by displaying the prompt:

Origin/ZAxis/3point/Entity/View/X/Y/Z/
Prev/Restore/Save/Del/?/<World>:

We will be using the ZAxis option for changing the current UCS. The complete interaction routine between AutoCAD and yourself is as follows:

AutoCAD screen prompt	Your response
Command:	Type UCS (RETURN)
Origin/ZAxis/3point/ Entity/View/X/Y/Z/ Prev/Restore/Save/Del/ ?/<World>:	Type ZAxis (RETURN)

Origin point <0,0,0>:   Type INT (RETURN) (for
                                an intersection OSNAP
                                operation).

of: Move pointing device until
                                'osnap' target sight
                                surrounds the base corner
                                of the 3D shape. Then
                                PICK (Fig. A6.33).

Point on positive   Type @0,-1,0 (RETURN)
portion of the Z axis
<0,0,1>:

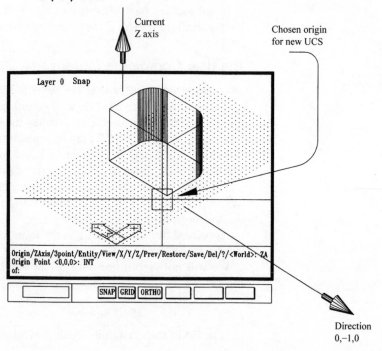

Figure A6.33.   Changing
the UCS.

Your UCS icon should now be shown as in Fig. A6.34, indicating the new
position and X, Y axes orientation for the current UCS. (Fig. A6.34 also
indicates the new current direction of the Z axis, which is parallel to a
direction of 0, –1, 0 relative to the previous X, Y, Z axes.)

A new plan view

Now that we have a new Z axis, we may view our object in its new plan view
form. Use the VPOINT command again, but this time enter a value of:

0,0,1   (RETURN)

Your new plan view should now be displayed as in Fig. A6.35.

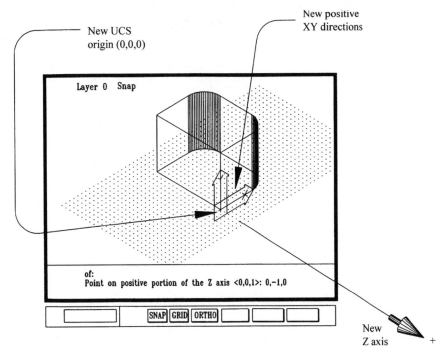

Figure A6.34.   New UCS.

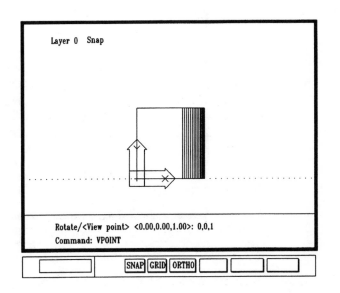

Figure A6.35.   New plan
view.

Adding text

It was stated at the start of the exercise that we will eventually be drawing a watering-can. Thus we will put an appropriate title on our object using an AutoCAD TEXT routine as follows:

AutoCAD screen prompt	*Your response*
`Command:`	Type TEXT (RETURN)

`Start point or Align/`
`Centre/Fit/Middle/Right/`
`Style:`
	Type 16,56 (RETURN)

`Height <3.0>:`	Type 16 (RETURN)
`Rotation angle <0>:`	RETURN (to accept 0 default).
`Text:`	Type CAN (RETURN)

Your display should now be as in Fig. A6.36, with the object's name CAN written with its start point (lower left corner of text) at the X, Y coordinates 16, 56. Remember, these coordinate values are relative to our new current UCS position.

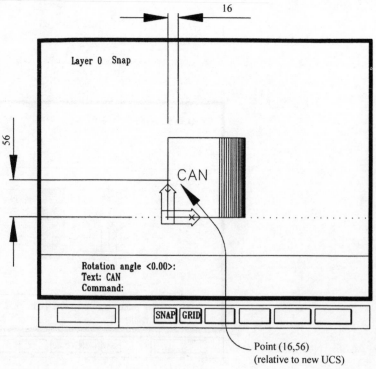

Figure A6.36.   Use of TEXT.

A base for a spout

At this point we will draw a base for the spout of our watering-can. To do this we will need to alter our thickness value.

Select the SETVAR command and set a new THICKNESS value of –160 by using the same routine as we did in the section 'Setting the thickness' (see page 51).

Draw a line from 0, 0 to –60, 0 using any of the accurate techniques previously discussed. (Remember, these are X, Y coordinates from the current UCS. No Z coordinates are supplied. This assumes the specified points are at zero Z from the UCS point.)

Now draw a LINE from –60, 0 to 0, 60.

Your display should now be as in Fig. A6.37.

Select ZOOM and use the PREVIOUS option to go back to your previous 3D viewpoint display. (If you have done any additional zooming at the plan-view stage, you will need to keep repeating the ZOOM PREVIOUS routine. This takes you back through a 'memory stack' of previous views until you arrive at the one you require.)

Your display should be as Fig. A6.38 with the two most recently-drawn lines having a 3D thickness equal to the width of the gradually-evolving watering can.

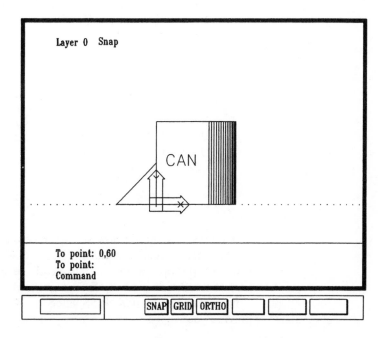

Figure A6.37.

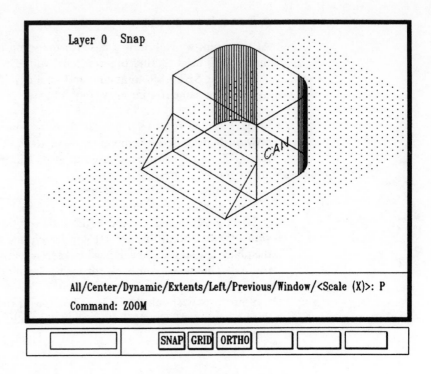

Figure A6.38.   Retrieved
3D display via ZOOM
(PREVIOUS) command.

Resetting the UCS and DRAWing an ARC

We will now create a handle for our can by drawing an ARC, but we must first reset our UCS and our THICKNESS.

Reset the UCS as follows:

AutoCAD screen prompt	*Your response*
Command:	UCS (RETURN)
Origin/ZAxis/3point/ Entity/View/X/Y/Z/Prev/ Restore/Save/Del/?/ <World>:	O (RETURN)
Origin point <0,0,0>:	120,0,-60 (RETURN)

Your display should now show a repositioned UCS icon to a new point on the base of the can (as in Fig. A6.39). Note that, by selecting the ORIGIN (O) option, the UCS is merely repositioned in 3D, with the direction of the Z axis (and the X, Y axes) remaining unaltered.

Now reset the THICKNESS value to −40 by using the same routine as on previous occasions.

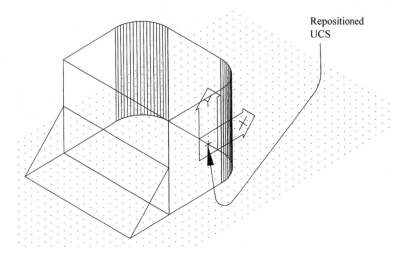

Repositioned
UCS

Figure A6.39.

Reset the VPOINT value to 0, 0, 1 and thus return to the plan view of our can (Fig. A6.40).

We will now select the ARC command and draw the handle as follows:

AutoCAD screen prompt	*Your response*
Command:	Type ARC (RETURN)

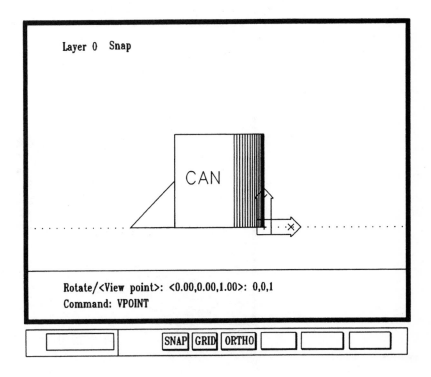

Figure A6.40.

`Centre/<Start point>:`

Type 0,0
(RETURN) (i.e. ARC
starts at 0, 0 X, Y
point from current
UCS).

`Centre/End/<Second point>:`

Type 60,60
(RETURN) (i.e.
second point of
ARC is 60, 60
X, Y from current
UCS).

`End point:`

Type 120
(RETURN) (i.e. ARC
ends at 0, 120
X, Y point from
current UCS).

Your plan view should now appear as in Fig. A6.41.

In this case, we constructed the arc by specifying three known points on its circumference. There are several other ways of drawing arcs. All alternative methods are described in Lesson 1 of Part B.

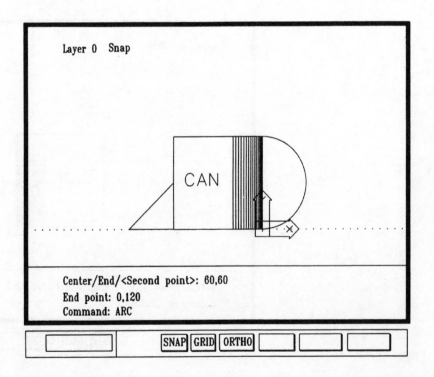

Figure A6.41.

New reset VPOINT to –1, –1, 1 to view our can, with its new handle, in 3D (Fig. A6.42).

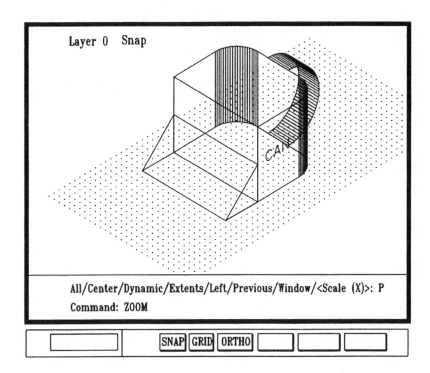

Layer 0   Snap

C·A·N

All/Center/Dynamic/Extents/Left/Previous/Window/<Scale (X)>: P
Command: ZOOM

SNAP GRID ORTHO

Figure A6.42. Retrieved 3D display via ZOOM (PREVIOUS) command.

Drawing the spout

The can needs a spout. To begin constructing this we need to change the UCS again. Do so as follows:

AutoCAD screen prompt	*Your response*
Command:	Type UCS (RETURN)
Origin/ZAxis/3point/ Entity/View/X/Y/Z/Prev/ Restore/Save/Del/?/ <World>:	Type 3 (RETURN)
Origin point <0,0,0>:	Type INT (RETURN) (for an intersection OSNAP operation).

`of:`	Move pointing device until OSNAP target sight surrounds Point A on Fig. A6.43. Then PICK.
`Point on positive portion of the X axis <1,0,0>:`	Type INT (RETURN)
`of:`	Move pointing device until OSNAP target sight surrounds Point B on Fig. A6.43. Then PICK.
`Point on the positive-Y portion of the UCS X-Y plane <0,1,0>:`	Type END (RETURN) (for ENDPOINT OSNAP operation).

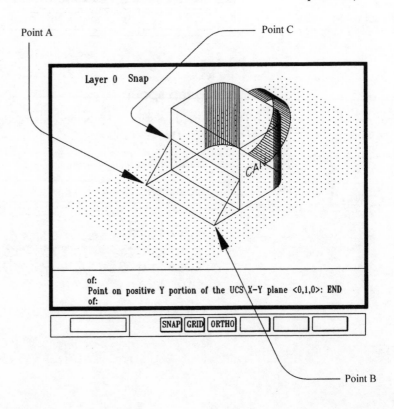

Figure A6.43. UCS 3POINT procedure.

of: Move pointing
                                             device until
                                             OSNAP target
                                             sight surrounds
                                             Point C on Fig.
                                             A6.43. Then
                                             PICK.

This time we have defined our UCS (repositioned and with a new Z axis) by specifying three known points which lie on the new XY plane. This is the 3POINT (or 3) option of the UCS command. The new UCS is indicated by the position and orientation of the UCS icon in Fig. A6.44. The direction of the new Z axis is also indicated in Fig. A6.44.

Now set the THICKNESS value to 160 via the same routine as on previous occasions.

Select the CIRCLE command and draw a circle whose centre point is specified as 80, 40 and whose radius is 16. The result is shown in Fig. A6.45. We have effectively drawn the neck for the spout of our can. It is in the form of a circle of radius 16 drawn in the current XY plane, with a centre point X = 80, Y = 40 from the current UCS, and a 3D thickness of 160 in the direction of the current Z axis. The principle is illustrated in Fig. A6.46.

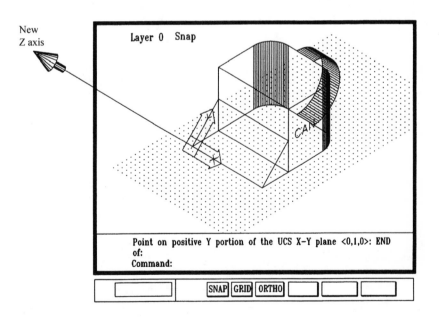

Figure A6.44.   New UCS.

Drawing the sprinkler

In order to draw the sprinkler on top of the neck of the spout, we will need to reset the UCS and the THICKNESS values once more. Do this as follows:

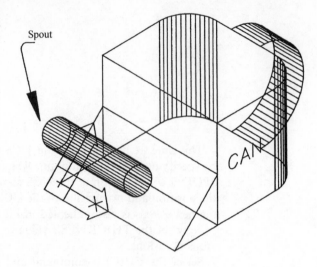

Spout

Figure A6.45.

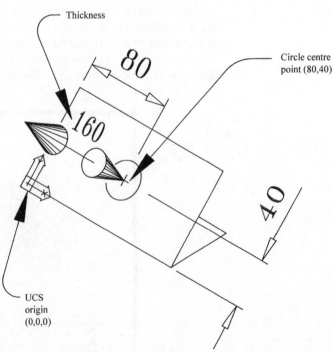

Thickness

80

160

Circle centre
point (80,40)

40

UCS
origin
(0,0,0)

Figure A6.46.

1. Select the O (origin) option of the UCS command. Use the same routine
   as in the section 'Resetting the UCS and DRAWing an ARC' (see page
   68) and enter an Origin Point value of 80, 40, 160. This takes the current
   UCS to the top centre of the neck (as shown in Fig. A6.47).
2. Use the SETVAR command to alter the THICKNESS setting to 16.
   Now select the CIRCLE command. Specify a centre point of 0, 0 and a
   radius of 40. This creates the 3D profile of the sprinkler (as shown in Fig.
   A6.48).

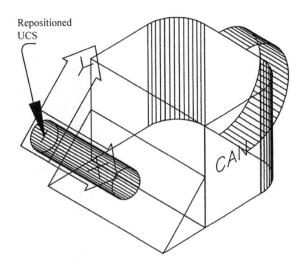

Repositioned
UCS

Figure A6.47.

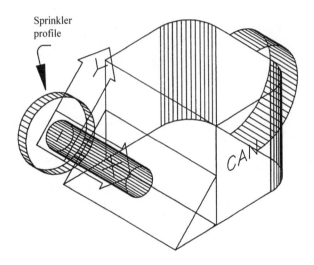

Sprinkler
profile

Figure A6.48.

Polar array of circles

We will put some holes in the sprinkler using a circular ARRAY.

Firstly, obtain the current plan view of the can by resetting VPOINT to 0, 0, 1. This gives you a view looking perpendicularly towards the sprinkler and along the axis of the spout (Fig. A6.49).

Draw another CIRCLE, of radius 4 and with centre 0, 24 from the current UCS (Fig. A6.50).

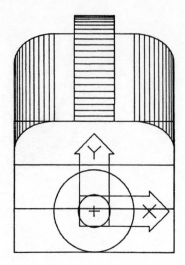

Figure A6.49.

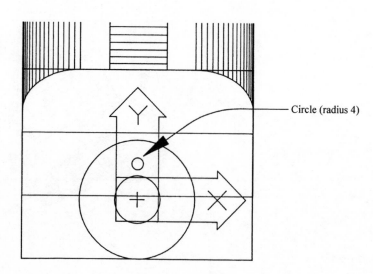

Circle (radius 4)

Figure A6.50.

Now draw an **ARRAY** of radius 4 circles around the current UCS zero datum, via the following routine:

AutoCAD screen prompt	Your response
Command:	Type ARRAY (RETURN)
Select objects:	Move pointing device until cursor pickbox touches the radius 4 circle. Then PICK.

Rectangular or polar array (R/P):	Type P (RETURN) (thus selecting a polar, i.e. a circular, array).
Centre point of array:	Type 0,0 (RETURN)
Number of items:	Type 12 (RETURN)
Angle to fill (+CCW,-=CW) <360>:	RETURN (to accept 360 degrees default angle).
Rotate objects as they are copied? <Y>:	RETURN

Your display should now be as in Fig. A6.51.

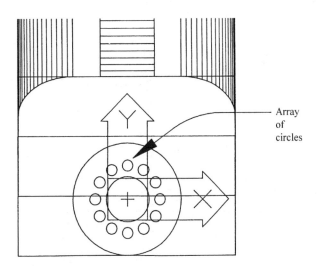

Array of circles

Figure A6.51.

Hidden line removal

Use ZOOM PREVIOUS to observe your completed can in 3D. The drawing would be much clearer if the hidden lines were removed. Type the command:

HIDE   (RETURN)

Your improved display should be as in Fig. A6.52.

Multiple views (viewports)

From Version 10 onwards, you may obtain multiple views of your drawing on a single screen. Type the command:

VIEWPORTS   (RETURN)

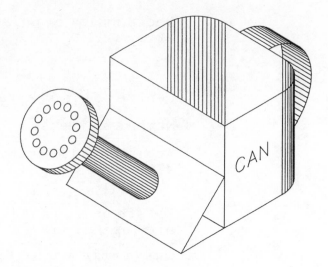

Figure A6.52.   3D view
(hidden lines removed).

AutoCAD then responds with the screen prompt:

```
Save/Restore/Delete/Join/Single/?/2/
<3>/4:
```

Respond to this by typing:

4   (RETURN)

Your screen display will then be partitioned into four equal rectangular portions (called *viewports*), with the 3D view of your can shown in each (Fig. A6.53).

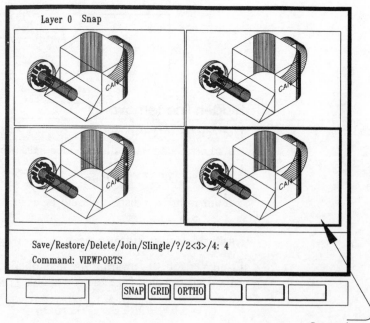

Figure A6.53.   Viewports.

Current viewpoint

You may alter the displays individually, so that each viewport could contain a different view of your can (see Fig. A6.54). If you move your pointing device, you will see that only one viewport displays the moving cursor in its cross-hairs form. This is the *current viewport*, and is the only one which may be worked on until a new current viewport is selected. The current viewport is further distinguished with a thicker border. When the cursor enters any of the non-current viewports, it becomes a small arrow. To change to a new current viewport, simply move the cursor inside the viewport you wish to be the next current one, and PICK.

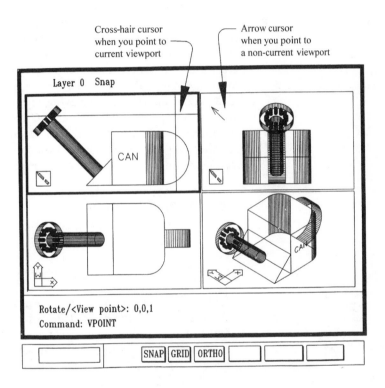

Figure A6.54.

Once you have selected your current viewport, you may treat this as your working drawing and subsequently apply any AutoCAD commands and draughting routines to this viewport in just the same way as if you had only a single view displayed. However, you should appreciate that it is only the view of your drawing that varies between viewports. If you edit, or add to, the geometry of the design, or change any settings, all views will be accordingly updated.

Reset the UCS to be the same as the WCS again, by selecting the UCS command, followed by the W option. Then, making each viewport current in turn, decide on suitable VPOINT settings or ZOOM procedures to display four viewport displays giving an overall display similar to that shown in Fig. A6.54.

Ending your drawing

Finally, type the command:

END   (RETURN)

As previously explained, this saves our current drawing to disk and takes us out of AutoCAD (or in this case, having already done some SAVEs, it updates the files CAN.DWG and CAN.BAK on the floppy disk in Drive A according to the current state of the drawing).

You should now be back in the operating system environment from which you first entered AutoCAD. You may now remove the floppy disk from its drive if you wish. Remember, this disk contains your AutoCAD drawing in the form of two files: CAN.DWG and CAN.BAK.

As previously stated, whenever you wish to retrieve your created drawing onto AutoCAD, you may do so by accessing AutoCAD via the procedure previously adopted, and then selecting the OPEN command. When AutoCAD responds by displaying the Open Drawing dialog box, you may enter your drawing filename (A:CAN in this case) using the procedure previously described in the section 'Opening existing drawings' (see page 22). Alternatively, for earlier releases, you may select the Edit an Existing Drawing option from the AutoCAD menu.

Other saving commands

For future drawing work it is useful to be aware that, along with SAVE and END, two other commands are available for saving your drawing work:

1. SAVEAS   This invokes the same dialog box display as the SAVE command, and requests the name of the drawing to save. In the case of the SAVEAS command, if you enter a new drawing name, AutoCAD saves the file and sets the current drawing to that new filename. This is in contrast to SAVE, which would save the file under the new name, but retain the original name of the current drawing.
2. QSAVE   This gives a quick saving facility. When you action this command, AutoCAD assumes that you wish to save the file to the current drawing name and does so accordingly, without requesting a filename.

Note: Remember that none of the SAVE, SAVEAS or QSAVE commands take you out of AutoCAD as the END command does. Thus, if you have completed your drawing, saved it to its current filename, and wish to remain in AutoCAD, you can execute the NEW command to begin a new drawing straightaway. Also, when the END command takes you out of AutoCAD, it always saves the file to the current drawing name.

Part B

2D draughting on AutoCAD

This part of the book contains ten lessons (Lessons 1 to 10 inclusive) which cover the principles and techniques required to become proficient in the use of AutoCAD at the level of basic 2D draughting.

Note: Before attempting any of the lessons in Part B, it is essential that you complete all the exercises in Part A. You are also advised to refer to Appendix B (covering menu options) before commencing Part B.

Lesson 1

Basic techniques

The object of this lesson is to enhance the draughting techniques covered in the practice exercise of Part A of this book, by introducing some more commands and enlarging on the options of the commands already used.

Starting up

Switch on your computer and, if you are going to save your drawing work directly to floppy disk, insert this in the appropriate drive once the system is 'booted-up'. Access AutoCAD via the operating system as described in Part A. Select the NEW command to begin a new drawing (or, if you are using a version of AutoCAD issued prior to Release 12, select the Begin a New Drawing option of the AutoCAD menu). Then enter any new drawing name you wish, with regard to the drive/directory on which the drawing will be saved, for example:

```
A:JSMITH1
```

Then PICK the OK box.

Drawing set-up

With reference to Part A, make the following drawing settings:

LIMITS	0, 0 (lower left corner)
	750, 500 (upper right corner)
SNAP	Set snap spacing to 10
GRID	Set grid spacing to 10. OFF
CTRL-B	Sets SNAP to OFF

The LINE command

The following LINE exercise serves as a revision of techniques encountered in Part A by using a variety of drawing modes, and also introduces some new options of the LINE command.

Proceed as follows:

AutoCAD screen prompt	*Your response*
Command:	Select LINE
From point:	Type 30,130 (RETURN)
To point:	Type @50,-100 (RETURN)
To point:	Type @120<90 (RETURN)
To point:	Type CTRL-B (to toggle SNAP ON) or PICK SNAP from Windows status bar.
To point: <Snap on>	Move cursor until top status line shows 98.99<45. Then PICK.
To point:	Type CTRL-D (to toggle COORDS ON).
To point: <Coords on>	Move cursor until top status line shows 410.260. Then PICK. (Your display should now be as Fig. L1.1.)
To point:	Type CTRL-G (to toggle GRID ON) or PICK GRID from Windows status bar.
To point: <Grid on>	Move cursor to Point A in Fig. L1.2. Then PICK.
To point:	Move cursor to Point B in Fig. L1.2. Then PICK.
To point:	Move cursor to Point C in Fig. L1.2. Then PICK.
To point:	Move cursor to Point D in Fig. L1.2. Then PICK.

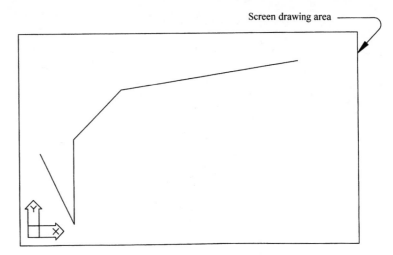

Figure L1.1.

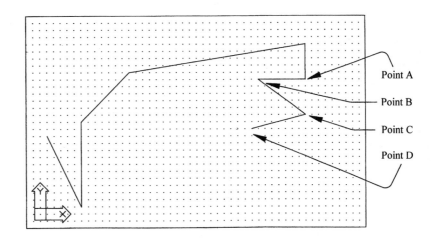

Figure L1.2.

To point:	Select the U (i.e. UNDO) option of the LINE command (e.g. by typing:
	U RETURN
	or via screen menu/ toolbar). (The last line you drew will be erased.)
To point: u	Select the U option again. The last-line-but-one you drew will be erased and your display should now be as Fig. L1.3.

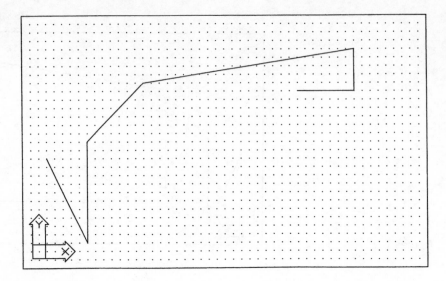

Figure L1.3. Two lines
undone.

To point: u   Select the C (i.e. CLOSE)
                                     option of the LINE
                                     command (e.g. by typing:

                                        C   RETURN

                                     or via screen menu/
                                     toolbar).

To point: c

Command:

Your display should now be as in Fig. L1.4.

CTRL key settings

We have already used some examples of making quick changes to drawing
mode settings by pressing the CTRL key and another key simultaneously. In
most cases the action results in 'toggling' a setting to ON or OFF from its
current state. (This may be done in mid-command if required.) The most
important examples are:

CTRL-B   Toggles SNAP ON/OFF

CTRL-C   Cancels your current command sequence and retrieves
          the Command: screen prompt

CTRL-D   Circular toggle for coordinate display: polar, dynamic
          WY, static XY, as described in Part A

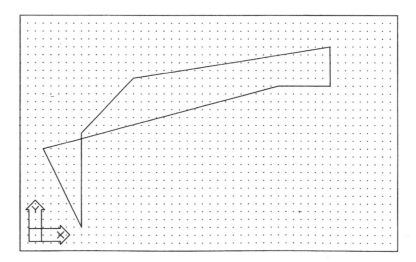

Figure L1.4. Lines closed.

CTRL-E   Circular toggle for Isoplane setting in isometric
          drawings (see Lesson 8)

CTRL-G   Toggles GRID ON/OFF

CTRL-O   Toggles ORTHO mode ON/OFF. For example, when
          ORTHO is ON, lines are automatically drawn
          vertically or horizontally from their start point

Note: If you are using AutoCAD Windows, you may use screen pointing
to PICK: SNAP, GRID, ORTHO or the coordinate displays as an alternative to CTRL-B, CTRL-G, CTRL-O and CTRL-D, respectively.

The CIRCLE command

In Part A we drew some circles by specifying CENTRE POINT and
RADIUS (the radius value being specified either via numerical input at
the keyboard or by 'dragging' the radius to size with the pointing device
and cursor). The other methods of drawing circles are:

- Specifying CENTRE POINT and DIAMETER (D option)
- Specifying 3 POINTS on the circumference of the circle (3P option)
- Specifying 2 ENDPOINTS for the diameter of the circle (2P option)
- Specifying TANGENTS to TWO EXISTING OBJECTS and the
  CIRCLE RADIUS (TTR option)

As in the previous LINE exercise, the following CIRCLE exercise will
make use of a number of different drawing modes. Start the new exercise by
ERASING some items of the LINE exercise to achieve the display in Fig.
L1.5, and switching GRID to OFF via CTRL-G. Note that, after each circle
has been drawn, the command is repeated by executing RETURN.

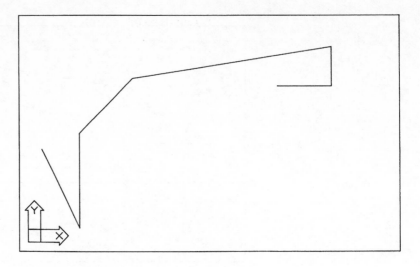

Figure L1.5.

Proceed as follows:

AutoCAD screen prompt	*Your response*
Command:	Select CIRCLE
3P/2P/TTR/<Centre point>:	Specify circle centre point of 220, 130
Diameter/<Radius>:	Type 40 (RETURN) (This creates a circle of 40 RADIUS and gives a display as Fig. L1.6a.)
Command:	RETURN (to reselect CIRCLE).
3P/2P/TTR/<Centre point>:	Type @ (RETURN) (Thus retrieving the last point specified— i.e. 220, 130—as the centre point of the new circle).
Diameter/<Radius>:	Select DIAMETER (D option), for example by typing:
	D RETURN
	or via screen menu/ toolbar).

Diameter: Type 40 (RETURN)
                                       (This creates a circle
                                       of 40 DIAMETER,
                                       and gives a display as
                                       in Fig. L1.6b.)

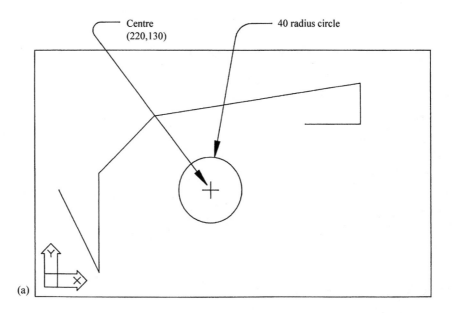

Centre
(220,130)   40 radius circle

(a)

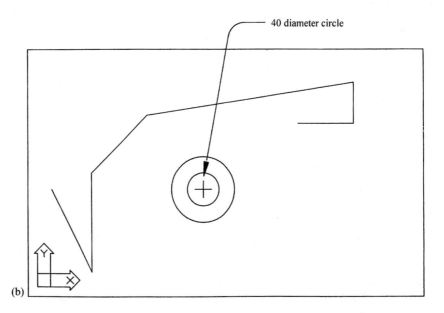

40 diameter circle

Figure L1.6.   (a) Drawing
a circle via default
Centre/Radius option; (b)
drawing a circle via
Centre/Diameter option.   (b)

`Command:`	RETURN
`3P/2P/TTR/<Center point>:`	Select 3P option (e.g. by typing:
	3P RETURN
	or via screen menu/ toolbar).
`First point:`	Move cursor approximately to Point A in Fig. L1.7. Then PICK.
`Second point:`	Move cursor approximately to Point B in Fig. L1.7. Then PICK.
`Third point:`	Move cursor approximately to Point C in Fig. L1.7. Then PICK.
`Command:`	RETURN
`3P/2P/TTR/<Center point>:`	Select 3P option as previously.

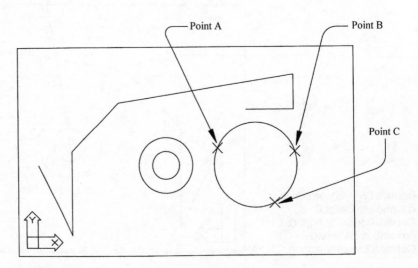

Figure L1.7.   Drawing a
circle via 3P option.

First point: Type TAN (RETURN)

to   PICK Line D with
                                OSNAP target sight
                                (Fig. L1.8a).

Second point: Type TAN (RETURN)

to   PICK circle E with
                                OSNAP target sight
                                (Fig L1.8a).

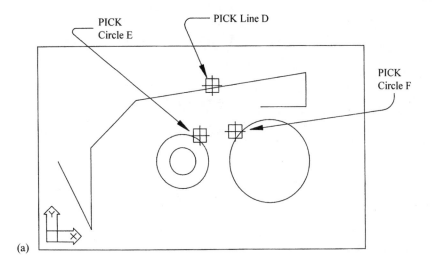

(a)

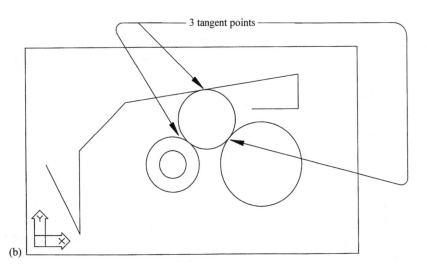

(b)

Figure L1.8. (a) 3P circle technique (using OSNAP TAN to a line and two circles); (b) completed 3P circle.

Third point:	Type TAN (RETURN)
to	PICK circle F with OSNAP target sight (Fig. L1.8a). (Your display should now be as Fig. L1.8b.)
Command:	RETURN
3P/2P/TTR/<Center point>:	Select 3P option again.
First point:	Type TAN (RETURN)
to	PICK circle E with OSNAP target sight (Fig. L1.9a).
Second point:	Type TAN (RETURN)
to	PICK Line H with OSNAP target sight (Fig. L1.9a).
Third point:	Type TAN (RETURN)
to	PICK Line J with OSNAP target sight (Fig. L1.9a). (Your display should now be as Fig. L1.9b.)
Command:	RETURN
3P/2P/TTR/<Center point>:	Select 2P option.
First point on diameter:	Type 100,50 (RETURN)
Second point on diameter:	Move cursor approximately to Point K in Fig. L1.10. Then PICK.
Command:	RETURN
3P/2P/TTR/<Center point>:	Select TTR option.

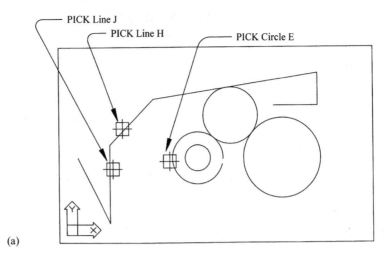

(a)

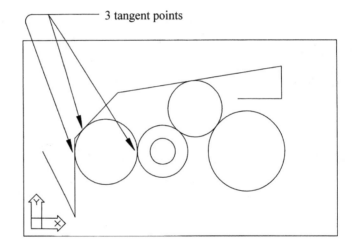

(b)

Figure L1.9.   (a) 3P circle technique (using OSNAP TAN to a circle and two lines); (b) completed 3P circle.

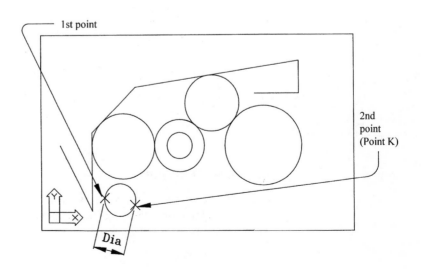

Figure L1.10.   2P circle technique.

```
Enter Tangent spec:
```
Note OSNAP target sight automatically displayed. Move this to PICK Circle L in Fig. L1.11a.

```
Enter second Tangent spec:
```
Move OSNAP target sight to PICK Line M (Fig. L1.11a).

```
Radius:
```
Type 100 (RETURN) (Fig. L1.11b)

```
Command:
```

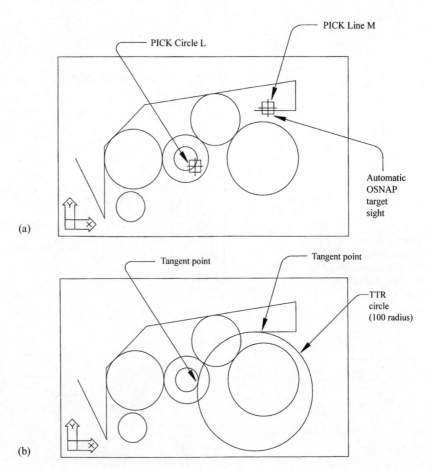

Figure L1.11.   (a) TTR circle technique; (b) completed circle display.

(a)

(b)

The UNDO marker

As this stage of our drawing, we will use the UNDO command to set a 'marker'. The purpose of this will become apparent later in the lesson. For now, just proceed as follows:

1. Select the UNDO command
2. Select the MARK option, e.g. by typing: M (RETURN), or via the screen menu/toolbar

The ARC command

An arc is part of a circle. In AutoCAD, there are many arc options, which are determined via different combinations of a number of standard parameters.

In the following exercise, we will draw four arcs by specifying:

1. Three points on the arc circumference (3P)
2. A start point, centre point, and endpoint (S, C, E)
3. A start point, centre point, and included angle (S, C, A)
4. A start point, centre point, and length of chord (S, C, L)

The exercise assumes a basic format in which the ARC command is successively repeated via RETURN, and the different types of arc parameters are specified at the keyboard (the procedure would vary slightly for screen menu selection). As with the previous LINE and CIRCLE exercises, a mixture of different drawing modes are employed. (Note that, after two parameters have been specified, the third arc parameter may be dragged to size via cursor if required.)

Start the exercise by ERASING all the existing objects (i.e. erase all the lines and circles in Fig. L1.11b). Then, using CTRL-D to change the screen coordinate display mode when required, proceed as follows:

AutoCAD screen prompt	*Your response*
`Command:`	Select ARC
`Center/<Start point>:`	Type 170,150 (RETURN) (Thus START POINT is specified.)
`Center/End/<Second point>:`	Type 200,220 (RETURN) (Thus SECOND POINT is specified.)
`End point:`	Move cursor to 80, 180 (watch arc being dragged to its END POINT. PICK. See 3P ARC drawn (Fig. L1.12a).

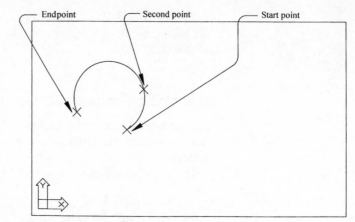

(a)

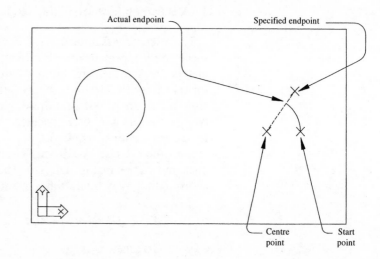

(b)

Figure L1.12.   (a) Drawing an arc to 3 points (default option); (b) drawing an arc via Start/Centre/End; (c) drawing an arc via Start/Centre/Angle;

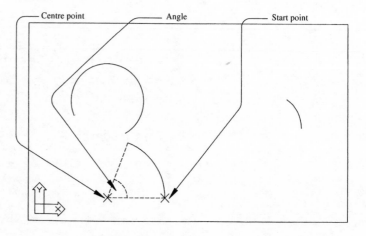

(c)

Command:	RETURN
ARC Center/<Start point>:	Type 480,160 (RETURN) (Thus START POINT is specified.)
Center/End/<Second point>:	Type C (RETURN) (or use option menu/ toolbar).
Center:	Type @-60,0 (RETURN) (Thus CENTRE POINT is specified.)
Angle/Length of chord/ <End point>:	Move cursor to 470, 230 (watch arc being dragged to its END POINT. PICK. See S, C, E arc drawn. (Actual end point lies on line joining point 470, 230 to centre point.) (Fig. L1.12b)
Command:	RETURN
Arc Center/<Start point>:	Move cursor to 240, 40. PICK. (Thus START POINT is specified.)
Center/End/<Second point>:	Type C (RETURN)
Center:	Move cursor to 140, 40. PICK. (Thus CENTRE POINT is specified.)
Angle/Length of chord/ <End point>:	Type A (RETURN) (or use options menu/ toolbar).
Included angle:	Type 70 (RETURN) (Thus the ARC ANGLE is specified. See S, C, A arc drawn.) (Fig. L1.12c)

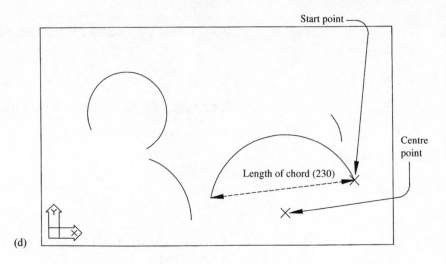

(d)

Figure L1.12.   (d) drawing an arc via Start/Centre/ Chord Length; (e) completed arc exercise.

(e)

Command:	RETURN
Arc center/<Start point>:	Type 500,100 (RETURN) (Thus **START POINT** is specified.)
Center/End/<Second point>:	Type C (RETURN)
Center:	Type 390,50 (RETURN) (Thus **CENTRE POINT** is specified.)
Angle/length of chord/ <End point>:	Type L (RETURN)

Length of chord:	Type 230 (RETURN) (Thus CHORD LENGTH is specified. See S, C, L arc drawn.) (Fig. L1.12d)
Command:	

Your display of arcs should now be as Fig. L1.12e.

The PAN command

PAN is a display facility which allows you to view your drawing at a new position without changing magnification. As with the ZOOM command, it is you, the viewer, who has moved position—the drawn objects do not alter their coordinate positions after a PAN operation.

Proceed with a PAN routine as follows:

AutoCAD screen prompt	*Your response*
Command:	Select PAN.
Displacement:	Move your cursor approximately to point A in Fig. L1.13a. PICK.
Second point:	Move your cursor approximately to point B in Fig. L1.13a. PICK.
Command:	

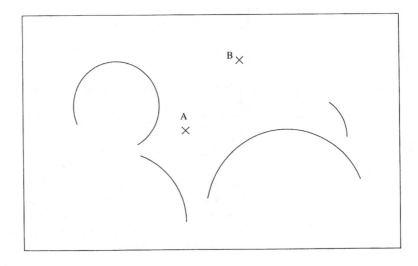

Figure L1.13. (a) Panning;

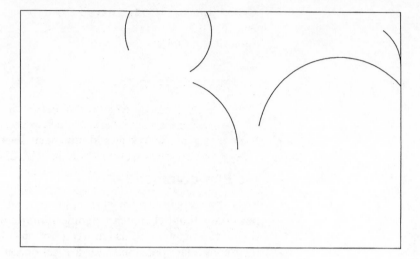

Figure L1.13.   (b) panned display.

Your panned display should now be as in Fig. L1.13b.

Note: If you are using later releases of AutoCAD Windows, you may use the drawing area scroll bars as an alternative to the PAN command.

U, UNDO and REDO

The U and UNDO commands comprise a useful tool which allows you to record all your drawing steps on a memory stack, and go back through the stack to any earlier stage. The U command has only the simplest facility of the UNDO command—that of retrieving previous drawing stages in single reverse order steps. The UNDO command has more complex facilities, e.g. that of taking you back to a previously MARKed stage of the drawing (see 'The UNDO marker', page 94).

Proceed as follows:

1. Select the U command. (The previous PAN operation will be undone, thus retrieving Fig. L1.12e.)
2. RETURN, to repeat the U command. (Another step will be undone, thus retrieving Fig. L1.12c.)
3. RETURN again. (Thus undo to Fig. L1.12b.)
4. Select the REDO command. (This will 'undo-the-last-undo' operation, thus taking you back to Fig. L1.12c again.)
5. Select the UNDO command. Then select the BACK option. You will now be taken back to the stage of the drawing which was given a 'marker' via the MARK option of the UNDO command. Thus Fig. L1.11b will be retrieved.)

While very useful, the UNDO facility can be demanding on computer memory, and thus may be switched off, if required, via the CONTROL option of the UNDO command.

Drawing regeneration

When a drawing is regenerated, AutoCAD recalculates the geometric data for all drawn entities according to current settings. This may be time-consuming. Thus frequent regenerations may not always be desirable.

A regeneration may be forced via the REGEN command, or it may occur as an automatic facility of certain commands. For example, some ZOOM options automatically invoke a regeneration.

Further ZOOM options and the VIEW command

In Part A, we used the ZOOM command via three of its options, namely WINDOW (W), ALL (A) and PREVIOUS (P). In the next exercise, we will use three more ZOOM options and also use the VIEW command (by which we may name, save and restore any chosen zoomed view).

Proceed as follows:

1. Select ZOOM. Then type:

    .25X   (RETURN)

   This procedure may be used to magnify or diminish your screen display to a stated scale. In this case, your display should now be diminished to a scale of 0.25, or a quarter (Fig. L1.14).
2. Select the VIEW command. Select the SAVE option. Then type any view name, such as:

    TESTVIEW   (RETURN)

   Thus our scaled view is now saved under the chosen name.

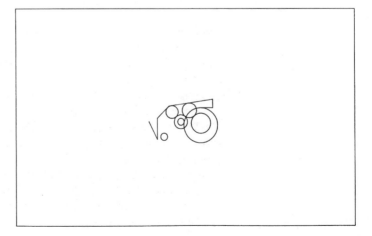

Figure L1.14.   ZOOM .25X.

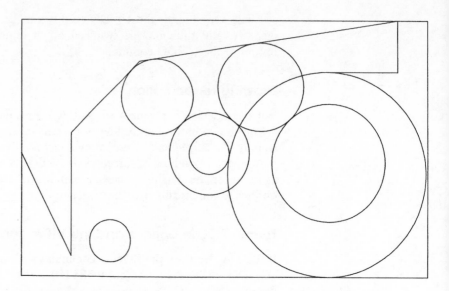

Figure L1.15.   ZOOM
EXTENTS.

3. Select the ZOOM command. Select the EXTENTS (E) option. Our
drawing will now be magnified with its full extent filling the screen
(Fig. L1.15).
4. Reselect the ZOOM command. Select the DYNAMIC (D) option. This
combines the ZOOM and PAN principle in a single operation. The first
effect of selecting the DYNAMIC option is that you will see your drawing on a diminished display along with a number of coloured box windows, namely: a white box showing the drawing limits; a red box
showing the generated area; a green box showing your current display
area (immediately prior to selecting the DYNAMIC option); a view box
with a 'x' at its centre (this is initially the same size and position as the
current view, but when you move your pointing device the view box
moves to take up the position at which you intend to pan your display).
The four boxes, with the view box being panned, are shown in Fig.
L1.16a. If you pan your view box outside the red box, an 'hour glass'
icon appears, to show that a regeneration would occur if you completed
the command at this panned position. When you have panned the view
box approximately to the position shown in Fig. L1.16a, then PICK.
Now move your pointing device to observe the view box enlarging or
diminishing, depending on direction of movement. Adjust the box size
approximately to the diminished size shown in Fig. L1.16b, and
RETURN. Your resulting display should be similar to Fig. L1.16c.
(Note that the diminished view box area now fills the screen, giving a
magnified zoom effect.)
5. Select the VIEW command. Select the RESTORE (R) option. Then type
the viewname chosen in (2):

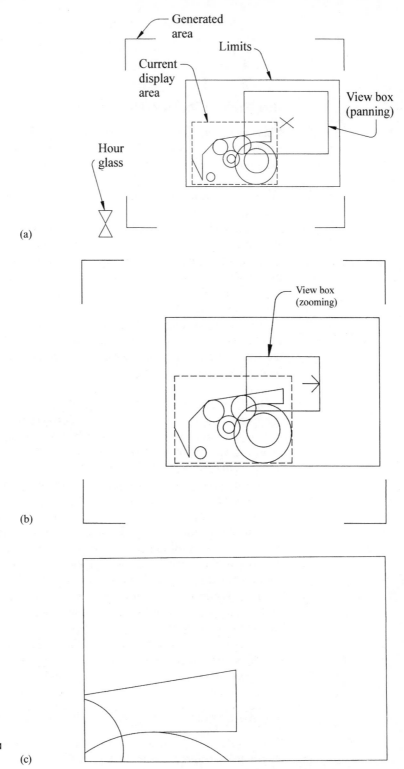

Generated area

Limits

Current display area

View box (panning)

Hour glass

(a)

View box (zooming)

(b)

Figure L1.16.   ZOOM DYNAMIC. (a) View box being panned; (b) view box diminished; (c) diminished view box area fills screen.

(c)

TESTVIEW   (RETURN)

The view previously saved in (2) should now be restored to the screen (Fig. L1.14).

The Aerial View facility

This useful device is available only if you are using AutoCAD in the Microsft Windows or Windows NT environment. Aerial View is a navigational tool that displays a view of the drawing in a separate window, enabling the user to quickly locate, and move to, a specific area. If you leave the Aerial View window open as you work, you can ZOOM and PAN without entering a command or choosing a menu option.

Aerial View is accessed by PICKing the Aerial View icon from the Tool Windows Flyout palette of the Standard toolbar (Release 13 onwards).

Having thus displayed the Aerial View window, you may ZOOM or PAN by PICKing either of these options from the Aerial View window menu bar. If you select ZOOM, you may PICK two opposite corners of a Zoom box within the Aerial View window. The area you specified then becomes the current screen display in the main drawing area window. If you select PAN, then a Pan box is created the same size as the current view box. This may be moved around inside the Aerial View window with your pointing device, before PICKing a chosen position to see a panned view in the main drawing display.

One of the most versatile options of Aerial View is the LOCATE facility. A typical screen display during the locate routine is shown in Fig. L1.17. You will see that the Aerial View window contains a magnified view of the main drawing display. Depending on your Release of AutoCAD, this magnified display may be obtained either by pressing the CTRL key and the PICK button of your pointing device simultaneously, or by PICKing LOCATE from the Options menu of the Aerial View window. A small cross-hairs cursor then appears in the main drawing area window. You may move this cursor around with your pointing device and observe the magnified display being simultaneously and dynamically panned to the equivalent position of the cursor in the Aerial View window. When you have achieved the magnified view your require, you may PICK to retain this view. The size of magnification may be adjusted via a small dialog box which is activated by selecting the Locator Magnification option from the Options menu of the Aerial View window.

Being a 'Microsoft-type' window, the Aerial View window may be moved to any required area of the screen, and may be resized using the standard Windows procedures described in Appendix B.

Infinite construction lines (XLINEs) and RAYs

From Release 13 onwards, you can create construction lines of infinite length in one direction (called A RAY) or in both directions (called an

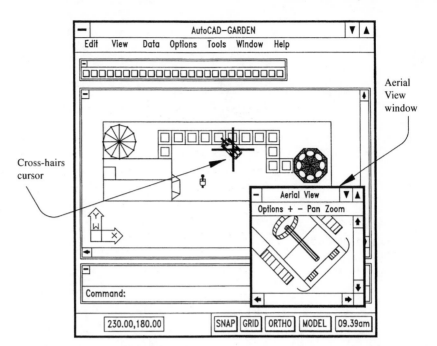

Figure L1.17. Aerial View
(Locate option).

XLINE). These infinite lines may be used as a reference for creating other objects. For example, you can use construction lines to create temporary intersections for use with object snapping, or as projection lines for creating multiple views of the same item. Infinite lines do not change the total area of the drawing. Thus their infinite dimensions have no effect on display routines such as zooming. You may edit infinite lines via commands such as COPY and ROTATE, in the same way as any other object.

If you have Release 13 onwards, proceed as follows:

1. ZOOM to an unused area of the screen.
2. Select the XLINE command.
3. AutoCAD responds by displaying a `From point:` prompt.
4. Respond by moving your pointing device approximately to the 'From point' shown in Fig. L1.18, and PICK.
5. AutoCAD responds by display a `Through point:` prompt.
6. Respond by moving your pointing device approximately to one of the 'Through points' shown in Fig. L1.18.
7. AutoCAD then continues to repeat the `Through point:` prompt after each successive point is defined. PICK two more 'Through points' similar to those in Fig. L1.18.
8. Finally RETURN, to complete the XLINE command. Your display should be similar to Fig. L1.19.

The sequence of operations in the RAY command is exactly the same as that for XLINE, but infinite ray lines radiate from the 'From point' in one direction only. The equivalent display which could be expected for RAY lines is shown in Fig. L1.20.

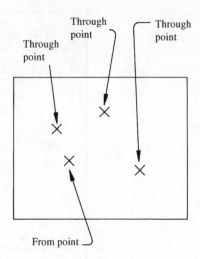

Figure L1.18.
Construction line (XLINE)
procedure.

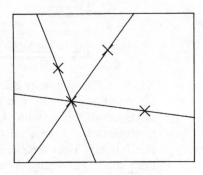

Figure L1.19.   Completed
XLINE display.

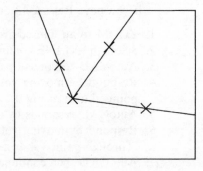

Figure L1.20.   Equivalent
RAY display.

End of lesson

If you wish to end your AutoCAD session at this stage, use the END command to save your current drawing and exit AutoCAD.

If you wish to continue with more AutoCAD work, use one of the SAVE commands (i.e. SAVE, SAVEAS or QSAVE) and begin another drawing via the NEW command.

Lesson 2

Draughting aids and set-up

Configuring AutoCAD

When you configure AutoCAD you effectively customize it to suit the particular makes and models of hardware items that you are running the AutoCAD program on (graphics screen, plotter, digitizer, etc.). To do this you must select specific *device drivers* for your hardware equipment. A device driver is a 'tailor-made' software file which translates AutoCAD graphics codes into codes which control a specific piece of hardware. For example, you would need to select the unique device driver for a Canon BJC800 inkjet plotter if you wished to use this type of plotter with AutoCAD. The AutoCAD package contains a range of device drivers for popular makes and models of hardware. If you wish to use AutoCAD on a hardware device not directly supported by AutoCAD, a special device-independent driver called the ADI (Advanced Draughting Interface) is supplied with the package. This enables hardware manufacturers to produce their own device drivers which will communicate with AutoCAD via the ADI driver.

Configuration procedures commence automatically when AutoCAD is first installed. Once configuration is completed, the device driver files (all those with the extension .DRV) may be removed from the computer hard disk if required, until any new hardware device is introduced.

Thus, all the previous exercises have assumed that AutoCAD is already configured for your hardware devices. If your device driver files are still on hard disk you may use the CONFIG command to reconfigure AutoCAD at any time. Practice configuration routines may thus be done during your training. However, *an AutoCAD configuration routine should only be undertaken in the presence of an experienced system user.*

Prototype drawing

When you begin a new AutoCAD drawing you are really editing an existing *prototype* drawing which already has certain settings (LIMITS, SNAP value, etc.). The standard default prototype is on a drawing file called

ACAD.DWG, which normally is automatically invoked after you specify the name of your new drawing. Alternatively, you may use your own prototype instead of ACAD.DWG.

Proceed with a prototype drawing exercise as follows:

1. Enter AutoCAD and begin a new drawing for floppy disk, with a name such as:

   A:SETTINGS

2. Use the commands LIMITS, SNAP and GRID to make settings with values similar to those in Lesson 1.
3. Leaving GRID ON, END the drawing.
4. Now automatically invoke these settings on another new drawing (e.g. called JSMITH2) by re-entering AutoCAD, selecting the NEW command, PICKing the entry box to the right of Prototype in the resulting dialog display, deleting any existing text, and entering:

   A:SETTINGS

   Then PICK the entry box to the right of New Drawing Name, and enter an appropriate name such as:

   A:JSMITH2

   Then PICK the OK box.

   A new drawing is thus created on floppy disk called JSMITH2, using the previous drawing SETTINGS as the prototype.
5. Note that your new drawing already has GRID ON, as set by the prototype drawing. Move your cursor and use the top coordinate display to check that your SNAP and GRID values are the same as those set in the prototype drawing.

Layers

Using layers is like doing each different part of your drawing on a separate transparent sheet. Being transparent the sheets (or *layers*) could be stacked in a pile to see the complete drawing, but the top sheet (or *current layer*) is the only one you could actually draw on at any one time. Alternatively, you could take sheets out of the stack, or put them back again whenever you like, to view different combinations. (This is called 'turning layers OFF or ON'.) Layering is thus a useful tool for logically structuring your drawing by grouping related objects on the same layer. Also, different colours and linetypes may be specified for each layer.

In AutoCAD the number of layers you may have on a single drawing is unlimited. They may be created at any stage in your drawing and be given any name you wish. (Names can be up to 31 characters long, containing any combination of letters and/or numbers. The name may also contain the characters '$', '-' and '_' but not the characters '.' ',' or ';'.)

The most important options in the LAYER command are:

- ?   Gives a list of existing layers and their settings
- SET (S)   Specifies the CURRENT layer you will draw on
- NEW (N)   Creates new layers
- ON/OFF   Turns specified layers on or off
- COLOR (C)   Specifies the colour of objects on a layer
- LTYPE (L)   Specifies the linetype for a layer, e.g. CONTINUOUS, HIDDEN, CENTER
- FREEZE (F)   Makes a specified layer invisible and prevents its entities being regenerated. This saves time by 'ignoring' these entities every time the drawing is regenerated
- THAW (T)   'Unfreezes' a specified layer, i.e. restores visibility of layer entities and sets them to be regenerated
- LOCK (LO)   Allows you to keep specified layers visible while making them unaffected by editing procedures. For example, items drawn on a layer which is locked would not be erased if they were contained in a window during object selection in the ERASE command
- UNLOCK (U)   Unlocks specified layers which are currently locked

Exercise in layers

The following exercise assumes the use of standard options (selected via keyboard or screen/tablet menus). Alternatively, layer settings may be actioned via a dialog box procedure. The latter approach is discussed after the initial exercise.

Proceed as follows:

1. Select the LAYER command. If this is done by keyboard, the traditional procedure outlined below will result.
2. Observe the options displayed. Select the NEW (N) option.
   We will now create two new layers called HIDE and CTR. Thus type:

   HIDE, CTR   (RETURN)

3. Select the option: ?. Observe the default input: < * >. This means 'all layers'. RETURN to accept this default. Observe the list of layers (Fig. L2.1). (Note that 'Layer 0' is listed along with your two new ones. Layer 0 is the single existing layer on the standard default prototype drawing.)

Layer name	State	Color	Linetype
0	On	7 (white)	Continuous
HIDE	On	7 (white)	Continuous
CTR	On	7 (white)	Continuous
Current layer: 0			

Figure L2.1.

4. Select the LTYPE (L) option. Then type in the name of the linetype:

> HIDDEN   (RETURN)

Now type:

> HIDE   (RETURN)

(thus specifying the HIDDEN linetype on layer HIDE).

5. Select the LTYPE option again and specify CENTER linetype on layer CTR, as in (4).
6. Now select ?, then * as before, to see the revised layer list.
7. Select the COLOR (C) option and specify colour RED on layer HIDE and then GREEN on layer CTR (the same way as you specified the linetypes).
8. Select ? and * again. See the further revised list (Fig. L2.2).

Layer name	State	Color	Linetype
0	On	7 (white)	Continuous
HIDE	On	1 (red)	Hidden
CTR	On	3 (green)	Center
Current layer: 0			

Figure L2.2.

9. Do a RETURN to exit the LAYER command.
10. On layer 0 (current layer) draw any LINE similar to 'a' in Fig. L2.3.
11. Reselect LAYER. Select the SET (S) option. Enter HIDE as the new current layer. HIDE is now the current layer (as shown at top left of screen). Exit the LAYER command as before.
12. Draw any CIRCLE similar to 'b' in Fig. L2.3. (Note that it has been automatically displayed with the HIDDEN linetype as specified for layer HIDE.)
13. Now use the S option of LAYER again to set CTR as the new current layer, and then draw a LINE similar to 'c' in Fig. L2.3. (Note that this line has the CENTER linetype, as specified for layer CTR.)
14. Now reset layer 0 as the current layer. Select the OFF option of the LAYER command and specify HIDE as the layer name to turn off. Observe the new display with layer HIDE turned off. Turn off layer CTR the same way. Observe the new display. Use the ? option to see the revised layer settings.
15. Use the ON option of the LAYER command to turn layers HIDE and CTR on again. See the resulting display.
16. Exit the LAYER command.

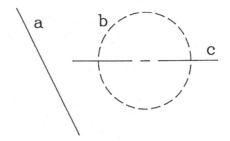

Figure L2.3.

Controlling layers via dialog box

The Layer Control dialog box may be displayed by selecting the DDLMODES command (e.g. by the keyboard). Alternatively, it may be obtained directly via your pointing device by PICKing LAYERS from the Data menu (MSDOS and Windows) or the Object Properties toolbar (AutoCAD Release 13 Windows onwards).

Proceed as follows:

1. Obtain the Layer Control dialog box by one of the procedures outlined above.
2. If you have worked through the previous layers exercise you should see a display similar to Fig. L2.4a. Note that our three existing layers: 0, HIDE and CTR are listed, along with their current settings, in the largest text box.
3. Create a new layer called NEWLAY by typing this name in at the Layer Name edit box (refer to Fig. L2.4a), and then PICKing the NEW box with your pointing device. The new layer name will then be added to the list of existing layers in the box above, along with its default settings: ON, Color: WHITE, and Linetype: CONTINUOUS.

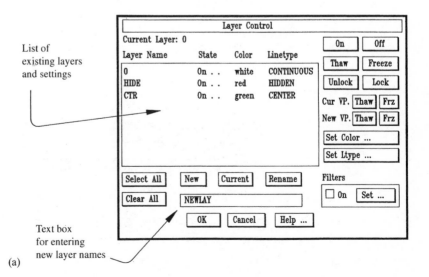

Figure L2.4. (a) The Layer Control dialog box;

(a)

4. We will now change the current settings of the new layer. Select the new layer by PICKing NEWLAY from the list of layers with your pointing device. The selected layer name and its current settings will then be highlighted.

5. Switch the selected layer, NEWLAY, off by PICKing the OFF button in the dialog display. Note that the ON/OFF setting for NEWLAY has been correspondingly changed in the list of layers. Switch NEWLAY back on again by PICKing the ON box.

6. Change the colour of NEWLAY by PICKing the SET COLOR box. This actions the display of a sub-dialog box in the form of a palette of colours. PICK a suitable colour and then PICK the OK box. You will thus be returned to the Layer Controls dialog box with the new colour name shown against NEWLAY in the list of layers.

7. A similar sub-dialog box procedure is available for changing the line-type setting of a selected layer. Set NEWLAY to a new linetype by PICKing the SET LTYPE box.

8. Set the new layer to be the current one by PICKing the CURRENT box. NEWLAY will then appear against the CURRENT LAYER title.

9. Now select one of the existing layers (0, HIDE or CTR) as in (4), and change its settings as in (5)–(8).

10. Make 0 the current layer again. Switch all layers on by PICKing the SELECT ALL box, and then PICKing the ON box.

11. PICK the OK box. This retains the settings made and takes us out of the Layer Control dialog box display.

Layer Control via toolbar icons

In the Windows version of AutoCAD you can also action layer routines described previously by PICKing appropriate icons in the Object Properties toolbar. An explanation of these icons is shown in Fig. L2.4b.

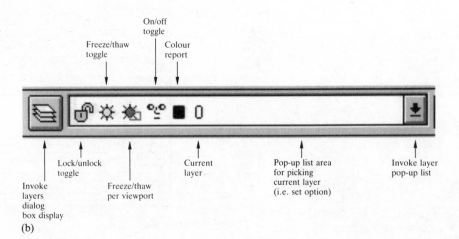

Figure L2.4. (b) Object Properties toolbar.

(b)

Layer filters

If you are working with a large number of existing layers it is sometimes convenient to get selected group listings of layers according to common properties. This may be done via the Filters Set box in the Layer Control dialog box display. You would consequently be taken through a sub-dialog box procedure, via which you could make your required layer filter settings. Only those layers which conformed to the current filter settings would then appear in the layer list of the Layer Control dialog box when the Filters box is set to ON. Using this facility you could, for example: get a list of all layers set to COLOR RED; all layers which are set to ON and have CENTER LINETYPE; all layers having names beginning with the letters PIPE . . . ; and so on.

LTSCALE

The LTSCALE command allows adjustment of segments and gap lengths for broken linetypes such as HIDDEN and CENTER.
    Proceed as follows:

1. Select LTSCALE.
2. The default scale factor value is 1. Enter a higher value (say 3). Observe the new appearance of the linetypes.
3. Reselect LTSCALE and enter a smaller value (say 0.4). See the effect.
4. Reset LTSCALE back to 1.

The LINETYPE and COLOR commands

Linetypes and colours of objects may be controlled independently of layers via the LINETYPE and COLOR commands. For example, if you selected the COLOR command and entered RED as the chosen colour, all subsequent objects would be drawn in red (whatever colour is specified on the current layer) until a new colour is set by reselecting COLOR.
    Thus, to avoid confusing effects, you should not attempt to use these two commands in conjunction with layer techniques. In this book, we will be using layers to structure our drawings and will therefore assume that colours and linetypes will be set via the LTYPE and COLOR options of the LAYER command and not via the LINETYPE and COLOR commands, which will be permanently set at BYLAYER (the default setting which automatically adopts the linetype or colour set for the current layer).

The POINT command

This command records the location of a specified point on your drawing. Although not forming part of any construction, it can be a useful tool, particularly as a 'node' from which to construct other objects. This is explained later. Proceed as follows.

Select the POINT command and PICK a point similar to 'd' in Fig. L2.5. Do a REDRAW to see your point displayed. (Usually, it will be shown as a small dot.)

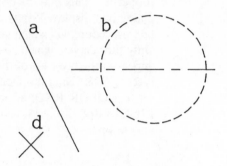

Figure L2.5.

System variables (the SETVAR command)

The SETVAR command allows you to make 'semi-permanent' settings to a range of *system variables*. For example, one system variable is called PICKBOX, which allows adjustment to the size of the pickbox edit cursor. Proceed as follows.

Select SETVAR, then enter PICKBOX as the system variable. The default pickbox size is 3. Enter 25 as the new value. Now select an edit command such as ERASE and move your pointing device. Note the enlarged pickbox. Cancel the erase command via CTRL-C. Reselect SETVAR and reset PICKBOX back to 3.

The PDMODE system variable controls the type of display for specified POINTS. Options include: dot (.), vertical cross (+), diagonal cross (×), vertical bar (|), nothing (OFF). Also the PDSIZE system variable controls the size of the points displayed. Proceed as follows.

Select SETVAR and specify PDMODE as the system variable. Enter 3 as the pdmode value. When out of the SETVAR command, select the REGEN command. Note that your point is now displayed as a diagonal cross (×) as in Fig. L2.5.

Some system variables are 'read only', i.e. they cannot be changed via SETVAR. For example, the system variable CLAYER automatically changes the screen display of the current layer setting whenever this is changed.

Note: From AutoCAD Release 12 onwards, you may bypass the SETVAR command if you wish, and access the system variable directly by entering its name at the Command: prompt).

The OSNAP command

We did some 'osnapping' (object snapping) in Part A, though not via the OSNAP command. Using the OSNAP command you can make 'semi-per-manent' settings which enables the cursor to 'snap on' to parts of existing objects which lie inside a target sight box (see page 39).

Proceed as follows:

1. Select the OSNAP command, then type:

   END,INT,TAN   (RETURN)

   as the object snap modes.

2. Select the LINE command. Move the cursor. Note that the osnap target sight has appeared. Keep moving the cursor until the leftmost intersection of circle b and line c lies somewhere inside the target sight, then PICK. Note that the start point of the line has snapped-on exactly to the intersection. Now move the cursor until the top endpoint of line a is somewhere inside the target sight. PICK.

3. Staying in the LINE command, move the cursor until the top of circle b is somewhere inside the target sight. PICK. Then RETURN to exit the LINE command. Note that the line has snapped exactly to the end of line a and tangentially to circle b (Fig. L2.6).

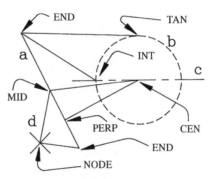

Figure L2.6.

4. Select the APERTURE command. (This enables you to adjust the target sight size.) The default size is 10. Enter 50 as the new value. Select any drawing command, e.g. CIRCLE, and move the cursor. Note the larger osnap target sight. Cancel your command via CTRL-C. Now use APERTURE again, to reset the target sight size back to 10.

5. Select OSNAP. Then select NONE, e.g. by typing:

   NONE   (RETURN)

   This switches off the osnap modes.

Object snapping inside other commands

In Part A, we invoked OSNAP temporarily inside other commands without using the OSNAP command. The following exercise serves as a revision to Part A, and also introduces some more OSNAP modes. (*Note*: Although the instructions indicate keyboard inputs, the osnap options can also be actioned inside other commands via screen menus, cursor menus and toolbars. Refer to Appendix B.)

Proceed as follows:

1. Select LINE. Move the cursor. (Note that there is no target sight, as OSNAP is switched off.) Type:

   END   (RETURN)

2. Move the cursor (note that the target sight has appeared) until the lower end of line a is somewhere inside the target sight. PICK. Type:

   NODE   (RETURN)

3. Move the resulting target sight until point d is somewhere inside it. PICK. Type:

   MID   (RETURN)

4. Move the target sight to cover any part of line a. PICK. Type:

   CEN   (RETURN)

5. Move the target sight to cover any part of the circumference of circle b. PICK. Type:

   PERP   (RETURN)

6. Move the target sight to cover any part of line a. PICK.
7. RETURN to exit the LINE command. Your display should be as Fig. L2.6.
8. Draw a CIRCLE similar to circle e in Fig. L2.7. Then select the LINE command, and type:

   TAN   (RETURN)

9. Move the target to cover the lowest circumference region of circle b. PICK. Type:

   TAN   (RETURN)

10. Move the target sight to cover the lowest circumference region of circle e. PICK.
11. RETURN to exit the LINE command. Note the line drawn tangentially to circle b and circle e (Fig. L2.7).
12. From Release 13 onwards you can object snap to *apparent intersections* of objects which appear to intersect (such as in some 3D views) or which would intersect if they were extended.

    If you have Release 13, select the LINE command, PICK a 'From point' at a convenient position leftward of line a in Fig. L2.6. Then type:

    APINT   (RETURN)

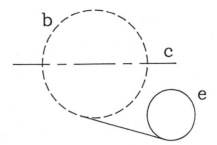

Figure L2.7.

Then PICK line a in Fig. L2.6. Repeat the APINT routine and PICK line c.

Then RETURN to complete the LINE command and see the end-point of the line drawn at the apparent intersection of lines a and c.

Introduction to POLYLINE (PLINE) and EXPLODE

A POLYLINE (or PLINE) is a profile of lines and/or arcs which is considered as a single object.

Proceed as follows:

1. ZOOM to an unused area of the screen. Ensure that SNAP and GRID are ON, with values of 5 and 10 respectively.
2. Select the PLINE (or POLYLINE) command. PICK a point such as h in Fig. L2.8. Moving the cursor rightwards from point h, PICK four more points at the appropriate grid dots in Fig. L2.8 to draw the polyline shown. Then RETURN to exit the PLINE command.

Figure L2.8.

3. Select ERASE and PICK the polyline on any of the four line segments. Complete the ERASE command. See that the complete polyline (all four line segments) has been erased at once. Select OOPS to retrieve the polyline.
4. The EXPLODE command may be used to 'unattach' the entities making up a polyline. Select EXPLODE. PICK the polyline on any of the four line segments. Now select ERASE and PICK any of the line segments. Complete the ERASE command. See that only the single selected line has been erased. Select OOPS to retrieve the erased line.

Rotated grid

Start this exercise by drawing an ARC with a START point at point i (Fig. L2.9), CENTRE at point h and included ANGLE of 25 degrees. The arc should be as in Fig. L2.9. Then proceed as follows:

1. Select SNAP. Select the ROTATE option. PICK point h as the base point. Enter 25 as the rotation angle. See the grid rotated at 25 degrees.
2. Complete Fig. L2.10 using the LINE command and PICKing at the appropriate grid dots shown.
3. Use the ROTATE option of SNAP again, to rotate the grid back to an angle of 0. Then switch off GRID via CTRL-G.

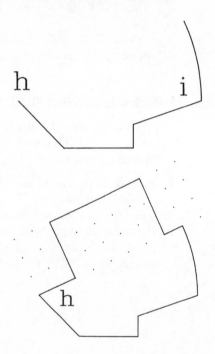

Figure L2.9.

Figure L2.10.

The UCS facility

UCS was used in Part A as an essential tool for 3D modelling work. The UCS facility may also be very useful in 2D work. Proceed as follows:

1. Select the UCS command. Select the 3POINT option. PICK point j (Fig. L2.11) as origin. PICK m as 'point on positive X axis'. PICK k as 'point on positive XY plane'. See the repositioned UCS icon.
2. Draw a CIRCLE, specifying its centre point by typing:

    36,8.5   (RETURN)

Then specify a radius value of 6 to complete the circle command. See the completed circle as in Fig. L2.12, noting that the X, Y coordinate values of 36, 8.5 are assumed to be relative to the current UCS.

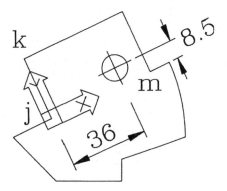

Figure L2.11.

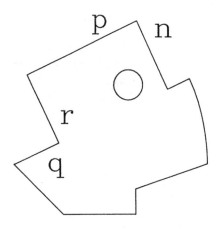

Figure L2.12.

3. Go back to the World Coordinate System (WCS) by selecting the UCS command again, and selecting the W option. See the UCS icon shifted to its original position.

4. Now complete this exercise by drawing a 10 radius FILLET, PICKing lines approximately at points n then p as in Fig. L2.12 (switch SNAP OFF via CTRL-B if convenient). Draw another 10 radius FILLET, PICKing points approximately at q then r (refer back to Part A concerning the FILLET command if necessary). Your drawing should now be as in Fig. L2.13.

Introduction to internal BLOCKS

Like polylines, BLOCKs are compound items considered as single objects. Blocks are created from existing objects and may be stored and then repeatedly inserted at varied scales. To store a block, you may give it any name you wish. We will call our block ITEM.

Proceed as follows:

1. Select the BLOCK command. Then, for the blockname, type:

    ITEM   (RETURN)

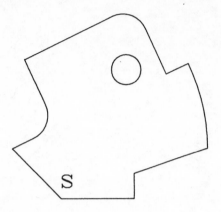

Figure L2.13.

Then (with SNAP ON) PICK point s (Fig. L2.13) as basepoint. Now select all objects in Fig. L2.13 (e.g. via a window). RETURN when all items have been selected. This completes the BLOCK command, and the selected items disappear.

2. Select the INSERT command. Then, for the blockname, type:

ITEM   (RETURN)

AutoCAD then asks for an insertion point. PICK any point. Now type:

1   (RETURN)

for the X scale. Now RETURN to accept the default value of 1 for the Y scale. Type:

0   (RETURN)

for rotation. Your block ITEM (consisting of the objects in Fig. L2.13) should now be displayed at the chosen insertion point.

3. Select ERASE. PICK any part of your inserted block. Complete the ERASE command. Note that the entire block of items has been erased at once. Retrieve the block via the OOPS command.

4. Like polylines, blocks may be 'exploded' back to their composite elements. Select the EXPLODE command. PICK any item in the block. The items are now exploded (or 'unblocked'). Select ERASE again and PICK any time on the former block. Complete the ERASE command and note that only the selected item of the former block has been erased.

5. Now use the INSERT command again, to insert your block ITEM at another convenient point, this time specifying values of 1, 0.75 and 0, for X scale, Y scale and rotation respectively (Fig. L12.14). Then INSERT the block again with values of 0.5, 1.25 and 0, for X scale, Y scale and rotation respectively (Fig. L12.15).

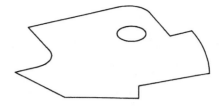

Figure L2.14.

Figure L2.15.

Introduction to standards libraries

Any existing drawing may be inserted onto your current drawing via the INSERT command. The elements of the inserted drawing then become a BLOCK on your current drawing. Thus it is possible to compile any number of drawings for standard items, store them on disk as a library, and then insert any of these standards on any current drawing whenever you wish, so avoiding repetition of drawing work on standard shapes.

Proceed as follows:

1. SAVE your current drawing.
2. Begin a NEW drawing called NUT to be stored on floppy disk (e.g. specify the drawing name as A:NUT).
3. Using SNAP and GRID of value 1, ZOOM to a convenient area of the screen to see the grid dots clearly. Then use LINE and ARC commands to complete the drawing shown in Fig. L2.16. Select the BASE command. PICK the basepoint as in Fig. L2.16. Then SAVE the drawing.
4. Reload your previous drawing (via the OPEN command).
5. Select the INSERT command. Then, for the blockname, type:

    A:NUT   (RETURN)

(assuming that your floppy disk drive is Drive A; otherwise modify to suit).

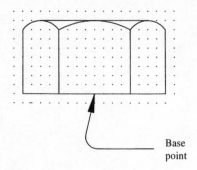

Figure L2.16.

Base
point

Then PICK an insertion point at about point t in Fig. L2.17 and enter values of 1, 1, 0 for X, Y scales and rotation respectively. See the inserted block as in Fig. L2.17.

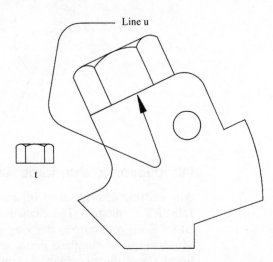

Line u

t

Figure L2.17.

6. NUT is now a block on your drawing. Select INSERT again. Then, for the blockname, type:

NUT   (RETURN)

Then type:

MID   (RETURN)

to invoke ONSAP MID, and PICK any point on line u (Fig. L2.17) as the insertion point. Then enter 2.5 for the X and Y scales, and 25 as rotation..Your drawing should now be as Fig. L2.17.

End of lesson

Lesson 2 is now completed. END the drawing.

Lesson 3

Editing techniques

We have already used some edit commands, namely ERASE, FILLET and ARRAY. In this lesson we will use some more edit commands and options.

Selecting objects for editing

There are several methods of selecting objects which you want to edit. The default option gives a message: Select objects:. The most useful responses to this are as follows.

OBJECT POINTING

This is the default option. It allows you to select any object by pointing to it with the small PICKBOX cursor and then PICKing it. You may then select any number of other objects the same way, before ending the selection procedure with a RETURN.

WINDOW (W)

If you enter W after the Select objects: prompt, you may select any number of objects at once by placing a window around them. All objects which are *entirely within the window* are selected.

CROSSING (C)

This option also uses a window, but selects all objects which are *either inside or crossing the window frame*.

LAST (L)

This selects the last object drawn.

PREVIOUS (P)

This selects all objects which were selected in the most recent previous editing operation.

REMOVE (R)

This option allows you to remove objects from a selection set (e.g. if they have been mistakenly selected for editing). 'Removed' objects are selected as above and will not then be affected by the edit command.

FENCE (F)

This allows you to select objects by drawing a series of joined line segments (like a polyline) through them. All objects which cross, or intersect, this 'polyline' are selected.

WPOLYGON (WP)

This is similar to WINDOW, but selects all objects inside an enclosing polygon.

CPOLYGON (CP)

As WPOLYGON, but objects are selected if they are either inside, or crossing, the polygon.

Filtering selection sets

As with layers, you can filter out selection sets so that they contain only those items which have specified common properties. For example, if you actioned the ERASE command, and placed a window around a number of items for selection, you could have your selection filters set so that only those items in the window which were, say, CIRCLES and coloured GREEN would actually be selected.

Selection set filtering may be invoked during the operation of any edit command by PICKing Selection Filters from the Assist menu (MSDOS) or the Select toolbar (Windows).

The COPY and MOVE commands

COPY allows you to replicate selected objects at another position on your drawing. MOVE is similar to COPY, but does not retain the original objects.

Proceed as follows:

1. Begin a new drawing using suitable settings (which you may have already actioned on your own prototype drawing—see Lesson 2).
2. Using the LINE command and a suitable SNAP value, accurately draw the L-shape in Fig. L3.1. (PICK at the appropriate GRID dots shown. These are spaced at 10 units.)
3. Select the COPY command. Select the WINDOW (W) option. Place a window around the L-shape (as we did during the ERASE procedures in

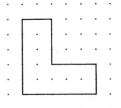

Figure L3.1.

Part A). After PICKing the window corners, RETURN to complete the selection routine.

Noting the <Basepoint or displacement>: prompt, move your cursor to anywhere on or near the shape (e.g. lower left corner of the L) and PICK a base point. Now move the cursor to another point on the screen for the second point of displacement. PICK. See the L-shape copied (e.g. as in Fig. L3.2).

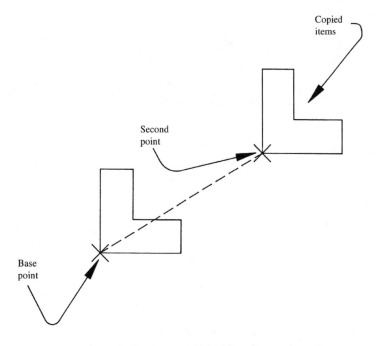

Figure L3.2.   The COPY command.

4. Select the MOVE command. Place a window around your new L-shape. RETURN to complete the selection procedure. Move the cursor and PICK a convenient base point as for the COPY procedure. Move the cursor to another point on your screen and PICK a second point of displacement. Note that the new L-shape has been moved to another position (e.g. as in Fig. L3.3).

5. Select the ERASE command. Select the PREVIOUS (P) option (thus selecting the new L-shape again). RETURN to complete the selection procedure. Note that the new L-shape is now erased.

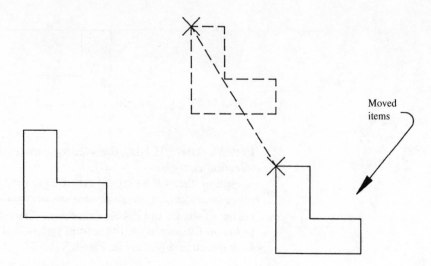

Moved
items

Figure L3.3.   The MOVE
command.

The ROTATE command

Proceed as follows.

Select ROTATE. Select the WINDOW option and select your L-shape as before. RETURN to complete the selection procedure. Point to the lower left corner of the L for the base point. PICK. Now type:

45   (RETURN)

for the rotation angle. See the rotated shape (Fig. L3.4).

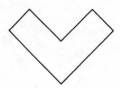

Figure L3.4.

The SCALE command

Proceed as follows.

Select SCALE. Select the PREVIOUS option (thus selecting the entire L-shape again). RETURN to complete the selection procedure. Point to the lowest corner of the rotated L-shape as the base point. PICK. Now type:

.5   (RETURN)

as the scale factor. Note the reduced size (Fig. L3.5).

Complete the exercise by scaling the L-shape back to its original size (i.e. this time enter a scale factor of 2).

Figure L3.5.

The STRETCH command

Proceed as follows:

1. ROTATE the L-shape back to its original position and place a 10 radius FILLET at the upper corner of the L-base (Fig. L3.6a).
2. Select the STRETCH command. Select the CROSSING (C) option. Put a window CROSSING horizontal lines a and b but ENCLOSING the 10 radius fillet and the rightmost vertical line (Fig. L3.6b). After PICKing the window corners, RETURN to complete the selection routine. Move the cursor to a convenient base point (e.g. lower-right corner). PICK. Move the cursor horizontally rightwards by 30 units. PICK.

    Note that the base of the L-shape has been stretched by 30 units.
3. Now stretch the vertical part of the L-shape by 10 units. Your drawing should then be as in Fig. L3.7.

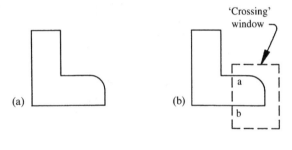

Figure L3.6.

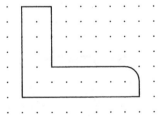

Figure L3.7.

The TRIM command

Proceed as follows:

1. Draw a CIRCLE of 40 radius, centre at point c (Fig. L3.8).
2. Select the TRIM command. Observe the `Select cutting edge(s):` prompt. Point to vertical edge d as the first cutting edge. PICK. Point to vertical edge e as another cutting edge. PICK.

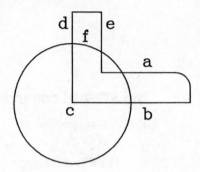

Figure L3.8.

Then RETURN to complete the selection of the cutting edges. Observe the `Select object to trim:` prompt. Point to the circumference of circle, approximately at f in Fig. L3.8. PICK. Note that the circle has been trimmed between the two selected cutting edges. RETURN to complete the TRIM command.

3. Now perform some more TRIMs to achieve the drawing shown in Fig. L3.9.

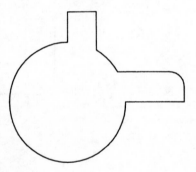

Figure L3.9.

The OFFSET command

Proceed as follows:

1. Select the OFFSET command. Then type:

    10   (RETURN)

for the offset distance.

Note the `Select objects to offset:` prompt. Point to anywhere on the circumference of the largest arc. PICK. Note the `Side to offset:` prompt. Point to anywhere INSIDE the largest arc. PICK. Then RETURN to complete the OFFSET command.

2. Now perform an OFFSET at a distance of 15 units OUTSIDE the largest arc. Your drawing should then be as in Fig. L3.10.

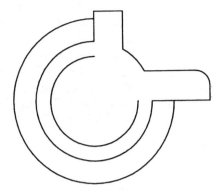

Figure L3.10.

The EXTEND command

Proceed as follows:

1. Select the EXTEND command. Note the `Select boundary edge(s):` prompt. Point to vertical line e (Fig. L3.11) as boundary edge. PICK. Then RETURN to complete the boundary edge selection. Note the `Select object to extend:` prompt. Point to the circumference of the largest arc, approximately at point g. PICK. Note that the arc has been extended to the selected boundary edge. RETURN to complete the EXTEND command.
2. Now EXTEND horizontal line. a to touch the smallest arc (Fig. L3.11).

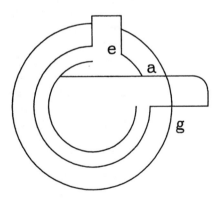

Figure L3.11.

The CHAMFER command

Proceed as follows:

1. Select the CHAMFER command. Select the DISTANCES option, e.g. by typing: D (RETURN). Then type:

   5   (RETURN)

   as the first chamfer distance.

Now RETURN to accept the default value of the second chamfer distance (i.e. the same as the first chamfer distance—5 units in this case). This brings you out of the CHAMFER command.

2. Reselect CHAMFER. Point to horizontal line b (Fig. L3.12). PICK. Note the resulting chamfer.
3. Now draw a 7.5 chamfer at the corner of vertical line e and horizontal line i (Fig. L3.12).

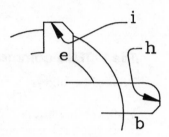

Figure L3.12.

Further exercise in FILLET

Proceed as follows:

1. Draw a 30 radius ARC as in Fig. L3.13, with an included angle 330 degrees, centre 100 units leftward from the centre of the existing arcs, and start point as shown.
2. Select FILLET. Then select the R option and enter a radius value of 20, as in previous exercises.
3. Reselect FILLET. Point to the upper-right circumference of the 30 radius arc. PICK. Now point to the largest arc at the upper-left circumference. PICK. Note the fillet drawn between the two arcs (Fig. L3.14).
4. Now draw a 40 radius FILLET between arc j and the lower-right of the 30 radius arc (Fig. L3.14).

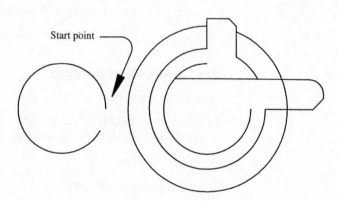

Start point

Figure L3.13.

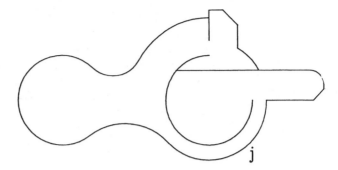

Figure L3.14.

The MIRROR command

Proceed as follows.

Select the MIRROR command. Select all of your objects via the WINDOW option. After PICKing the window corners, RETURN to complete the selection procedure. Note the `First point of mirror line:` prompt. Move the cursor to any point 10 units rightward of your drawn objects (e.g. as in Fig. L3.15). PICK. Note the `Second point:` prompt. Move the cursor to any point vertically below the first point (e.g. as in Fig. L3.15). PICK. Thus your 'mirror line' has been specified (although it is not displayed). Note the `Delete old objects?:` prompt. Respond by entering NO, e.g. by typing: N (RETURN).

See the mirrored display (Fig. L3.15). Do a suitable ZOOM routine to see your new display if necessary.

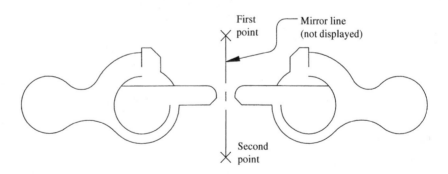

Figure L3.15.

The BREAK command

Proceed as follows.

ZOOM to see a display similar to Fig. L3.14 again, and select the BREAK command. Point to the 30 radius arc, approximately at point k (Fig. L3.16). PICK. Then point to the arc, approximately at point m. PICK. Note the broken arc (Fig. L3.17).

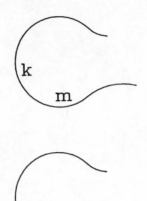

Figure L3.16.

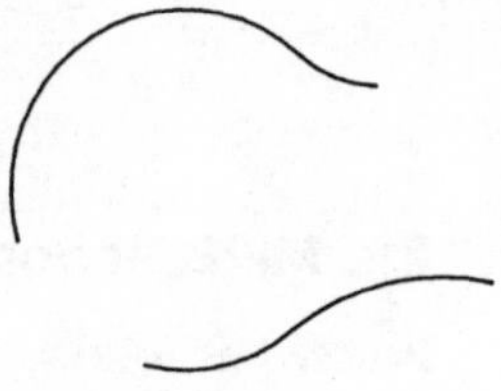

Figure L3.17.

The CHANGE command

CHANGE is a complex command with many options. This exercise involves a small sample of them.

Proceed as follows:

1. Select the CHANGE command. Point to line a (Fig. L3.18). PICK. Select the PROPERTIES option, e.g. by typing: P (RETURN). Select the LINETYPE option, e.g. by typing: LT (RETURN). Select the HIDDEN linetype, e.g. by typing: HIDDEN (RETURN). Then RETURN to complete the CHANGE command. Note that line a has changed to hidden linetype (Fig. L3.18).

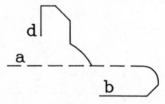

Figure L3.18.

2. The default option of CHANGE is 'Change point'. Reselect CHANGE. PICK lines a, b and d near the ends shown in Fig. L3.18. RETURN to complete the selection routine. Now point approximately to point n in Fig. L3.19. PICK. See the line ends changed to point n (Fig. L3.19).

    Note: If you only wish to change the properties of objects, the CHPROP (change properties) command may be used as an alternative to CHANGE. CHPROP bypasses the 'Change point' option and gives direct access to the PROPERTIES options.

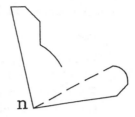

Figure L3.19.

Fillets and chamfers with the 'No trim' option

Sometimes you may wish to draw fillets and chamfers but retain the original construction elements. From Release 13 onwards you may achieve this via the 'No trim' option. The option may be demonstrated by a simple fillet exercise.

Proceed as follows:

1. ZOOM to an unused area of the screen.
2. Draw two lines similar to those in Fig. L3.20a.
3. Select the FILLET command. Select R and enter a convenient radius size for your lines.

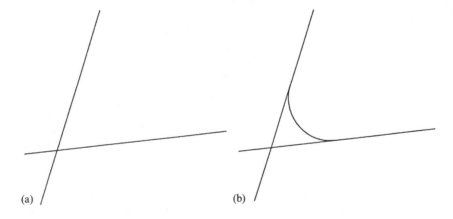

Figure L3.20. FILLET 'No trim' option. (a) Without fillet; (b) with fillet but original lines left untrimmed.

(a)   (b)

4. Reselect the FILLET command, e.g. via RETURN.
5. Select the TRIM option, e.g. by typing:

> T   (RETURN)

6. AutoCAD then displays the prompt: TRIM/NO TRIM:. Select the 'No trim' option, e.g. by typing:

> N   (RETURN)

7. PICK your two lines as in previous fillet routines, thus completing the FILLET command.
8. Your drawing should appear similar to Fig. L3.20b, with a fillet shown but the original lines left untrimmed.

Further exercise in ARRAY

Proceed as follows:

1. ZOOM to an unused area of the screen and, with SNAP ON, draw a CIRCLE of radius 5 units and centre point near the top of the screen. Then draw a vertical LINE starting FROM the centre of the circle, and length 10 units upwards (Fig. L3.21a).

Figure L3.21. (a) Initial shape; (b) polar array (rotated objects); (c) polar array (objects not rotated); (d) rectangular array.

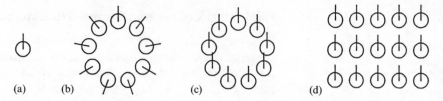

(a)   (b)   (c)   (d)

2. Select the ARRAY command. Select the circle and the line (e.g. by PICKing each, or via WINDOW). RETURN to complete the selection procedure. Select the POLAR option, e.g. by typing: P (RETURN). Note the `Center point of array:` prompt. Move the cursor to the point 40 units vertically below the centre of the circle. PICK. Then, for the number of items, type:

> 9   (RETURN)

Next, for the angle to fill, type:

> 360   (RETURN)

Note the `Rotate objects as they are copied:` prompt. Respond by entering YES, e.g. by typing: Y (RETURN).
See the polar array of objects, as in Fig. L3.21b.

3. Go back to the display in Fig. L3.21a again via the U or the UNDO command. Reselect the ARRAY command and repeat the previous polar array procedure exactly, except for your final response to the `Rotate objects as they are copied:` prompt. This time, enter NO to this prompt, and thus see the display in Fig. L3.21c.

4. Go back to the display in Fig. L3.21a again via U or UNDO. Reselect the ARRAY command. Select the circle and line again. RETURN to complete the selection procedure. Select the RECTANGULAR option, e.g. by typing: R (RETURN).
Note the `Number of rows:` prompt. Type:

> 3   (RETURN)

Note the `Number of columns:` prompt. Type:

> 5   (RETURN)

Note the `-- distance between rows:` prompt. Type:

> 20   (RETURN)

Note the Distance between columns: prompt. Type:

15   (RETURN)

See the rectangular array of objects, as in Fig. L3.21d (PAN upwards, or ZOOM to suit if necessary).

Trimming to an extended cutting edge

This useful technique is available for Release 13 onwards. If your system is in this category, proceed as follows:

1. ZOOM/PAN to an unused area of the screen.
2. Draw two lines similar to those in Fig. L3.22a.

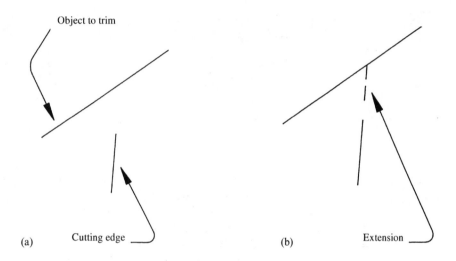

(a)   Cutting edge   (b)   Extension

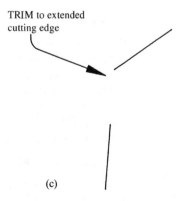

(c)

Figure L3.22.

3. Select the TRIM command. PICK the lower line as the 'Cutting edge'. RETURN.
4. Select the EDGE option, e.g. by typing:

     E   (RETURN)

5. Select the EXTEND option, e.g. by typing:

     E   (RETURN)

(Fig. L3.22b).
6. PICK the upper line on its left-hand side as the 'Object to trim'. RETURN.
7. Your display should be similar to Fig. L3.22c, with the upper line trimmed to the extension of the lower line.

Editing with GRIPS

The GRIPS facility has been available from AutoCAD Release 12 onwards. If your system is in this category, proceed as follows:

1. ZOOM/PAN to an unused area of the screen (changing LIMITS if necessary). Then draw two LINES and one CIRCLE similar to Fig. L3.23a. (Choose any sizes you wish, but keep in the approximate proportions shown.)
   Set to a suitable SNAP value for your screen display.
2. Access the GRIPS system variable (e.g. via the SETVAR command). Ensure that the GRIPS system variable is set to a value of 1, which means that grips are activated.
3. While AutoCAD is currently displaying the Command: prompt, PICK the two lines and circle in turn. Note the grip boxes displayed on the objects (Fig. L3.23b).
4. Now move your cursor until the pickbox exactly covers grip box a (Fig. L3.23c). PICK. Move the cursor approximately to point b (Fig. L3.23c). PICK. See the lines stretched to the new point, as in Fig. L3.23d (STRETCH is the default GRIP mode).
5. Move the cursor until the pickbox exactly covers grip box c (Fig. L3.23c). PICK. Then select MIRROR GRIP mode, e.g. by typing: MI (RETURN). Move the cursor to point b (Fig. L3.23c). PICK. Note the objects mirrored about line cb (Fig. L3.23e).
6. Move the cursor until the pickbox exactly covers grip box d (Fig. L3.23c). PICK. Then select ROTATE GRIP mode, e.g. by typing: RO (RETURN). Then, for the rotation angle, enter:

    90   (RETURN)

Thus see the objects rotated through 90 degrees about the circle centre grip box (Fig. 3.23f).
7. Similarly, experiment with the grip modes: MOVE, COPY and SCALE.

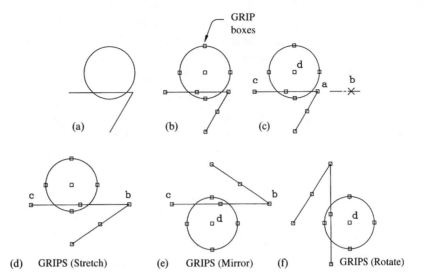

Figure L3.23.

(a)   (b)   (c)

(d)   GRIPS (Stretch)   (e)   GRIPS (Mirror)   (f)   GRIPS (Rotate)

NOUN/VERB selection

This facility allows you to select objects before you select your required edit command, and is available from AutoCAD Release 12 onwards. If your system is in this category, proceed as follows:

1. Although you may use GRIPS and NOUN/VERB selection concurrently, we will avoid confusion between them by deactivating GRIPS for this exercise. Do this by accessing the GRIPS system variable (e.g. via the SETVAR command), and setting the GRIPS system variable to a value of 0.
2. By default, NOUN/VERB selection is activated. However, you may check this by accessing the Entity Selection Settings dialog box, e.g. by typing:

   DDSELECT   (RETURN)

   In the resulting dialog display, note the square 'checkbox' to the left of the mode title: 'Noun/Verb Selection'. If this checkbox is 'crossed', NOUN/VERB selection is currently activated and should be left in this state. If it is empty, PICK the checkbox to toggle NOUN/VERB selection activated, and thus see the checkbox crossed. Then PICK the OK box.
3. While AutoCAD is currently displaying the Command: prompt, PICK the circle and line cb from the previous exercise concerning GRIPS.
4. Now select the COPY command. Note the prompt: 2 FOUND. Complete the COPY command by PICKing a convenient 'Base point' and 'Second point', in turn, to copy the (already selected) line and circle to a suitable location on the screen.

5. Experiment with some more edit commands (such as ERASE, MOVE, MIRROR) on existing drawn objects in this lesson, using NOUN/VERB selection.

Selection by groups

This facility is available from Release 13 onwards. A *group* is a named selection set of objects. Members of a group remain related to each other for repeated editing purposes at any stage of the drawing, unlike ordinary members of a selection set, which are related only when selected during a single command. Once created, the complete group may be selected during any edit command by selecting the GROUP option and supplying the name of the group to be edited. Despite the group relationship, a degree of access to individual entities is retained. This is illustrated in Fig. L3.24, which shows a named group of objects which have been copied via the COPY command, followed by an EXTENSION operation applied to an individual group member.

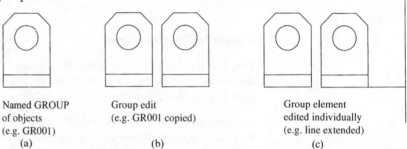

Named GROUP   Group edit   Group element
of objects   (e.g. GR001 copied)   edited individually
(e.g. GR001)   (e.g. line extended)
     (a)   (b)   (c)

Figure L3.24.

A group of objects may be created by selecting the GROUP command, supplying a name for the new group, specifying if the group is to be selectable, and selecting the objects you wish to be members of that group. When groups are selectable, selecting a single member of the group also selects all the members of the group. Groups are selectable only if the system variable PICKSTYLE is set to a value of 1 or 3. (This is relevant to the section on the BHATCH command in Lesson 6.)

An object can be a member of more than one group. You can cycle through the various groups to which a selected object belongs by holding down the CTRL key and repeatedly pressing the PICK button to observe the successively highlighted groups.

As with blocks and polylines, a group may be broken up via the EXPLODE command.

The AutoCAD/Windows Clipboard

This section is relevant only if you are using AutoCAD in the Microsoft Windows or Windows NT environment.

The Windows Clipboard was mentioned in Chapter 1 of Part A. It is a common facility for users of all the different software packages (not just

AutoCAD users) who are working under the Windows operating system. Items from any of the Windows applications can be placed onto the Clipboard. Users of any other application on the Windows system can then take these items from the Clipboard and 'paste' the items onto their own work.

In AutoCAD, if you select any drawn objects destined for the Clipboard, and then select CUT from the Standard toolbar, the selected objects will be deleted from your drawing and stored on the Clipboard. Alternatively, if you select your drawing objects and then select COPY from the Standard toolbar, your selected objects will be copied to the Clipboard. The drawing objects on the Clipboard are then available for a user of, say, the wordprocessing package Word for Windows, to paste onto a Word text file.

Similarly, a Word file could be placed on the Clipboard for you, the AutoCAD user, to paste onto your drawing. This can be done by selecting Paste from the Standard toolbar.

Ideally such imported files will be in AutoCAD format. However, AutoCAD can also accept other formats, such as Windows Metafile (WMF), via conversion routines during pasting.

You might also use these Clipboard facilities to copy or transfer drawing objects between different AutoCAD drawing files. However, this facility is also available by using BLOCKS (see Lesson 2 and Lesson 10).

End of lesson

Lesson 3 is now completed. END your drawing.

Summary exercises: Lessons 1–3

Before commencing the next lesson, apply the knowledge you have gained and skills you have developed in the preceding lessons to produce the drawings shown in the following figures. Use the grid dots shown, as an aid to size and proportion. Respective grid sizes and smallest size increments are shown below. The centres of circles, and arcs drawn via the ARC command, may be assumed to be at the most logical XY position in the size increment shown. (This does not necessarily include those which would be subsequently created via the COPY or ARRAY commands.) The minimum FILLET radius value is 10 in all cases.

- *Exercises 1–4*
  Grid: 20
  Lowest size increment: 5
- *Exercises 5–7*
  Grid: 40
  Lowest size increment: 10

PLOTting your drawings

When you have completed these drawings, you may wish to PLOT some, or all, of them to a hard copy device such as a pen plotter or laser printer.

This is achieved via the PLOT command which, from Release 12 onwards, activates a dialog box routine for you to make specifications

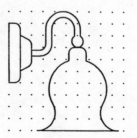

Exercise 1.

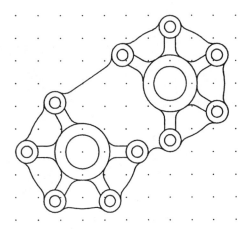

Exercise 2.

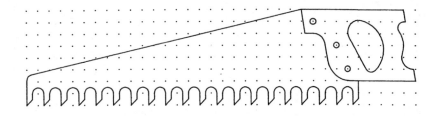

Exercise 3.

and settings according to the type of plot required. AutoCAD allows you to specify the area of your drawing you want plotted via the following options:

- DISPLAY   Plots the area of your drawing currently displayed on screen
- EXTENTS   Plots all the drawn objects to their extents
- LIMITS   Plots the entire drawing area specified in the LIMITS setting
- VIEW   Plots the drawn objects contained within the area of a named VIEW. The VIEW command is discussed in Lesson 1
- WINDOW   Plots the drawn objects contained within a specified size of window

The settings made, and dialog undertaken, during the PLOT routine will be governed by the drawing application and the make/model of the hardware device for which your system is configured. However, important parameters specified during the plot command routine include:

- For pen plotters, the allocation of screen colours to specific pen numbers if multi-pen plots are required
- Scaling requirements (such as a quoted ratio between AutoCAD drawing units and corresponding millimetres distance on the plotter, or the use of

Exercise 4.

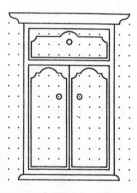

Exercise 5.

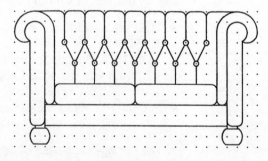

Exercise 6.

the FIT option which automatically fits the specified display area to the size of the particular plotter being used)

• Whether hidden line removal is required. (Hidden line removal will not be required in these exercises, but is relevant to 3D work in Part C)

• Whether a PLOT FILE is required. This can be a useful device for some applications. If you do request a plot file, the plot to hard copy is not actually undertaken at the time of the PLOT command. Instead, the plot

Exercise 7.

data is stored to a named file on disk (automatically given the extension .PLT). The hard copy plot may then be repeatedly undertaken on any subsequent occasion via the PRINT command in the operating system. Thus, for example, it would be possible to execute the hard copy plot on any other compatible system (whether or not that system has AutoCAD installed).

Lesson 4

Dimensioning and units

The UNITS command

In this book, all examples of coordinates, distances, and angles are assumed to be in decimal notation. In some disciplines other notations are required, and the UNITS command may be used to set the required notation.

UNITS may also be used to set the PRECISION of displayed values in exercises such as dimensioning. In this exercise we will use the UNITS command to set the precision of coordinates and angles.

Begin a new drawing for floppy disk storage. Then proceed as follows.

Select the UNITS command. Select Option 2 (decimal system). AutoCAD then asks for the precision by prompting: `Number of digits to right of decimal point:`. Respond to this by typing:

> 3   (RETURN)

You will then be asked for the required system of angle measure. Select Option 1 (decimal degrees). Next, AutoCAD asks for the angular precision by prompting: `Number of fractional places for display of angles:`. Respond to this by typing:

> 0   (RETURN)

Then, in response to the prompt: `Direction for angle 0:`, specify a '3 o'clock' datum by typing:

> 0   (RETURN)

Finally, AutoCAD asks: `Do you want angles measured clockwise?` Respond by typing:

> N   (RETURN)

Starting your drawing

1. Set SNAP ON to a value of 5. Set suitable values for LIMITS and GRID for the drawing shown in Fig. L4.1.

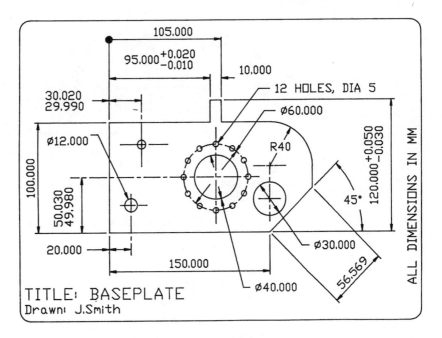

Figure L4.1.

2. Set up three layers: one with CONTINUOUS linetype for main outlines; another with CENTER linetype for centre lines; a third with CONTINUOUS linetype to contain the dimensions. Specify a different colour for each layer, use any layer names you wish, and set all layers to ON.
3. Using the appropriate layers, draw the main outlines and the centre lines of the component shown in Fig. L4.1, but *do not attempt to include the dimensions yet* (estimate sizes not shown).
4. Set the layer you created for dimensioning, as the current layer.

Dimension settings

Note: The following exercise assumes the traditional approach of entering the DIM mode to access dimensioning commands. However, with Release 13 onwards this is not essential. For example, the dimension command LINEAR can be actioned by selecting the command DIMLINEAR without entering DIM mode, the dimension command RAD can be actioned via DIMRAD, and so on.

1. Select the DIM command to access the AutoCAD dimensioning mode.
2. Select STATUS to see the display of current dimension SYSTEM VARIABLES settings. We will adjust some of these settings for our drawing. Fig. L4.2 shows what they control.

Note: In AutoCAD Release 12 onwards, you may also control dimension variables via the creation of *dimension styles*, by using a system of dialog, and sub-dialog, boxes which are accessed via the DDIM command. That

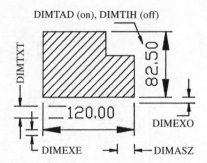

approach is discussed later in this lesson, as an alternative to the following instructions.

3. Select DIMASZ (to adjust arrow size). For its new value type:

    6   (RETURN)

4. Similarly:
    – Select DIMTXT (to adjust dimension text height), and enter a new value of 7
    – Select DIMEXO (to adjust extension line offset), and enter a new value of 3
    – Select DIMEXE (to adjust tail length of extension line beyond dimension line), and enter a new value of 3
    – Select DIMTAD (to specify that text will be placed above dimension line). Select the ON option
    – Select DIMTIH (text inside extensions horizontal). Select the OFF option.
5. Select STATUS again. Observe the new settings. Look for DIMASO. Check that this is set to ON. If it isn't, select DIMASO and then select the ON option. (DIMASO is discussed later in this lesson.) Select REDRAW.

Basic dimensioning

Note: If you are using Release 13 onwards, you may create horizontal and vertical dimensions via the single command LINEAR (or DIMLINEAR if you don't enter the DIM mode), instead of using HOR and VER.

1. We will begin dimensioning by drawing the 150 horizontal dimension in Fig. L4.1. Proceed as follows.
    Select HOR (or LINEAR). Move the cursor to touch corner a (Fig. L4.3) as 'First extension line origin' (use SNAP ON or OSNAP for accuracy). PICK at corner a. Similarly, PICK corner b as '2nd extension line origin'. Move the cursor to approximately the same height as point c for 'Dimension line location' (horizontal position does not matter). Then PICK. AutoCAD now calculates the dimension length (150.000 in this case) and displays this as the default dimension text. RETURN to accept this default text.

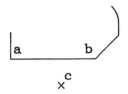

Your 150.000 dimension should now be automatically displayed similar to that shown in Fig. L4.1. If you do not like the look of the position of the dimension, select UNDO (while remaining in DIM mode) and do the dimension again. (Note that there is no OOPS facility with dimensions.)

2. Repeat the HOR (or LINEAR) procedure for the 20.000 dimension. The effect is untidy, so UNDO and repeat, but instead of doing a RETURN for the default 20.000 text, press SPACE BAR instead, then RETURN. This suppresses the text and gives lines/arrows only. Now select LEADER. Take the cursor to the point of the left arrow for the 'Leader start'. PICK. Take the cursor horizontally leftwards to a suitable length for the end of the leader. Then RETURN to accept the default text of 20.000. See your leader dimension as in Fig. L4.1.

3. Use HOR (or LINEAR) for the 10.000 dimension, PICKing left and right top corners of the 10 unit width as first and second extension line origins respectively. Note that the text and arrows have been forced outside the extensions. (The text has been forced rightwards due to the stated order of picking the extension origins.)

4. Now select VER (or LINEAR). Draw the 100.000 vertical dimension in a similar manner to that adopted when using HOR for the 150.000 dimension.

5. Select RAD to draw the 40 radius dimension. Take the cursor to this arc and PICK it approximately at point d (Fig. L4.4a). RETURN to accept the default text. The result is untidy, so UNDO and repeat, but instead of RETURNing for default text, type:

    R40   (RETURN)

6. Select DIA to draw the 60.000 diameter dimension. PICK this circle anywhere on its circumference. RETURN to accept the default text. The result is untidy, so UNDO and repeat, but PICK the circle approximately at point e (Fig. L4.4b), then press SPACE BAR, and RETURN to suppress text. Select LEADER. PICK point e as the leader start point. Draw the leader as shown in Fig. L4.1, PICKing when the leader is to change direction, then moving the cursor horizontally rightwards, PICKing the end point of the leader, then RETURNing, and finally RETURNing again to accept the default text (Q60.000).

Now draw the dimension for the 40.000 diameter hole by the same method.

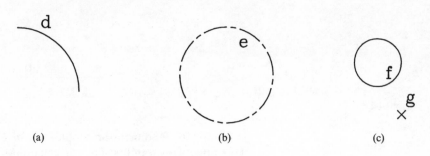

(a)   (b)   (c)

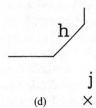

Figure L4.4.   (d)   ×

7. Select LEADER. Draw a leader as in Fig. L4.1, for the 12 equi-spaced holes, proceeding as before, but instead of RETURNing for the default text, enter the note shown, i.e. type:

12 HOLES, DIA 5   (RETURN)

8. Select DIA to draw the 30.000 diameter dimension. PICK this circle approximately at point f (Fig. L4.4c). RETURN to accept the default text. Observe the prompt: TEXT DOES NOT FIT. ENTER LEADER LENGTH FOR TEXT. Take the cursor approximately to point g. PICK. See the diameter dimension with automatic leader and text, as in Fig. L4.1. Now select DIA again to draw the 12 diameter dimension. Proceed as for the last diameter. Note the different type of text display for very small circles.

   Note: If horizontal bars are not automatically drawn on the leaders, add these at the end of the lesson using the LINE command.

9. Select ALIGN. Then RETURN to get the SELECT option. Move the cursor and PICK any point on the slanted line h (Fig. L4.4d). Move the cursor approximately to point j for the dimension line location. PICK. Then RETURN to accept the default text.

Toleranced dimensions

Proceed as follows:

1. Select DIMLIM. Select the ON option (thus specifying tolerances to be displayed as UPPER and LOWER LIMITS).

Select DIMTP, to specify plus tolerance. Type

.02   (RETURN)

Select DIMTM, to specify minus tolerance. Type

.01   (RETURN)

Select STATUS to see the new settings. Select REDRAW. Use HOR and LEADER to draw the 30.020/29.990 dimension in the same manner as previously employed for the 20.000 horizontal dimension, RETURNing at the end of the LEADER routine to accept the default text. The upper and lower limits will automatically be displayed (see Fig. L4.1).

2. Select DIMTOL. Select the ON option (thus specifying tolerances to be displayed in PLUS/MINUS fashion). Reset DIMTP to 0.05 and reset DIMTM to 0.03.

REDRAW, then use VER to draw the 120 vertical dimension. The plus/minus tolerances will automatically be displayed (see Fig. L4.1).

3. Now draw the other toleranced dimensions.

Associative dimensions

By default, each dimension is *associative*, i.e. its text, leaders and arrows are considered as a single block item. Proceed as follows:

1. Depart from the dimensioning mode by selecting EXIT.
2. Select ERASE and PICK any point on the vertical 120 toleranced dimension. Complete the ERASE command. Note that, being associative, all the dimension (i.e. text, leaders, arrows) is erased.
3. Go back to dimensioning mode via DIM. Select DIMASO. Select the OFF option, thus setting future dimensions to be non-associative. Making the required tolerance settings, redraw the 120 vertical dimension. Select EXIT. Repeat the ERASE routine on the 120 dimension. Note that, being non-associative, only the one selected part of the dimension is erased. (Note that the other dimensions remain associative, since they were drawn before DIMASO was set to OFF.) Select OOPS to retrieve the erased item.
4. Go back to dimensioning mode via DIM. Reset DIMASO back to ON.

ANGLE dimensions

Proceed as follows.

Set DIMLIM and DIMTOL to OFF. Select ANG. Move the cursor to line k (Fig. L4.5). PICK. Move the cursor to line h. PICK. Move the cursor approximately to point m to specify a point for the angle arc to cross. PICK. Move the cursor approximately to point n for text location. PICK. See the 45 degree angle dimension displayed, as in Fig. L4.1.

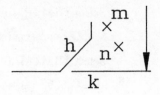

Figure L4.5.

Arrow blocks

You can customize your own arrow shapes by creating libraries of arrow blocks. Here we will use a standard arrow block called DOT to draw the 105.000 dimension in Fig. L4.1. Proceed as follows:

1. Select DIMBLK1 to set the first arrow block. Set a new value by typing:

    DOT   (RETURN)

2. Select DIMSAH. Select the ON option, thus specifying separate arrow blocks. Select STATUS to see the new settings. (Note that DIMBLK2 has no value shown. This means that the second arrow block is set for the normal default arrow-head.)
3. Now use HOR to draw the 105.000 horizontal dimension. Note the 'dot and arrow' result (Fig. L4.1).
4. Reset DIMSAH to OFF. Reset DIMBLK1 back to normal arrow display by selecting DIMBLK1, and then entering a full-stop, i.e. type:

    .   (RETURN)

Editing dimensions

Certain editing techniques are available for associative dimensions. Proceed as follows:

1. Select NEWTEXT. We will change the text from '105.000' to '(105)' (including brackets). Thus, for the new text, type:

    (105)   (RETURN)

    Now PICK the 105.000 dimension for editing. Then RETURN. Note the revised text.

2. Set DIMLIM to ON. Set DIMTP to 0.04. Set DIMTM to 0.02. Select UPDATE (this may be used to update selected dimensions to current settings). Move the cursor to the 10.000 horizontal dimension in Fig. L4.1. PICK. Note that the selected dimension has been updated to the new settings.
3. Now depart from dimension mode by selecting EXIT.

The TEXT command

The TEXT command was used in Part A, and will be enlarged upon in Lesson 5. For now, we will use the TEXT command to add some simple notes to our dimensioned drawing. Proceed as follows.

1. Select the TEXT command. Move the cursor approximately to the lower left of the note 'TITLE: BASEPLATE' (see Fig. L4.1). PICK. Then, for the text height, type:

   20   (RETURN)

   Then RETURN to accept the default rotation (zero). For the required text, type:

   TITLE: BASEPLATE   (RETURN)

   See the required text displayed as in Fig. L4.1.
2. Repeat the TEXT command to add the note beneath 'TITLE: BASEPLATE' (see Fig. L4.1), using your own name, text height of 15 units, and zero rotation.
3. Now add the note 'ALL DIMENSIONS IN MM' (see Fig. L4.1), using text height of 15 units, and rotation of 90 degrees.

Dimension Styles and dialog boxes (DDIM command)

For AutoCAD Releases 12 and 13 onwards you may organize your dimensioning procedures by creating a library of Dimension Styles (similar to Text Styles, as later discussed in Lesson 5), via the DDIM command. This activates a system of dialog boxes, from which you may make settings for dimension variables required for each new style being created.

Each dimension style is given a name of your choosing, and is specified via parameters such as we have previously used in this lesson, e.g. arrow size, text height, type of tolerance, etc. Once you have created a new dimension style, this is added to the library and automatically becomes the current style. You may then go on to create more new styles, and, on any subsequent occasion, reset any existing style as the current one by selecting it from the dialog box.

By default, your AutoCAD drawing will initially have only one dimension style. As for text styles, this is called Standard, to which you may thus use the DDIM command to add any number of new dimension styles.

Dialog box user interface procedures for creating Dimension Styles were subject to revision between Releases 12 and 13. The following exercise covers the Release 13 procedure. If you are using Release 13 onwards, proceed as follows:

1. ERASE the 150.000 horizontal dimension and the 100.000 vertical dimension from your drawing.
2. Access the DDIM command to see the resulting Dimension Styles dialog box displayed (Fig. L4.6). We will use this to create a new dimension style called 'NEWSTYL'.
3. PICK the Name edit box in the dialog display. Then enter:

   NEWSTYL

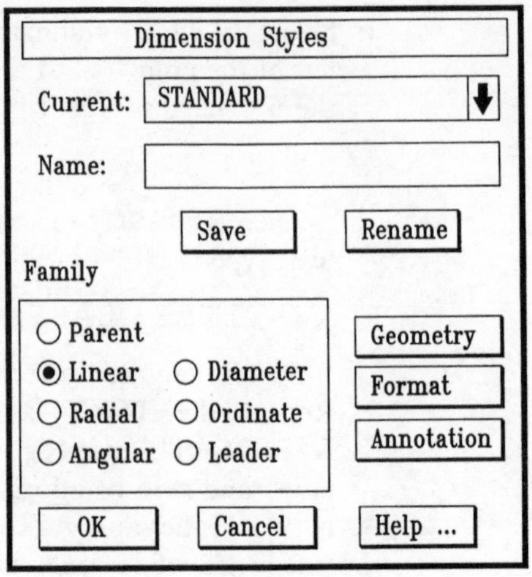

Figure L4.6. The
Dimension Styles dialog
box.

4. In the Family area of the dialog display, PICK the Linear circular button. (It will then be shown filled-in, meaning 'switched on'.)
5. Now PICK the Geometry box in the dialog display. See the resulting Geometry sub-dialog box. We will use this to set values for the variables DIMEXE and DIMEXO, and DIMASZ in our new dimension style.

   PICK the Extension box in the dialog display, and then enter a value of 6.

   PICK the Origin Offset box, and then enter a value of 10.

   In the Arrowheads area of the dialog box, PICK the SIZE edit box and enter a value of 8. Then select Closed Filled for both 1st and 2nd Arrowheads via the appropriate scroll boxes.

   PICK the OK box and thus see the Dimension Styles dialog box redisplayed.
6. PICK the Annotation box in the dialog display. See the resulting Annotation sub-dialog box display. We will use this to make settings for DIMTXT, DIMTOL, DIMTP and DIMTM.

   In the Text area of the dialog box, PICK the Height box, and then enter a value of 6.

   PICK Bilateral from the Method scroll box (thus specifying '+/−' type tolerancing).

   PICK the Upper Value box, and then enter a value of 0.06.

   PICK the Lower Value box, and then enter a value of 0.04.

   PICK the OK box and thus see the Dimension Styles dialog box redisplayed.
7. PICK the Format box in the dialog display. See the resulting Format sub-dialog box display. We will use this to make settings for DIMTAD and DIMTIH.

   PICK the Fit scroll box, and select Best Fit.

   In the Horizontal Justification area, select Centred from the scroll box.

In the Vertical Justification area, select Above from the scroll box.

Do not PICK the Inside Horizontal or Outside Horizontal boxes (thus these boxes will remain blank, and dimension text will not be horizontal on any non-horizontal dimensions).

PICK the OK box and thus see the Dimension Styles dialog box redisplayed.

8. In the Dimension Styles dialog box, PICK the Save box.
9. Complete the DDIM routine by PICKing the OK box in the Dimension Styles dialog box.
10. Now select the LINEAR dimension command (either by selecting LINEAR while within the DIM mode, or by selecting DIMLINEAR from outside the DIM mode), and redraw the 150.000 horizontal dimension to the settings of the current style NEWSTYL. The dimension should appear as in Fig. L4.7.

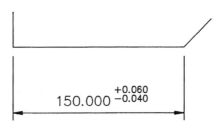

Figure L4.7.

11. Finally, create another new dimension style called NEWSTYL2, using suitable settings, to redraw the 100.000 vertical dimension as toleranced to 100.030/99.950 (to be displayed in the stated Limits fashion). For your own practice, and to reflect the smaller space, use generally smaller values for your size settings than we specified in style NEWSTYL.

Note: When a number of different dimension styles have been created, the user can select any existing style to become the current one by PICKing the scroll area of the Current box in the Dimension Styles dialog box. This causes a list of the existing styles to pop up. The list may be scrolled until the required style name is found. When the selected name is PICKed, this style becomes the current one.

Summary exercises

Use the techniques gained in the previous exercises to draw, and fully dimension, the items shown in Figs L4.8 and L4.9.

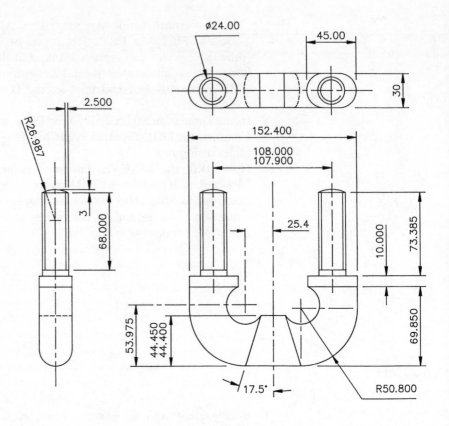

Figure L4.8.

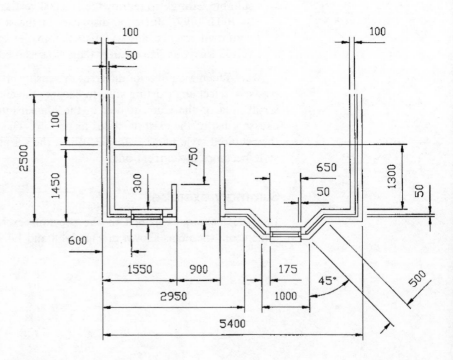

Figure L4.9.

Lesson 5

Text and style

The TEXT and DTEXT commands

When you use the TEXT command, your writing does not appear on the screen until you have completed the command with a RETURN. When using the DTEXT command, your text dynamically appears on the screen as you type it at the keyboard. The DTEXT command also allows successive lines of text during a single command operation.

Begin a new drawing. Then proceed as follows.

Select the DTEXT command. Move the cursor and PICK a start point somewhere on the screen. Then, for text height, type:

    25   (RETURN)

Then, for rotation, type:

    0   (RETURN)

Now start typing the first line of text shown in Fig. L5.1 by keyboard, noting the square dtext cursor leading the text as it dynamically appears on the screen (see Fig. L5.2). Complete this line of text with a RETURN at the keyboard, and note that the dtext cursor has 'carriage returned' ready to start the next line of text (see Fig. L5.3).

Paint all timbers (3 COATS).
Pre-coat lead flashings.
Allow for the FULL RANGE of
polyester powder finish.

Figure L5.1.

Figure L5.2.

Paint all timbe□

Paint all timbers (3 COATS).

Figure L5.3.

□

155

Complete the remaining lines of text in Fig. L5.1 as before. When you have 'carriage returned' the dtext cursor after the last line of text, do an extra RETURN to exit the DTEXT command.

Methods of displaying text

By default, AutoCAD text is displayed left justified at its start point, as defined in Fig. L5.4a.

Proceed as follows:

1. Select either the TEXT command or the DTEXT command. Then select the RIGHT (R) option. PICK a suitable start point. Do RETURNs to accept the default height and rotation. Then write the text shown in Fig. L5.4b. Note the 'right justified' effect of the completed text display. (Using the DTEXT command, the right justified effect does not occur until the command is completed.)
2. Similarly, use the options CENTRE, MIDDLE, FIT and ALIGN, in turn, to create the text shown in Figs L5.4c, L5.4d, L5.4e and L5.4f, respectively. (For the FIT and ALIGN options, PICK two points in each case, at a suitable distance apart for 'First text line point' and 'Second text line point'.)

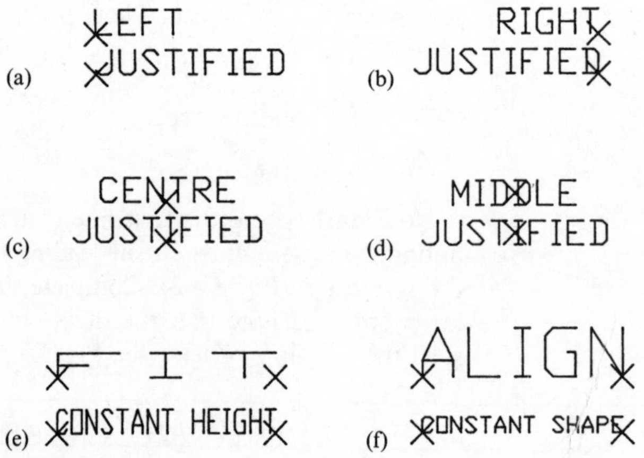

Figure L5.4.

Special characters

You may include some characters which are not on the keyboard by using '%%' codes:

%%c   Diameter symbol (Ø)
%%d   Degree symbol (°)
%%p   Plus/minus symbol (±)

For example, using the default options of TEXT or DTEXT, and suitable start point, type the following text at the keyboard:

```
MAXIMUM TEMPERATURE 375%%d CELSIUS
%%p2.5%%d
```

After completing the command, your text should appear as shown in Fig. L5.5.

Now create the text shown in Fig. L5.6.

Figure L5.5.

MAXIMUM TEMPERATURE 375° CELSIUS ±2.5°

Figure L5.6.

5 Holes ⌀25. Equi-spaced on 350 PCD (±.05)

Text styles

You may build up libraries of text STYLES. Each STYLE is defined by a number of different parameters, such as:

- The text HEIGHT
- The text FONT type (i.e. shape/pattern of text)
- The text WIDTH FACTOR
- The text OBLIQUING ANGLE

The text STYLE we have been using is called STANDARD. This is the only one supplied by AutoCAD, but you may create any number of others. Each STYLE is given its own name, which may be anything of your choosing. The STANDARD text style has a primitive FONT type called TXT. Several other FONTS are available (Appendix C).

Exercise in STYLE

Note: From Releases 12 and 13 onwards, the STYLE command invokes automatic dialog box displays. The exact sequence of events varies between releases and platforms, but the options and parameter requirements remain consistent.

In the following exercise, pull-down menus are not a suitable selection technique for the STYLE command, since that approach might not give enough versatility between stylenames and font types. (This statement applies for both MSDOS and Windows systems.)

Proceed as follows:

1. Select the STYLE command, e.g. by typing:

    STYLE   (RETURN)

    For the style name, type:

    WIDESLOPE   (RETURN)

    Then, select TXT as the font type. As the text height, type:

    30   (RETURN)

As the width factor, enter:

3   (RETURN)

As the obliquing angle, type:

20   (RETURN)

Then, keep to default values. When you have completed the STYLE command, WIDESLOPE will be the current text style.

2. Now select the TEXT or the DTEXT command and, in the new current text style, create the text shown in Fig. L5.7.

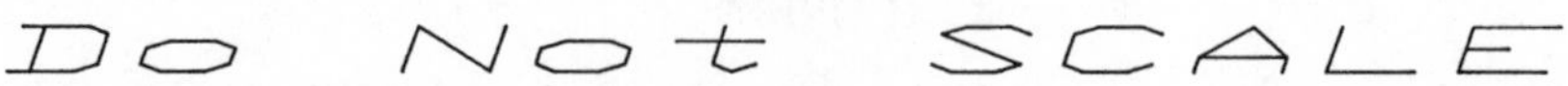

Figure L5.7.

3. Select the STYLE command again and create a text style called ITAL1, specifying the font type ITALICT and text height 25. Otherwise keep to default parameter values.

4. Now create another new style called ITAL2. Use ITALICT font type again, but this time specify a text height of 0. (This keeps the height variable, as in the STANDARD style.) Otherwise use default parameter values.

5. Create two more styles. Specify the parameters shown below, but other-wise use default values:

Style name: COPPERPLATE   Font: SCRIPTC   Height: 40
Style name: OLDENGLISH   Font: GOTHICE Height: 50

6. We now have a library containing six different text styles. List their names and parameters by selecting the STYLE command, and then selecting the ? option.

7. Being the last style created. OLDENGLISH is the current one. Set ITALS as the new current style by selecting either TEXT or DTEXT, then the STYLE (S) option.

Then, for the style name, type:

ITAL2   (RETURN)

For the text height, type:

45   (RETURN)

Then PICK a suitable start point and write the first line of text in Fig. L5.8. Then complete the command.

8. Similarly, create the second and third lines of text in Fig. L5.8, using styles ITAL1 and COPPERPLATE respectively.

9. Use the LINE command to draw a profile around the written text as shown in Fig. L5.8. (Estimate proportions.)

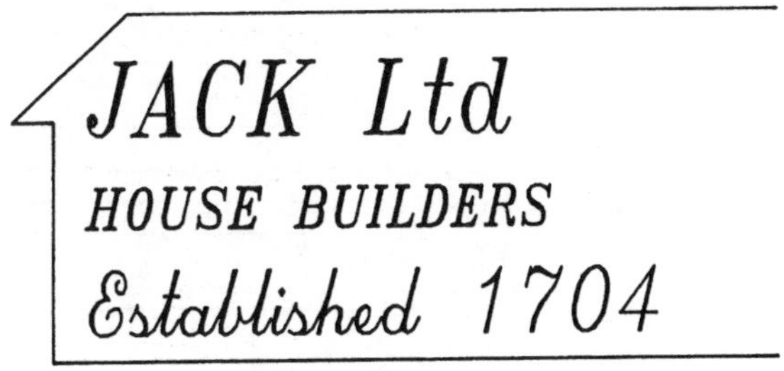

Editing text

You may alter some parameters of existing text using the CHANGE command. Here, we will change the STYLE of some existing text. Proceed as follows.

Select the CHANGE command. Point to the text line 'Jack Ltd'. PICK. Now keep doing RETURNs until prompted for a new style name. Then type:

OLDENGLISH   (RETURN)

Now keep RETURNing until the CHANGE command is completed. See the changed text (Fig. L5.9).

Figure L5.9.

The QTEXT command

QTEXT can improve efficiency on involved text sessions. Proceed as follows.

Select the QTEXT command. Select the ON option. Get a drawing regeneration by selecting the REGEN command. See the existing text shown as enclosing rectangles (Fig. L5.10). (This simplified display speeds up drawing work during periods when the actual display of existing text is not essential.) Restore text display by reselecting QTEXT, selecting the OFF option, and then selecting the REGEN command.

The MIRRTEXT system variable

Usually, when you create a mirror image of existing objects, you would not wish any existing text to be mirrored as well. The MIRRTEXT system variable can be of assistance in this situation. Proceed as follows:

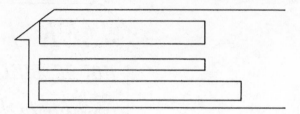

Figure L5.10.

1. Select the MIRROR command. Select all items (text and lines) in Fig. L5.9. PICK the two rightmost endpoints (marked '×' in Fig. L5.11) as points for the mirror line. Select the N (NO) option for deleting old objects. See the display as in Fig. L5.12a. (The unwanted reversed text is due to the MIRRTEXT system variable being set to its default value of 1.)
2. Use the U or the UNDO command to undo the mirror operation, and thus go back to the display in Fig. L5.9. Select the SETVAR command. Select MIRRTEXT as the system variable. Enter a value of 0 (thus suppressing mirrored text).
3. Repeat the MIRROR routine as before. See the display shown in Fig. L5.12b.

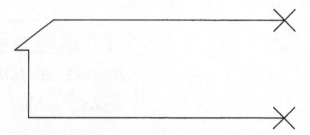

Figure L5.11.

Styles with symbol fonts

Specialist font types for symbols and non-roman text are available via the use of *character mapping*, shown in Appendix C.

Proceed as follows:

1. Create three new text styles with names GREEK, SUMS and SONGS, using font types GREEKC, SYMATH and SYMUSIC, respectively. Specify text height of 0 (i.e. variable height) in all cases. Otherwise keep to default parameter values.
2. Using TEXT or DTEXT, set the current text style as SUMS. Then using text height 25, and any convenient start point, type the lower case text shown in Fig. L5.13a, at the keyboard, followed by RETURN. After completing the command, your text should be displayed as shown in Fig. L5.13b. Check this result against the character mappings for the SYMATH font in Appendix C.

Figure L5.12.

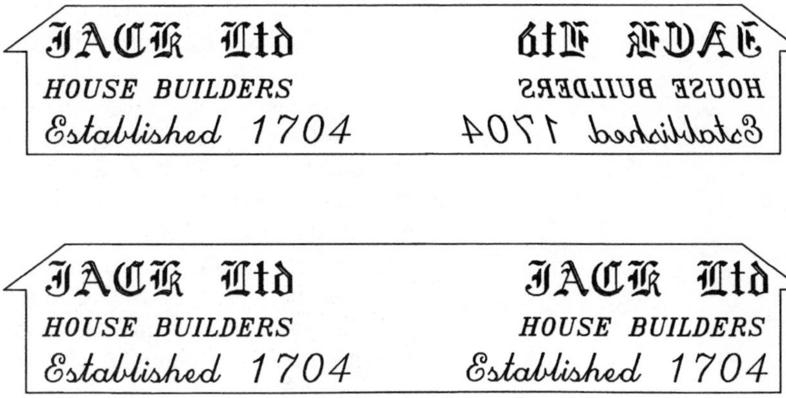

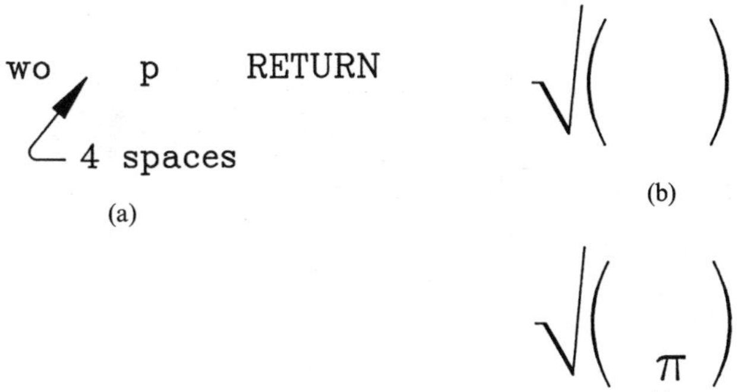

$$Radius\ of\ Sphere\ =\ \sqrt[3]{\left(\frac{3V}{4\pi}\right)}$$

(d)

$$Area\ =\ \underset{\delta\alpha\,\to\,0}{Lim}\left\{\sum_{0}^{\pi}sin\ \alpha\ \ \delta\alpha\right\}$$

$$=\ \int_{0}^{\pi}sin\ \alpha\ \ d\alpha$$

(e)

Figure L5.13.

3. Now set GREEK as the current text style and use character mapping to create a π with height 25 and a suitable start point to get a display like Fig. L5.13c.
4. Complete the display in Fig. L5.13d, using text style ITAL2 with suitable heights and start points. (Tidy up the text using MOVE if necessary, and assume that Figs L5.13b, c, d are zoomed to a higher magnification than previous diagrams.)
5. Using the text styles SUMS, GREEK, and ITAL2 with suitable heights and start points, create the text shown in Fig. L5.13e.
6. Now, using the text styles SONGS, OLDENGLISH and ITAL2, with suitable heights and start points, create the text shown in Fig. L5.14. Assist with the LINE command. (Assume that Fig. L5.14 is zoomed to a greater magnification than the previous diagrams which contained the text style OLDENGLISH.)

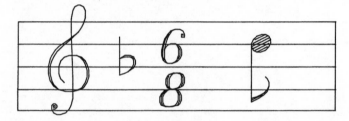

Figure L5.14.

Advanced text features

In later releases of AutoCAD, the following features have been included to enhance the text facilities we have been using in this lesson:

- A multi-line text facility (MTEXT command) supporting word wrap, alignment, tabs, styles and formatting
- Integrated, dialog-based wordprocessing with a standard editing, cut-and-paste and formatting control interface

- Integrated spell-checking (via the SPELL command), both for the word processor and for checking text on the whole drawing

These advanced wordprocessing, editing and spell-checking facilities may be actioned via the Edit Mtext dialog box, which may be displayed by PICKing the text icon in the Draw toolbar (see Fig. L5.15). This allows the user to pick a text area on the screen and make appropriate settings such as text style prior to commencing wordprocessing and editing.

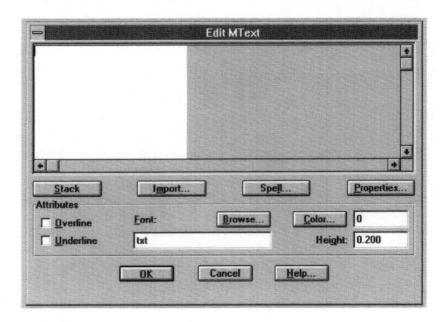

Figure L5.15. The Edit Mtext Dialog Box.

End of lesson

Lesson 5 is now completed. END the drawing.

Lesson 6

Further draughting

The ELLIPSE command

When you use the ELLIPSE command, you may enter the required parameters, from which AutoCAD approximates the ellipse geometry from a
series of ARCS, automatically formed into a special type of polyline. Being
a type of polyline, an AutoCAD ELLIPSE may thus be broken up into its
separate arcs via the EXPLODE command, if required. (*Note*: True elliptical curves are available on AutoCAD from Release 13 onwards.)

There are a number of methods for drawing ellipses, including the
ISOMETRIC CIRCLE routine, which is discussed in Lesson 8.

In the following exercise we will use three common ellipse options.
Proceed as follows:

1. The default method is to specify the *endpoints of one axis and the eccentricity of the other axis*, where the term 'eccentricity' may be taken as
   meaning 'half the length of an axis'.

   Begin a new drawing with SNAP and GRID set ON at 10 units. Select
   the ELLIPSE command. Move the cursor to an area of the screen and
   PICK three points at the appropriate grid points and in the order shown
   in Fig. L6.1. Thus one axis and an eccentricity have been specified, and
   the ELLIPSE should be displayed as in Fig. L6.1.
2. Now we will draw an ELLIPSE by specifying its *centre point and two
   eccentricities*.

   Reselect the ELLIPSE command. Select the CENTRE (C) option.
   Move the cursor and PICK a convenient centre point. Then PICK two
   eccentricity points in the order shown in Fig. L6.2. See the completed
   ellipse, as in Fig. L6.2.
3. Our third method will be to specify the *endpoints of one axis and a
   rotation*. The 'rotation' principle is explained in Fig. L6.3. The ellipse
   display is the view you would get if you looked normal to the diameter of
   a circular disc which had rotated through an angle about that diameter.
   The diameter of the circular disc is thus equal to the major axis of the
   ellipse seen.

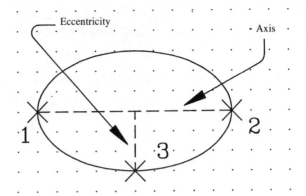

Figure L6.1.

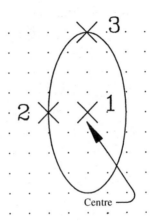

Figure L6.2.

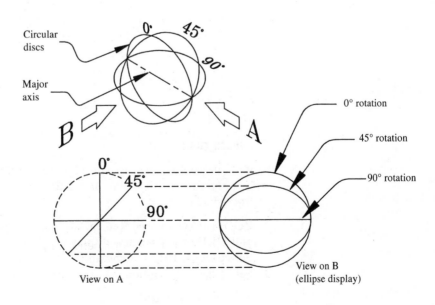

Figure L6.3.   Principle of
the ELLIPSE ROTATION
option.

Reselect the ELLIPSE command. PICK two axis endpoints as in Fig. L6.4. Then select the ROTATE (R) option. For the rotation angle, enter:

60   (RETURN)

The completed ellipse, and explanation, is shown in Fig. L6.4a.

Now draw ellipses with the same axis endpoints, but with rotations 0, 30, 45, 80 (see Fig. L6.4b).

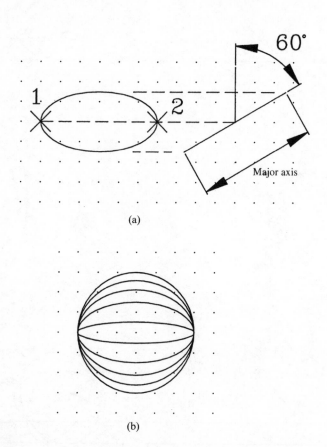

(a)

Figure L6.4.

(b)

Elliptical arcs

From Release 13 onwards, you can create elliptical arcs by selecting the ARC option of the ELLIPSE command.

Proceed as follows:

1. ZOOM/PAN to a convenient area of the screen. Set a suitable SNAP and GRID for your new display.
2. Select the ELLIPSE command.
3. Select the ARC option, e.g. by typing:

A   (RETURN)

4. Select the CENTRE option, e.g. by typing:

    C   (RETURN)

5. PICK a convenient ellipse centre point with your pointing device. Referring to Fig. L6.5, PICK a convenient axis endpoint horizontally rightwards of the centre point. Then PICK a convenient 'Other axis distance' vertically above the centre point.

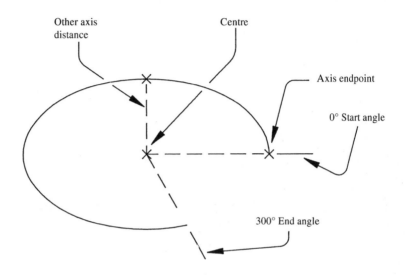

Figure L6.5.   ELLIPSE, ARC option.

6. AutoCAD then displays a prompt which defaults to a 'Start angle' option. Accept the default by typing in a start angle value of:

    0   (RETURN)

7. AutoCAD next displays a prompt which defaults to an 'End angle' option. Accept the default by typing in an end angle value of:

    300   (RETURN)

8. Your completed elliptical arc should appear similar to Fig. L6.5.

The POLYGON command

Like ellipses, an AutoCAD POLYGON is a special case of polyline which, once created, may thus be broken to its composite lines via the EXPLODE command, if required.

In this exercise we will draw three POLYGONS using different options. Proceed as follows:

1. Select the POLYGON command. Then, for the number of sides, enter:

    5   (RETURN)

Move the cursor and PICK a suitable centre point.
Now select the I (inscribing circle) option. Then, for radius, enter:

30   (RETURN)

See a pentagon drawn inside a 30 radius inscribing circle (not displayed), as in Fig. L6.6.

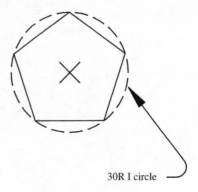

Figure L6.6.

30R I circle

2. Reselect the POLYGON command. Specify 6 sides. PICK a suitable centre point. Then select the C (circumscribed circle) option. Specify 30 radius.

See a 60 A/F (across flats) hexagon, as in Fig. L6.7. Note that the hexagon circumscribes a 60 radius circle (not displayed).
3. Reselect the POLYGON command. Specify 8 sides. Select the E (edge) option. PICK two edge endpoints as in Fig. L6.8.

See an octagon (edge-size 20) as in Fig. L6.8.

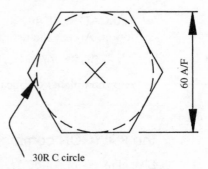

Figure L6.7.

60 A/F

30R C circle

Point filters, ORTHO and DIVIDE

Point filtering is a very useful technique, by which you can tell AutoCAD to ignore either the X or Y coordinate value (or Z value in 3D work) when you specify a point. The required value of the ignored X or Y (or Z) can then be added afterwards (using a different drawing mode if you wish).

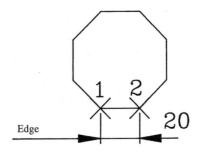

Figure L6.8.

Edge   20

Proceed as follows:

1. Using convenient locations and sizes, draw an ARC and a small CIRCLE similar to those in Fig. L6.9a.

Figure L6.9.   (a)   (b)

2. Select the LINE command. Then, in response to the `From point:` prompt, enter:

    `.Y`

(followed by RETURN if typed-in at the keyboard).
    Then, while still in the LINE command, use the END osnap to PICK the lower endpoint of the arc. (This is the *point filter* operation, which has specified the Y location of the start point, but left the X value, as yet, unspecified.) Note the `Need X:` prompt. Use the END osnap to PICK the top endpoint of arc (so that the line starts vertically at the bottom of the arc and horizontally at the top). In response to the `To point:` prompt, enter:

    `.X`

(followed by RETURN if typed-in at the keyboard).
    Then use the CEN osnap to PICK the centre of the circle. Note the `Need Y:` prompt. Use the END osnap to PICK the top of the arc (so that the line ends horizontally at the centre of the circle and vertically at the top of the arc). RETURN to complete the LINE command. The line should be as in Fig. L6.9b.

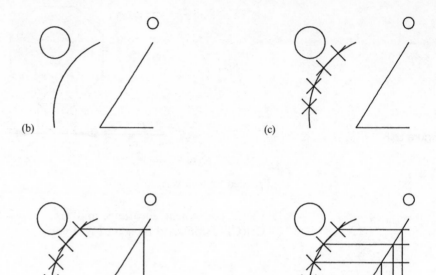

(b)

(c)

(d)

(f)

Figure L6.9.

3. Now use suitable point filters and osnaps to draw a circle whose centre is horizontally at the top endpoint of the arc and vertically at the lower endpoint of the arc, then a new line starting at the lower end of the first line and ending at the same height, directly beneath the top point of the first line (see Fig. L6.9c).

4. Use SETVAR to set PDMODE to a value of 3 (as discussed in Lesson 2).

5. Select the DIVIDE command. Move the cursor and PICK the arc. Then, in response to the Number of segments: prompt, enter:

5   (RETURN)

Note the NODE points which have appeared on the arc, dividing it into five equal segments (see Fig. L6.9d).

6. Use CTRL-O to toggle ORTHO mode ON. This allows only vertical or horizontal lines to be drawn. (Or pick ORTHO in the Windows status bar.)

7. Select the LINE command, then use the NODE osnap to PICK the top node as the start point of the line. Specify point filter .X in response to the To point: prompt and use osnap END to PICK the top end of the first line. PICK any nearby point in response to the Need Y: prompt. RETURN. See a new horizontal line (Fig. L6.9e). Now use ORTHO, osnaps INT and END and suitable point filters to draw the new vertical line shown in Fig. L6.9e.

8. Use ORTHO, and appropriate osnaps and point filters, to draw more 'ortho' lines as shown in Fig. L6.9f.

9. Use CTRL-O to switch ORTHO OFF. (Or pick ORTHO in the Windows status bar.)

The MEASURE command

The MEASURE command is similar to DIVIDE, but creates segments of stated length.

Proceed as follows:

1. ZOOM to a unused area of the screen and use the ARC command to draw a semi-circle of 50 radius, as in Fig. L6.10a.
2. Select the MEASURE command. Move the cursor and PICK the arc. RETURN. Then, in response to the Segment length: prompt, enter:

   35   (RETURN)

   See segment node points displayed as in Fig. L6.10a.
3. You may also place BLOCKS instead of nodes at segments using either DIVIDE or MEASURE.

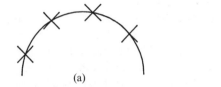

(a)

(b)

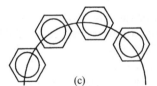

(c)

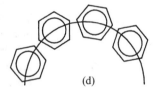

(d)

Figure L6.10.

With reference to Lesson 2, create a block called **POLYCIRC**, made up of a 10 radius circle and a concentric hexagon of 15 radius inscribing the circle (Fig. L6.10b). Use the BASE command to set the block base point at the centre of the 10 radius circle.

Select the MEASURE command. PICK the arc again. RETURN. Select the BLOCK (B) option. Then, for block name, enter:

   POLYCIRC   (RETURN)

Then, in response to the Align block: prompt, select the NO (N) option.

Finally, in response to the Segment length: prompt, enter:

   35   (RETURN)

See the blocks displayed, as in Fig. L6.10c.

4. Use either the U command or the UNDO command to undo the last MEASURE operation. Then repeat MEASURE on the arc, using the

previous parameters, except in this case select the yes (Y) option in response to the Align block: prompt (Fig. L6.10d).

Inquiry commands

LIST

The LIST command gives information about selected existing objects. Proceed as follows.

Select LIST and, for example, PICK the previous arc drawn. RETURN. Note the listed parameters of the arc on the text screen (layer, linetype, sizes, etc.). Select REDRAW to retrieve the graphics screen if necessary.

ID and DIST

The ID and DIST commands give information about specified points. Proceed as follows.

Select the ID command. PICK any point on the screen. Note the coordinate values of the specified point shown in the screen prompt area.

Select the DIST command. PICK any two points on the screen. Note the text display giving the distance, and angle, between the two points picked. (In the DOS system you may need to press the F1 key to see all of the text display, then F1 again, or REDRAW, to get back to the graphics display.)

AREA

The AREA command gives the enclosed area, and perimeter, between a number of specified points. Proceed as follows.

Select the AREA command. Move the cursor to a suitable part of the screen and PICK points at the grid dots, and in the order shown, in Fig. L6.11. (Grid dots are spaced at 10 units.) RETURN. See text display:

Area=3000.000. Perimeter=244.237

STATUS

We have already used STATUS while in the DIM mode for dimensioning work. If you select the STATUS command while not in DIM mode, a list of all the current mode settings for your drawing is displayed on the text screen (e.g. limits, snap and grid spacings, current layer, defaults, and extents). If necessary, the graphics screen is retrieved via REDRAW or the F1 key (DOS) or F2 key (Windows).

On-screen help

You can obtain on-screen information about any chosen command by selecting the HELP (or ?) command and then entering the name of that command. Alternatively, if you RETURN after selecting HELP, a list of all the AutoCAD commands is displayed.

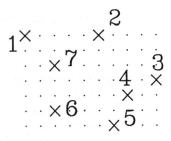

Figure L6.11.

Transparent routines

Some commands may be actioned 'transparently' (i.e. inside other commands) if an inverted comma is placed in front of the required command (e.g. you could action a PAN operation while inside another command by entering 'PAN or get help while within a command via 'HELP).

Proceed as follows:

1. Select the ZOOM command. Select option ALL (A).
2. Select the LINE command. PICK the start point of the line somewhere in the outer area of the screen. Before picking the end point, type:

        'ZOOM   (RETURN)

    This takes you into the ZOOM routine while you are still in the LINE command. Select the WINDOW (W) option of ZOOM. PICK two points to put a window around a small area approximately central to the screen. See the zoomed display while still in the LINE command. You are then taken back to the LINE routine. PICK the endpoint of your line somewhere in the zoomed view. RETURN to complete the LINE command.

The AutoCAD calculator (CAL command)

The CAL command may be used:

- As a simple calculator at the command line. For example, if you selected the CAL command, and then typed in:

        (3*(4+1))/2   (RETURN)

    AutoCAD would display the answer: 7.5.
- More significantly to the draughtsperson, as a construction tool, using a combination of mathematical operators and object snap modes. In these cases, CAL is often invoked transparently (i.e. within other commands, as described above).

    For example, if you wanted to draw a line to start halfway between the midpoint of an existing line and the centre of an existing circle, you could select the LINE command and then, in response to the From point: prompt, enter: 'CAL to action the CAL command transparently.

In response to AutoCAD's Expression: prompt you could then type:

(mid+cen)/2   (RETURN)

AutoCAD would then ask you to Select object for MID snap: and you could do so by PICKing the existing line with an automatically invoked OSNAP target sight.

You would then be asked to Select object for CEN snap:, and you could respond by PICKing the existing circle with the target sight.

AutoCAD would then draw the start point of the new line at the required position and take you back to the main command, for you to complete the new line.

The RENAME and PURGE commands

You may use the RENAME command to change the name of saved VIEWS, LAYERS, BLOCKS, etc. Also, if they are currently unused (e.g. a block is not inserted, or a layer is OFF with nothing drawn on it), you may get rid of them via the PURGE command (for AutoCAD releases prior to 13, this must be the first command selected on your current drawing session).

We will now use RENAME to change the name of our block POLYCIRC to a new name: HEXACIRC. Proceed as follows.

Select the RENAME command. Select the BLOCK option. Then, for the old view name, enter:

POLYCIRC   (RETURN)

Then, for the new block name, enter:

HEXACIRC   (RETURN)

Hatching routines

It is a common draughting procedure to fill an area with a type of pattern. This is called *cross-hatching*, or just *hatching*, and is done on AutoCAD via the HATCH command. The simplest type of hatch pattern available on AutoCAD is called U. (This is the User Defined hatch pattern. It merely consists of straight lines at a specified angle and distance apart. Also, please note, the U hatch pattern has absolutely nothing to do with the U or UNDO commands.) In addition, there are several other standard hatch patterns available to suit specific applications. These may be listed via the ? option of HATCH.

The completed hatched pattern is considered by AutoCAD as a single BLOCK of objects, which may thus be broken up into its composite entities via the EXPLODE command.

The following exercise uses the traditional HATCH command facilities. However, from Releases 12 and 13 onwards, you can adopt a far more versatile approach by using the BHATCH command, which is discussed at the end of this lesson.

Proceed as follows:

1. ZOOM to an unused area of the screen and draw a horizontal LINE 120 units long, then three more LINES to get the 100 size square shown in Fig. L6.12a. Draw a 20 radius circle at the centre of the square, with two centre lines, as in Fig. L6.12a. The following sections contain the drawing stages required to cross-hatch the area bounded by the square and the circle using the 'U' hatch pattern.

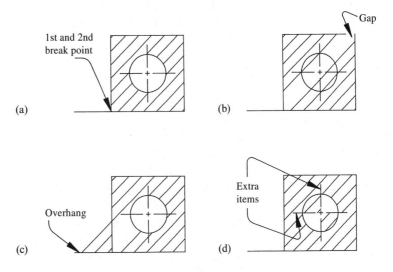

Figure L6.12.

2. The HATCH command (unlike BHATCH) recognizes only simple profiles, and will be confused by any gaps (Fig. L6.12b), overhangs (Fig. L6.12c) or extra items included during selection (Fig. L6.12d). To correct the overhang on the base, select the BREAK command. PICK anywhere on the 120 long horizontal base line. Then, to select first break point, enter:

   F   (RETURN)

   Then (via the SNAP or OSNAP), PICK the lower left corner of the square accurately). Keeping the same point, PICK again for the second break point. The horizontal base has now been broken into two parts (whose ends happen to be touching), namely two lines of lengths 20 and 100 (see Fig. L6.12a).

3. Select the HATCH command. Then select the U hatch pattern, e.g. by typing: U (RETURN). Then, for the cross-hatch angle, enter:

   45   (RETURN)

For the spacing, enter:

10   (RETURN)

Then, in response to the prompt: Double hatch area?, select the NO (N) option.

Then, in response to the Select objects: prompt, select only the five objects bounding the area to be hatched, i.e. the four 100 length lines and the circle. (In this case, individual selection via PICKBOX is probably most suitable, but whichever selection method you use, do not include the 20 length line or the two centre lines.)

Then RETURN to complete the object selection. The selected area should now be correctly cross-hatched, as in Fig. L6.12a.

4. Now draw a right-angled triangle, 160 wide, 80 high, as in Fig. L6.13a. Use TEXT or DTEXT (STANDARD style, 15 height, 0 rotation) to place the text: WEDGE somewhere totally inside the triangle.

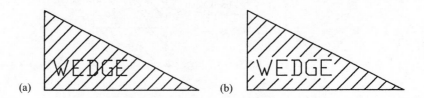

Figure L6.13.   (a)   (b)

Select HATCH. Enter the same parameters as previously (i.e. U pattern, 45 angle, 10 spacing, N for double hatch). Then select the three lines of the triangle only (not the text). RETURN to complete the hatching of the triangle. The text will be hatched through, as in Fig. L6.13a.

Select ERASE and PICK any part of the hatching pattern inside the triangle. RETURN. Being a BLOCK, the selected hatching will all be erased at once.

Repeat the last hatching routine with the same parameters, but this time select the text as well as the three triangle lines (e.g. by placing a window around all the items). The text will not be hatched through (see Fig. L6.13b).

Hatching PATTERNs and STYLEs

In the previous exercises we were hatching areas using the U HATCH PATTERN and the NORMAL HATCH STYLE. (NORMAL is the default hatch style.) Now we will do some hatching using other combinations of patterns and styles. Proceed as follows:

1. At a convenient area of the screen, draw items similar to those in Fig. L6.14a (largest radius, about 60 units). Ensure that the profiles contain no gaps or overhangs.

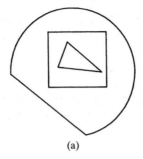

(a)

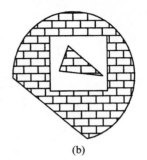

(b)

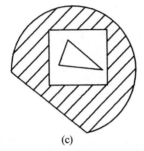

(c)

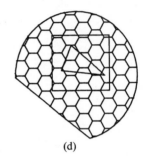

(d)

Figure L6.14.

2. Select HATCH. Then, for hatch pattern, enter:

BRICK   (RETURN)

For SCALE, enter:

30   (RETURN)

For ANGLE, enter:

0   (RETURN)

Then select all the items in Fig. L6.14a (e.g. by placing a window around them). RETURN to complete the selection.

See the hatching effect as in Fig. L6.14b (this is BRICK pattern, NORMAL style). Note that, for all patterns other than U, a SCALE value is entered instead of a spacing distance.

3. ERASE the brick hatching. Reselect the HATCH command. Then, for pattern, enter:

U,O   (RETURN)

Then specify the parameters: 45 angle; 10 spacing; N for double hatch.

Finally, select the items in Fig. L6.14a as before. See the hatching effect as in Fig. L6.14c (this is U pattern, OUTERMOST style).

4. ERASE the U,O hatching. Reselect the HATCH command. Then, for pattern, enter:

HONEY,I   (RETURN)

Then specify the parameters: 70 scale; 0 angle.

Finally, select the items in Fig. L6.14a again. See the hatching effect as in Fig. L6.14d (this is HONEY pattern, IGNORE style).

Hatching exercise

Draw the hexagon in Fig. L6.15 using the POLYGON command, with CENTRE option (choose suitable point) and 250 radius circumscribed circle.

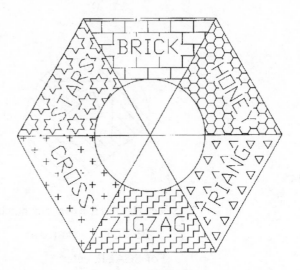

Figure L6.15.

Select the EXPLODE command. PICK the polygon (thus splitting it up into six separate lines).

Draw three lines accurately joining the opposite corners of the hexagon, then draw a 120 radius arc in each of the six resulting segments as shown.

Create the text shown at suitable heights and rotations.

Use suitable BREAK operations for hatching the segments.

Hatch each segment as shown in Fig. L6.15 using NORMAL (default) style, pattern as shown in text, 100 scale, and 0 angle.

The BHATCH command

BHATCH is an extremely versatile command which overcomes many of the limitations of the HATCH command. Using BHATCH, you can simply PICK any point in the area you wish to be hatched. AutoCAD then searches for the boundary of this area, and 'flood hatches' to that boundary. BHATCH was introduced with AutoCAD Release 12 and was further enhanced at Release 13. If you are using Release 12 onwards, proceed as follows:

1. ZOOM/PAN to an unused area of the screen.
2. Draw three LINES and two CIRCLES, giving a drawing display similar to Fig. L6.16a. (Don't worry about the overhangs on the lines—

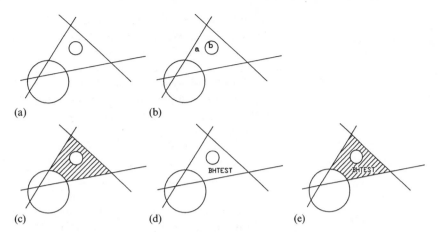

Figure L6.16. Hatching by the BHATCH command.

BHATCH can cope with them as they are.) Make a note of the approximate overall size of the drawing arrangement (e.g. via the coordinate display).

3. Select the BHATCH command. Thus see the Boundary (or Flood) Hatch dialog box appear on the screen (Fig. L6.17 shows the Release 13 revised version of this dialog box). Now move your cursor to the Pick Points box in the dialog display, and PICK. The dialog display then goes, and AutoCAD displays the prompt: Select internal point:.

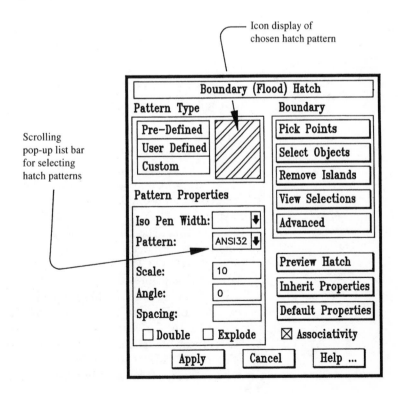

Figure L6.17. The Boundary (or Flood) Hatch dialog box.

Respond by PICKing a point inside the area enclosed by the lines and the larger circle. (This should be close to the 'boundary' of the area, e.g. as point a in Fig. L6.16b.) If you are using Release 12 you should then PICK for another 'internal point' inside the smaller circle, close to its circumference, e.g. as point b in Fig. L6.16b. (It is not necessary to pick point b if you have Release 13 onwards, since the circle will be detected as an 'island' to be flood-hatched around.) Now RETURN to complete the selection of internal points.

AutoCAD then redisplays the Boundary (Flood) Hatch dialog box.

From now on, the description of the BHATCH routine applies specifically to Release 13. If you have Release 12 you may achieve the same results by a slightly longer process involving two or three successive dialog displays, i.e. the Boundary Hatch dialog box, the Hatch Options dialog box, and the Stored Hatch Pattern icon display (for selecting predefined hatch patterns). In Release 13 the dialogs and icons are streamlined into a single display.

Proceed as follows. Respond to the redisplayed Boundary (Flood) Hatch dialog box by PICKing the User Defined box in the Pattern Type area of the dialog display.

PICK the Angle box, delete any existing text via keyboard, and enter:

45

Now PICK the Spacing box and enter a suitable value for the hatch spacings, with regard to the size of your drawing arrangement. Then PICK the Apply box in the dialog display.

This completes the BHATCH routine, and your display should be as Fig. L6.16c.

4. Now erase the hatching you have just produced (e.g. via ERASE LAST), and then use the TEXT or DTEXT command to add the text 'BHTEST' to a suitable height and position, similar to Fig. L6.16d.

5. Select the BHATCH command again, and repeat the procedure in (3) by PICKing the same (or similar) 'internal point' as before, and RETURNing to complete the selection of internal points.

Now, when the Boundary (Flood) Hatch dialog box has reappeared, PICK the Select objects box in the dialog display. The dialog box then goes, and AutoCAD displays the prompt: Select objects. Respond by PICKing the text 'BHTEST'. Then RETURN to complete the selection. The Bhatch dialog box will now be displayed again. Respond by PICKing the Apply box in the dialog display. This completes the BHATCH routine. (AutoCAD assumes the same hatch pattern requirements as previously.)

The resulting hatch display should be as Fig. L6.16e. (Note that the text 'BHTEST' is not hatched through.) Retain the drawing work shown in Fig. L6.16e for some hatch editing procedures after section (6).

6. Now repeat the hatching exercise from 'Hatching Exercise' (page 178), using the BHATCH command. This time you won't need to explode the polygon, or perform any 'breaks' in your lines. Also you may draw a

single circle of radius 120, instead of the six arcs drawn previously. The appropriate hatch patterns may be specified by PICKing the Pre-Defined box in the Pattern Type area of the Boundary (Flood) Hatch dialog box display. If you then scroll through the pattern names in the Pattern scrolling pop-up list bar and PICK the one you require, you will see an icon display of the selected hatch pattern in the Pattern Type area of the dialog display (refer to Fig. L6.17). You should then enter the required Scale and Angle via the appropriate boxes before PICKing Apply.

Associative hatching

This useful facility is available from Release 13 onwards. Associative hatching is related directly to the boundary geometry which it is hatched to. Thus if the boundary geometry is subsequently modified the associative hatching would be automatically updated to the new boundary. If BHATCH work is done under default settings of Release 13, and if the system variable PICKSTYLE is set to a value of either 2 or 3, the hatching will conform to the associative principle. (See Lesson 3 concerning PICKSTYLE in relation to GROUPS.)

Proceed as follows:

1. Redisplay the BHATCH drawing work relating to Fig. L6.16e.
2. Select the MOVE command and move the lowest line down to a position approximately as shown in Fig. L6.18.
3. See how the associative hatching has automatically updated to the modified boundary.
4. Similarly, MOVE the smaller circle down to approximately as shown in Fig. L6.18, and use the SCALE command to reduce the size of the larger circle.
5. Your display should now be similar to Fig. L6.18, with the hatching automatically updated to all the edit operations on the boundary.

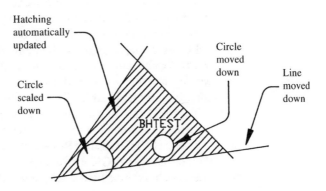

Figure L6.18. Associative hatching.

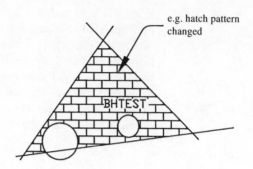

Figure L6.19.   HATCHEDIT
command.

The HATCHEDIT command

HATCHEDIT was also introduced at Release 13, and allows you to make quick modifications to existing associative hatching. Using menus, it may be selected from the Modify menu (MSDOS) or the Edit toolbar (Windows).

Proceed as follows:

1. Select HATCHEDIT.
2. PICK the hatching in Fig. L6.18.
3. The Boundary (Flood) Hatch dialog box is then displayed. PICK the Pre-Defined box. Scroll through the Pattern pop-up list and select a new hatch pattern. Then PICK the Apply box.
4. Your drawing should now have the new selected hatch pattern, as indicated in Fig. L6.19.
5. Experiment with some more HATCHEDIT routines, such as changing the predefined hatch scale, switching to user-defined hatching, altering hatch angles and altering spacing.

The 'internal point'

When you use BHATCH and specify an associative hatch boundary via the Pick Point procedure, the point you specify inside the area to be hatched is called the *internal point*. (For example, this would correspond to point a of our drawing in Fig. L6.16b.)

The internal point may be considered as the origin of the hatch pattern. If the boundary is edited so that the internal point no longer lies inside the hatch area, a different area may be hatched.

For example, suppose we had edited our drawing in Fig. L6.16b by moving the small circle over the internal point (see Fig. L6.20a). AutoCAD would then have assumed the small circle to be the new boundary and consequently hatched inside it (see Fig. L6.20b).

To avoid this unwanted effect, you may move the internal point of an existing associative hatch, as follows:

Select HATCHEDIT; PICK the existing hatch; select Pick Points from the dialog box; PICK a new internal point which avoids any 'new boundaries' such as the edited circle; select Apply.

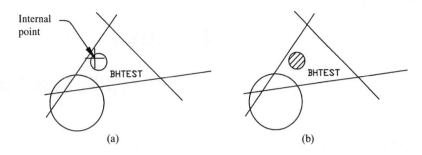

Figure L6.20.   (a) Small
circle moved to
encompass internal point;
(b) resulting hatch effect.

End of lesson

Lesson 6 is now completed. END your drawing.

Lesson 7

2D solid work, PLINE and SKETCH

The SOLID command

Begin a new drawing and then proceed as follows:

1. Select the SOLID command. PICK any four points such as 1, 2, 3 and 4 in Fig. L7.1a, in the order shown. RETURN after the fourth point is picked. See the solid area displayed, as in Fig. L7.1a.

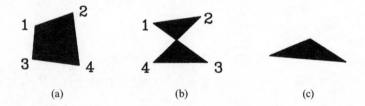

(a)   (b)   (c)

(d)

Figure L7.1.

2. Reselect SOLID. PICK four more points in the order shown in Fig. L7.1b. RETURN. Note the different effect achieved with the new order.
3. SOLID may also be used to draw solid triangles. Reselect SOLID. PICK any three points in any order you wish. RETURN after picking the third point. See a solid triangle such as in Fig. L7.1c.
4. Now, with SNAP and GRID set to 10, accurately draw the solid items shown in Fig. L7.1d. (PICK points at the appropriate grid dots shown.)

184

The TRACE command

Select TRACE. Then, for trace width, enter:

12   (RETURN)

Then PICK any convenient start point. (This is point 1 in Fig. L7.2.) Move the cursor horizontally rightwards, approximately to point 2 of Fig. L7.2 (say about 70 units). PICK. Then PICK more points similar to this in Fig. L7.2, and in the order shown. RETURN after picking the last point, thus completing the trace.

Figure L7.2.

Now draw some more traces with different widths and varying numbers of segments.

Note: Continued traces are not considered as single objects (as polylines and blocks are), but as individual segment items. For example, if you select ERASE, and PICK one of your traces, you will see that only one segment of the trace is selected.

The DOUGHNUT command

Proceed as follows:

1. Select the DOUGHNUT command. Then, for the inside diameter, enter:

    40   (RETURN)

    For the outside diameter, enter:

    90   (RETURN)

    Now PICK a convenient point for the centre of the doughnut. See the resulting doughnut displayed (Fig. L7.3a). Move the cursor and PICK another convenient centre point. Move the cursor and PICK another centre point. Then RETURN to complete the DOUGHNUT command. See three identical doughnuts displayed.
2. Draw some more doughnuts of differing numbers and sizes.
3. Now draw a solid circle of outside diameter 50 units, as in Fig. L7.3b, by specifying zero value for the inside diameter.

The PLINE (POLYLINE) command

As stated in Lesson 2, a polyline (or pline) is a continuous profile of line and/or arc segments which is considered as a single item.

(a)   (b)

Figure L7.3.

Proceed as follows:

1. Select the PLINE command. PICK any convenient start point. Then select the WIDTH option, e.g. by typing: W (RETURN). Then, for starting width, enter:

    5   (RETURN)

    Now RETURN to accept the default (thus specifying that the ending width will be the same as the starting width). Move the cursor upwards towards the right and PICK, to achieve a pline segment (width 5) similar to segment a in Fig. L7.4.

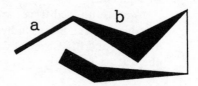

Figure L7.4.

    Select the WIDTH option again. Then RETURN to keep the starting width at 5. Then, for the ending width, enter:

    30   (RETURN)

    Move the cursor and PICK to achieve another pline segment, similar to segment b in Fig. L7.4. Move the cursor and PICK again to achieve a third pline segment. Then select the UNDO option, e.g. by typing: U (RETURN), and see that the third pline segment has now been erased. Now, while remaining in the PLINE command, continue to draw some more pline segments of varying starting/ending widths to achieve a polyline similar to that in Fig. L7.4. (The thinnest segment has zero width.) Complete the PLINE command by executing a RETURN after picking the final point.

2. With GRID and SNAP set to 10, select PLINE and, starting from the top left of Fig. L7.5, draw the top horizontal line segment rightwards with constant width 20 units and length 100 (length specified by PICKing at the appropriate grid point in Fig. L7.5). While still in the PLINE command, set the starting and ending widths to 20 and 5 respectively. Now select the ARC option, e.g. by typing: A (RETURN). Then PICK the arc end point accurately at point c in Fig. L7.5, and see the arc segment displayed. (We will not specify any more widths for segments on this

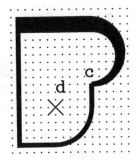

Figure L7.5.

polyline. By default, the remainder of the polyline will thus be drawn at a constant width of 5 units, i.e. the last width specified.)

Remaining in the PLINE command, select the LINE option, e.g. by typing: L (RETURN). Draw the vertical line segment downward from point c as shown in Fig. L7.5. Then select the ARC option. Then select the CENTRE option, e.g. by typing: CE (RETURN). PICK the arc centre accurately at point d in Fig. L7.5. Select the ANGLE option, e.g. by typing: A (RETURN). Then, for the arc angle, enter:

    −90   (RETURN)

Then, while still in the PLINE command, select the LINE option and draw the horizontal line segment at the base of Fig. L7.5. Complete the PLINE command by selecting the CLOSE option, e.g. by typing: C (RETURN).

3. Draw an accurate polyline as shown in the inner profile of Fig. L7.6 (200 by 100 rectangle, 50 mean radius arc at top left corner, three other corner arcs 20 mean radius, constant width 5 units).

After completing the PLINE command, select the OFFSET command. Then, for the offset distance, enter:

    15   (RETURN)

Now PICK any point *outside* the polyline as the offset side. RETURN to exit the OFFSET command. See the offset profile as in Fig. L7.6.

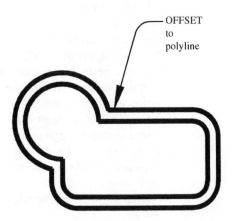

OFFSET
to
polyline

Figure L7.6.

The FILL command

1. Select the FILL command. Select the OFF option. Then select the REGEN command. Note that the existing 'solid' times are now shown 'hollow'. (This can be useful by speeding-up screen displays while working on another stage of the drawing.)
2. Draw some more simple solids traces, doughnuts, and 'thick' plines. Note the hollow display effect. Then select FILL again and select the ON option. Select REGEN. Note that the 'solid' items are now filled-in again.

The SKETCH command

The SKETCH command may be used for creating irregular profiles which would have been drawn freehand by traditional means (e.g. as in rough pencil sketching on paper).

Switch SNAP OFF, then proceed as follows:

1. Select the SKETCH command. Then, for record increment, enter:

    1   (RETURN)

    Now PICK a convenient point (this will be point e in Fig. L7.7). Note the PEN DOWN prompt. Move the cursor in the approximate direction of ef (Fig. L7.7), noting the irregular sketched profile forming. PICK at a point similar to f. Note the PEN UP prompt. Move the cursor to a point similar to g. PICK. Note the PEN DOWN prompt. Sketch a similar profile to that shown from point g. After PICKing the final point, exit from the SKETCH command by selecting the EXIT option, e.g. by typing: X (no RETURN required).
2. Reselect SKETCH. RETURN to accept the default record increment of 1. PICK a point similar to point h in Fig. L7.7. Move the cursor, thus sketching a similar profile to hk (do not PICK yet). Select the ERASE option, e.g. by typing: E (no RETURN required). Move the cursor back to about point j, noting the profile being erased. Move the cursor slightly forward again towards point k, to retrieve some of the erased profile. PICK. With the pen now up, move the cursor towards point k again (do not PICK). Select the CONNECT option, e.g. by typing: C (no RETURN required). Move the cursor back towards point j until it touches the end of the sketched profile. Note that the PEN DOWN prompt has automatically appeared. Move the cursor towards point k again, thus forming a new sketched profile connected to the end of the last one. PICK at about point k to end the new sketched profile. Leave the SKETCH command via the EXIT option as before.
3. Sketch another profile with a larger increment (say 10). See the coarser display.

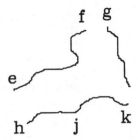

Figure L7.7.

Note: A SKETCHed profile is considered as a polyline of short line segments (line length set by the record increment value) if it is drawn when the system variable SKPOLY is set to a non-zero value. If you do not wish your sketched profiles to be polylines you should select SKPOLY (e.g. via the SETVAR command) and set it to 0.

Examples

Accurately draw the items shown in Fig. L7.8, using the grid dots shown and suitable snap values. (Assume that the GRID dots are spaced at 10, and the smallest increment in each item is 5 units.)

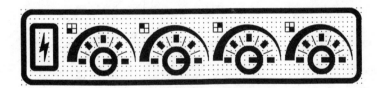

Figure L7.8.

Summary exercises: Lessons 4–7

Refer back to the two dimensioning exercises which concluded your work in Lesson 4 (i.e. Figs L4.8 and L4.9). In each case, OPEN the drawing and copy the geometry to another area of the drawing. Then edit the copied work to produce the drawings shown in Exercise 8 and Exercise 9.

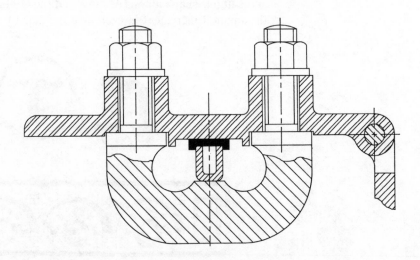

Exercise 8.

Estimate the sizes and scales of the additional items and hatch patterns shown. You can aid your completion of the assembly drawing in Exercise 8 by INSERTing the drawing called NUT (created in Lesson 2), as a BLOCK on your assembly drawing, with a suitable scale applied at insertion.

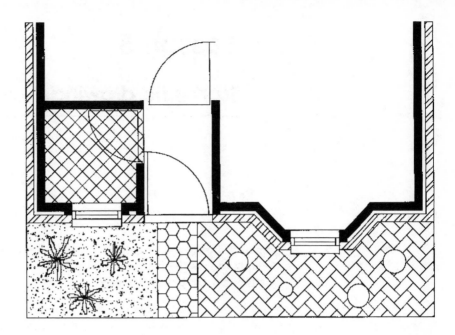

Exercise 9.

Lesson 8

Isometric drawing

Isometric drawing is essentially a two-dimensional drawing mode which attempts to give the impression of a 3D view of an item. This is achieved by adopting two basic principles:

- All horizontal edges are drawn at 30 degrees to the horizontal.
- All circles are drawn as ellipses in the appropriate choice of three *iso-planes*, namely: left, right and top. (Isometric arcs are also formed from ellipses, followed by suitable edit routines using commands such as TRIM.)

The importance of isometric drawing has now been much diminished with the advancement of CAD 3D modelling techniques. However, isometric drawing retains a role in some draughting applications. For example, if you require a reasonable approximation of a 3D effect in a single view (perhaps of a complex arrangement with awkward cutaways and hidden line removal) and are not concerned about automatic generation of other views or any perspective effect, then isometric drawing could sometimes be more efficient than 3D modelling as a draughting tool.

In the following isometric procedures, it must be emphasized that although we are giving the impression of 3D views, we will be drawing lines and ellipses by working *entirely within the 2D XY plane*. You should never attempt to mix isometric drawing with 3D modelling principles. Thus, in Lesson 8, we will never have occasion to use any of the AutoCAD 3D facilities, such as Z coordinates, 3D thicknesses, or 3D viewpoints (the AutoCAD VPOINT setting remaining constant at its default 'bird's eye' plan view: 0, 0, 1).

Proceed as follows:

1. Begin a new drawing. Select SNAP. Then select the STYLE (S) option. Now select the ISOMETRIC (I) option. Then, for vertical spacing, enter:

    10   (RETURN)

    Now move your pointing device. Note the special isometric cursor display.

192

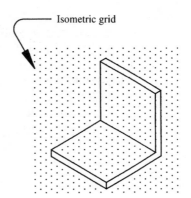

Isometric grid

Figure L8.1.

2. Set GRID ON with a value of 10. Note the isometric grid display.
3. Using the LINE command and the isometric SNAP/GRID facility, draw the L-shape (Fig. L8.1) in isometric (base: 100 by 100; height: 100; 10 thick). Then draw the model house shown in Fig. L8.2 (base: 100 by 100; total height: 100; roof: 40 deep; estimate other sizes).
4. Now draw an isometric cube of size 100 by 100 by 100.
5. Select the ELLIPSE command. Select the ISOCIRCLE (I) option. Then, for 'circle centre', take the cursor to the centre of the top face of the cube and PICK. Then select the DIAMETER option, e.g. by typing: D (RETURN). Then, for the isometric circle diameter, enter:

70   (RETURN)

Note the ellipse drawn on the top face of the cube, representing a 70 diameter isometric circle.
6. Select the ISOPLANE command. Select the LEFT option, e.g. by typing: L (RETURN). Move the cursor. Note the different type of cursor display for ISOPLANE LEFT. Now draw another 70 diameter 'isocircle' ellipse, proceeding exactly as in step (5), but in this case taking the cursor to the centre of the left face of the cube for the isometric circle centre.
7. Select ISOPLANE. Select the RIGHT option. Move the cursor and note the different cursor display for ISOPLANE RIGHT. Now draw another 70 diameter isometric circle exactly as on the previous occasions, except

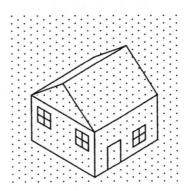

Figure L8.2.

in this case taking the cursor to the centre of the right face of the cube for the isometric circle centre.

You should now have drawn a 100 side isometric cube with a 70 diameter isometric circle at the centre of each visible face.

8. Select ISOPLANE. Select the TOP option. Draw a 70 diameter isometric circle on the top face of the cube, 10 units below the existing isometric circle, and on the same vertical axis. Then use the TRIM command to erase the lower part of this isocircle to its intersection with the upper isocircle. Now use similar procedures with the LEFT, then RIGHT, options of ISOPLANE, to complete the 'hollow box with holes' shown in Fig. L8.3.

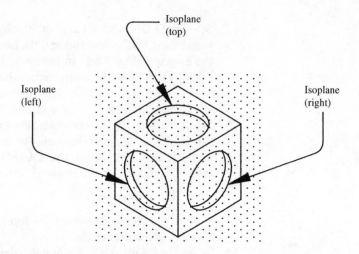

Figure L8.3.

You may also wish to take this a stage further by showing back edges that would be visible through these holes (assuming either a hole on every face of the cube, or no holes on the back faces).

9. Now draw the isometric items shown in Fig. L8.4. The main portions of each have maximum overall size 100 units. Minimum size increment is 10 units.

Try using ORTHO ON to help your drawing work (noting the different effect achieved when drawing in different isoplanes).

For isometric 'semi-circles' use temporary LINES along suitable major axes as cutting edges when TRIMming. (Alternatively, with Release 13

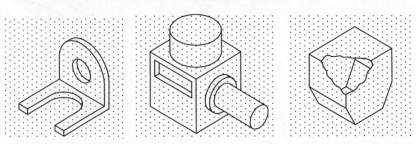

Figure L8.4.

onwards, you may use the ARC option of the ellipse command. See Lesson 6.)

For curved 'silhouette' edges use OSNAP INT and/or OSNAP TAN to connect isocircles and the temporary major axis lines. (*Note*: In some cases the nature of the ellipse construction causes OSNAP TAN to be unsuccessful. On such occasions use OSNAP END instead.)

Lesson 9

Polyline editing (PEDIT command)

Once you have created polylines, these may be edited via special techniques using the PEDIT (poly-edit) command. PEDIT is a complex command containing many different options which become essential tools in advanced draughting techniques. For this reason, a full lesson has been devoted to PEDIT procedures.

PEDIT options CLOSE and OPEN

Begin a new drawing. Set LIMITS to 0, 0 (lower left) and 3000, 2000 (upper right). Set SNAP and GRID ON at 10 units. Then proceed as follows:

1. Accurately draw the polyline shown in Fig. L9.1a, using a single PLINE command and with these parameters: linewidth 2; overall size 30 by 50 (to midpoint of linewidth); all arc radii 10; all other lengths in increments of 10 or 20; start point as in Fig. L9.1a.
2. Select the PEDIT command. Point to anywhere on the polyline and PICK. Select the CLOSE (C) option. Your polyline should now be closed as in Fig. L9.1b.
3. The OPEN (O) option of PEDIT 're-opens' a polyline where it was previously closed. Remaining in the PEDIT command, select the OPEN option. Your polyline should now be open again as in Fig. L9.1a.
4. Select the EXIT (X) option to complete the PEDIT command.

PEDIT options JOIN, WIDTH and UNDO

1. Using the LINE and ARC commands (not PLINE), draw a horizontal line rightwards from the top of the lower left end of the polyline, then an arc, radius 20, touching this line (see Fig. L9.2). Then complete the profile in Fig. L9.2 with another PLINE of varying linewidth. Estimate sizes and linewidths to scale. (The first polyline, the line, the arc and the second polyline should all touch each other accurately via either SNAP or OSNAP END.)

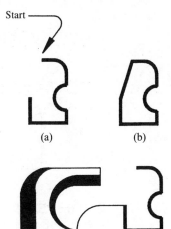

Start

(a)   (b)

Figure L9.1.

Figure L9.2.

2. We will now 'join' the line, arc and new polyline so that they become part of the first polyline. Select the PEDIT command. Then PICK the first polyline anywhere on its profile. Then select the JOIN (J) option. Then PICK the line, arc and new polyline in turn. RETURN. The four objects should now be one single polyline. (Note that the former line and arc have now assumed the linewidth of the original polyline.)

3. Remaining in the PEDIT command, select the WIDTH (W) option. Then, for the new linewidth, enter:

    0   (RETURN)

Note that the polyline now has a constant width of 0.

4. Remaining in the PEDIT command. Select the UNDO (U) option. Thus undo the last PEDIT operation (in this case, retrieving the previous linewidths).

5. Select the EXIT option to complete the PEDIT command.

Vertex editing

1. Select ZOOM, option ALL. Then use the WINDOW option of the ZOOM command to display a screen area approximately at the window corners 600, 600 (lower left) and 1400, 1400 (upper right).

2. Select the PLINE command and draw a polyline as in Fig. L9.3 (zero linewidth) with the following parameters:

    line from 660, 980 to 620, 980
    line to 620, 1060
    arc to endpoint 720, 1060 (or centre 670, 1060; angle −180)
    line to 900, 1060
    line to 770, 1130
    line to 730, 1130
    line to 1000, 1230

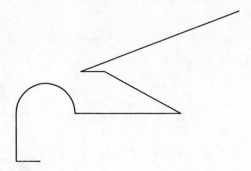

Figure L9.3.

3. Select the PEDIT command. The select the EDIT VERTEX option, e.g. by typing: E (RETURN). Note that a '×' marker has appeared at the first vertex of the polyline and the following options prompt has appeared:

```
Next/Previous/Break/Insert/Move/
Regen/Straighten/Tangent/Width/eXit:
```

4. Select the NEXT option from the above screen prompt, e.g. by typing: N (RETURN). Note that the '×' marker has moved to the second vertex on the polyline. Now RETURN and you will see that the marker has moved to the third vertex. Keep repeating the RETURN to see the marker moving to each successive vertex (see Fig. L9.4). Continue until you have reached the final vertex of the polyline.

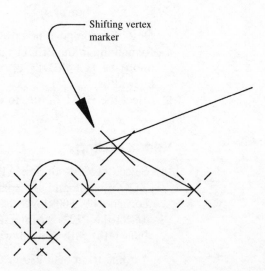

Shifting vertex marker

Figure L9.4.   Edit vertex (NEXT option).

5. Now select the PREVIOUS option, e.g. by typing: P (RETURN). This performs the same operation as NEXT, but in the reverse direction. Thus the '×' marker moves back to the previous vertex. Now repeatedly perform RETURNs, thus taking the marker back through the vertices, until the marker is again at the first vertex.

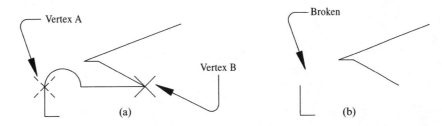

Figure L9.5. Edit vertex
(BREAK option).

6. Use the NEXT option to take the '×' marker to vertex A in Fig. L9.5a.
   Select the BREAK option, e.g. by typing: B (RETURN). Note the following screen prompt:

   `Next/Previous/Go/eXit:`

   Select NEXT from this prompt, thus taking the '×' marker to the
   next vertex. Then RETURN to take the marker forward again
   (bringing it to vertex B in Fig. L9.5a). We have thus specified A and
   B as the two vertices between which we will modify the polyline. Note
   that the `Next/Previous/Go/eXit:` prompt has reappeared.
   Now select GO from this prompt. This executes the chosen vertex-
   editing option (in this case, BREAK) between the two specified vertices.
   See that the polyline has been broken into two parts (each forming an
   individual polyline) with the 'gap' lying between vertices A and B (Fig.
   L9.5b). AutoCAD then returns to the main vertex-editing display
   prompt:

   `Next/Previous/Break/Insert/Move/`
   `Regen/Straighten/Tangent/Width/eXit:`

7. We will now UNDO the last BREAK operation. Select the EXIT
   option from the vertex editing prompt, e.g. by typing: X (RETURN).
   AutoCAD then takes you back to the main Pedit prompt:

   `Close/Join/Width/Edit vertex/Fit curve/`
   `Spline curve/Decurve/Undo/eXit:`

   Select the UNDO option from this prompt. The original polyline will
   now be displayed, as in Fig. L9.3.

8. Select EDIT VERTEX again, and use the NEXT option to take the '×'
   marker to vertex C in Fig. L9.6a. Then select the INSERT option, e.g.
   by typing: I (RETURN). This option allows you to add a new vertex to
   your polyline, and thus AutoCAD displays the prompt:

   `Enter location of new vertex:`

   Respond to this by entering:

   `730,1180`   (RETURN)

   Your polyline should now appear as Fig. L9.6b, with a new vertex at
   730, 1180 between vertex C and the next vertex. Now add some more
   vertices, approximately at the positions shown in Fig. L9.7.

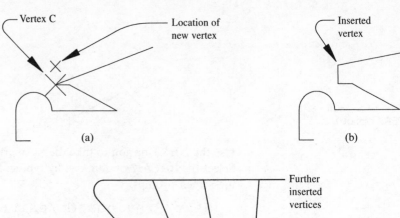

Figure L9.6.   Edit vertex
(INSERT option).

(a)

(b)

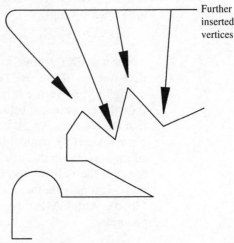

Figure L9.7.

9. Use the **PREVIOUS** option to take the '×' marker to vertex D in Fig. L9.8a. Select the **MOVE** option, e.g. by typing: M (RETURN). This allows you to reposition the currently-marked vertex, and thus AutoCAD displays the prompt:

        Enter new location:

Respond to this by entering:

        770,1060   (RETURN)

Your polyline should now appear as in Fig. L9.8b, with vertex B repositioned at 770, 1060.

10. Use the **NEXT** option to take the '×' marker to vertex E in Fig. L9.9a. Select the **STRAIGHTEN** option, e.g. by typing: S (RETURN). This draws a straight line between the current vertex and a second specified vertex, while deleting any other existing vertices or segments lying between them. As for the **BREAK** option, the second vertex is selected via the prompt:

        Next/Previous/Go/eXit:

Thus continue in the same manner as in (8), by selecting **NEXT**, performing RETURNs until the '×' marker reaches point F in Fig.

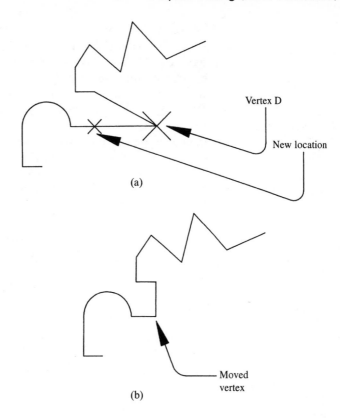

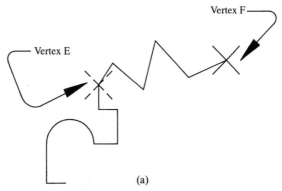

Figure L9.8.   Edit vertex (MOVE option).

Figure L9.9.   Edit vertex (STRAIGHTEN option).

L9.9a, and then selecting GO. Your polyline should now appear as in Fig. L9.9b, with a single 'straightened' segment between vertices E and F.

   Now use the same procedure to straighten the polyline between vertices G and H in Fig. L9.10a, thus modifying the polyline as in Fig. L9.10b.

11. Working from the `Next/Previous/Break/Insert/ Move/Regen/Straighten/Tangent/Width/eXit:` prompt, take the '×' marker to vertex J in Fig. L9.11a, and then select WIDTH from the same repeated prompt. The WIDTH vertex-editing

option allows you to alter the width of the single polyline segment which immediately follows the currently-marked vertex. After you have selected WIDTH, AutoCAD requests the starting width and the ending width required. Respond to this by entering values of 10 and 40 respectively. The new segment widths will not be displayed until the REGEN option is selected from the repeated vertex-edit prompt. After you have done so, your polyline should appear as in Fig. L9.11b.

12. Complete this exercise by selecting the EXIT option of the edit-vertex prompt, thus taking you back to the main Pedit prompt. Select the WIDTH option from this prompt, then enter a value of 0 for the new width. The polyline should now be returned to its previous state in Fig. L9.10b.

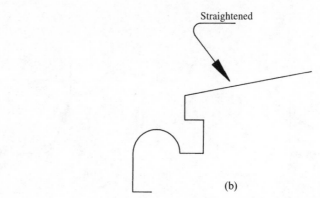

Figure L9.9.   Edit vertex (STRAIGHTEN option).

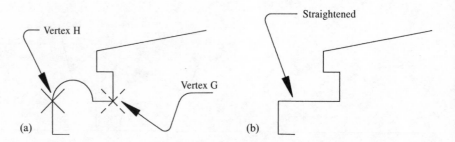

Figure L9.10.

Then leave the PEDIT command by selecting EXIT from the main Pedit prompt.

Using PEDIT to create curved profiles from existing polylines

Smooth curves may be computed from existing polylines via either the FIT or the SPLINE options of PEDIT.

The FIT option draws a smooth curve passing through all the vertices of the selected polyline. The fitted curve is made up of a series of joined arcs.

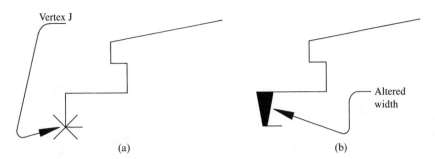

Figure L9.11.   Edit vertex
(WIDTH option).

(a)   (b)

Proceed as follows:

1. Select **PEDIT** and **PICK** the polyline created in the previous exercise. Then select the FIT option, e.g. by typing: F (RETURN). The edited polyline should now appear as in Fig. L9.12. The strange curve thus produced indicates that the FIT option does not always produce the desired effect. However, you may modify the curve to suit your requirements in the next stage.

2. Select **EDIT VERTEX**. Then use NEXT to take the '×' marker to vertex A in Fig. L9.13a. Now select the TANGENT option, and, in response to the prompt Direction of tangent:, take your cursor approximately to the position shown in Fig. L9.13a, then PICK. Note that an arrow marker has appeared through vertex A in the direction of the picked point. Now EXIT from EDIT VERTEX and select FIT again. Your modified curve should appear as in Fig. L9.13b, with the arc portion at vertex A now drawn tangentially to the arrow marker (which, although shown in Fig. L9.13b for explanation, is no longer displayed on the screen).

3. Let us assume that the edited curve remains unsatisfactory. We could perform further **TANGENT** routines as previously; but, in this case,

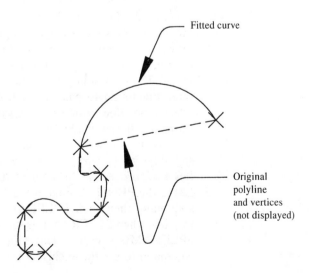

Figure L9.12.   PEDIT (FIT
option).

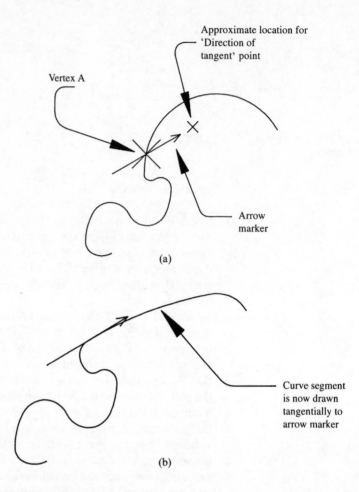

Vertex A

Approximate location for
'Direction of
tangent' point

Arrow
marker

(a)

Curve segment
is now drawn
tangentially to
arrow marker

(b)

Figure L9.13.   Edit vertex
(TANGENT option).

cancel the curve we have created and retrieve our original polyline by
selecting the DECURVE option, e.g. by typing: D (RETURN). Our polyline should now be displayed as previously in Fig. L9.10b.

4. Now, while remaining in the PEDIT command, select the SPLINE
option, e.g. by typing: S (RETURN). The resulting *spline curve* is shown
in Fig. L9.14. A spline curve differs from a FITted curve in that, rather
than attempting to pass through the vertices, the spline curve uses the
selected polyline as an enclosing frame. Under default settings, the spline
frame (i.e. the original polyline) is not displayed once the spline has been
created. If you wish to see the frame in conjunction with the created
spline curve, you may do so via the SPLFRAME system variable. In
this case, proceed as in the next stage.

5. Leave the PEDIT command via the EXIT option. Select the SETVAR
command, then enter SPLFRAME as the variable name. The frame is
invisible when SPLFRAME is set to 0 (default value) and is visible when
SPLFRAME is set to 1. Thus enter a value of 1. Now select the REGEN
command to see the enclosing frame (Fig. L9.15).

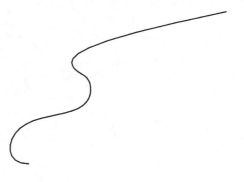

Figure L9.14.   PEDIT
(SPLINE option).

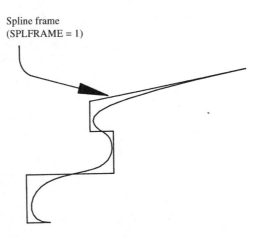

Spline frame
(SPLFRAME = 1)

Figure L9.15.

6. Assuming that the spline frame is not required to be permanently displayed, repeat the previous procedure to set SPLFRAME back to 0, then REGEN to make the frame invisible again.

7. *Note*: There are two more system variables which are of importance here.

   The SPLINETYPE variable affects the shape of the spline produced. If SPLINETYPE is set to 6 (the default) a *cubic B-spline* is formed. If it is set to 5, a *quadratic B-spline* is produced (this matches its frame more closely than the cubic type).

   The SPLINESEGS variable controls the fineness or coarseness of spline curves. The default setting is 8. If you set SPLINESEGS to a greater value than this, the resulting spline is made up from more line segment approximations, thus producing a more accurate, finer curve. However, this becomes more demanding on regeneration times.

   Both SPLINETYPE and SPLINESEGS are accessed via the SETVAR command. (SETVAR may be bypassed for Release 12 onwards.)

8. Now draw the polyline shown in Fig. L9.16a, with a total of five vertices: first vertex at 710, 820; last vertex at 1000, 1110; three intermediate vertices approximately at the positions shown in Fig. L9.16a. Then use the FIT option of the PEDIT command to produce the curve in Fig. L9.16b. (If your curve doesn't look correct, use appropriate PEDIT procedures to achieve the required shape.)

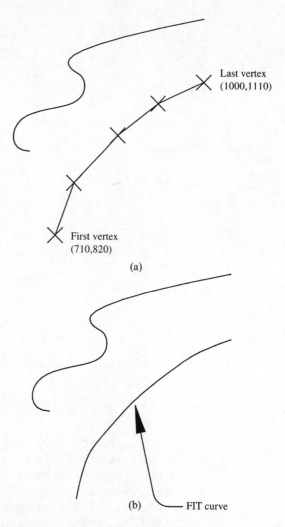

Figure L9.16.

9. To summarize our work on PEDIT, draw the items shown in Fig. L9.17. (Construct all curves via FIT or SPLINE from straight line segments of PLINES. Use the dimensions shown as a guide to proportions.)

Note that the first example is merely an extension of our previously created polyline curves, to make up a doorway with a decorative frame.

Advanced curve geometry

From Release 13 onwards, the curve techniques previously described, may be enhanced using NURBS (non-uniform rational B-splines) geometry and true ellipses. NURBS allow you to precisely define curves. This makes the creation, manipulation and editing of complex, curved shapes easy and accurate. The facility for creating true ellipses (in contrast to the approximations used via the ELLIPSE command) provides an additional aid in this process.

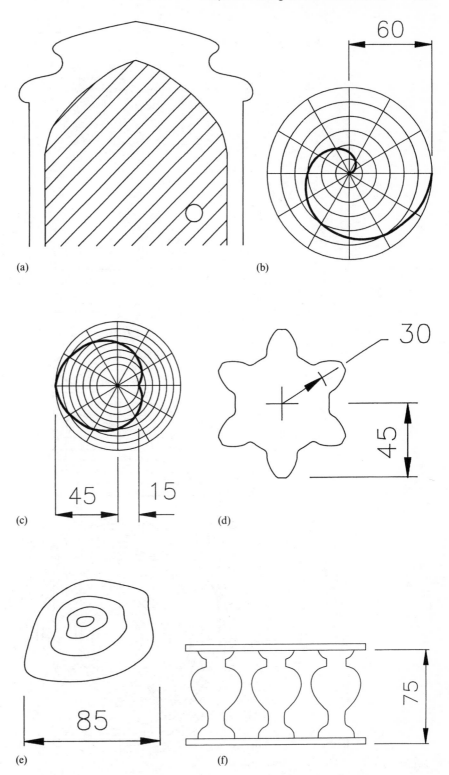

(a)

(b)

60

(c)

45   15

(d)

30

45

(e)

85

(f)

75

Figure L9.17.

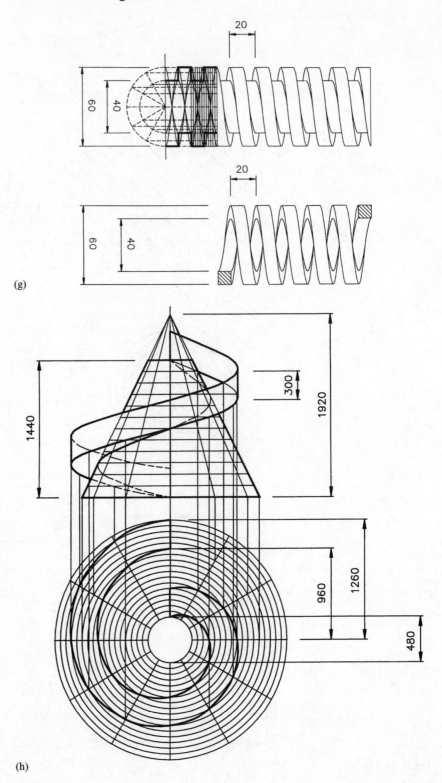

(g)

(h)

Figure L9.17.

Lesson 10

Blocks and attributes

BLOCKS have already been introduced in Lesson 2 and have also been referred to in the context of special cases such as associative dimensions and hatch patterns. As previously stated, a block is an arrangement of drawn objects which are considered by AutoCAD as a single composite item (although the objects making up the block do not have to be touching—as in the case of polylines). The purpose of this lesson is to enlarge on the BLOCK techniques already encountered, and introduce the concept of *attributes* which may be used to provide text display in conjunction with inserted blocks.

Proceed as follows:

1. Begin a new drawing and draw the item shown in Fig. L10.1 (overall dimensions: 100 by 100; chamfer: 40 by 40; fillet radius: 40; circle radius: 20). Estimate a suitable centre point for the circle.

2. Select the BLOCK command and, following the procedure outlined in Lesson 2, specify a blockname (e.g. THING), PICK the lower left corner of the item as the block basepoint, select every object (e.g. via the WINDOW option), and finally RETURN to complete the BLOCK command. Note that the drawing has disappeared. (If you restore it via OOPS, it won't be a block.)

3. Select the INSERT command and, following the procedure outlined in Lesson 2, enter your blockname, e.g.

   THING   (RETURN)

   Then PICK a convenient insertion point, and enter RETURN RETURN RETURN (thus specifying the default value of 1 for X and Y scales and default value of 0 for rotation). Note the inserted block (in this case, identical in appearance to your original drawing in Fig. L10.1).

4. Repeat step (3), but this time specify an X scale factor of 1.5, RETURN to set Y scale factor the same as X, and then RETURN to accept default zero rotation. Now repeat, but specify 2, 0.75 and 0 for X scale factor, Y scale factor and rotation respectively. Repeat again

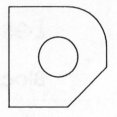

Figure L10.1.

but specify 1, 1 and 40 for X scale factor, Y scale factor and rotation respectively.

You should now have four blocks displayed, with the variations as shown in Fig. L10.2.

Note: If you are using AutoCAD Release 12 onwards, you may use a dialog box procedure for executing the inserts described in (3) and (4). This is invoked by the DDINSERT command.

5. Select an edit command, such as ERASE, MOVE or COPY. PICK the last inserted block on any one of its lines, arc or circle. Note that the complete block of items has been selected at once. Complete the edit command and then undo this edit routine via either the U command or the UNDO command. (Thus you should now be back where you were at Fig. L10.2.)

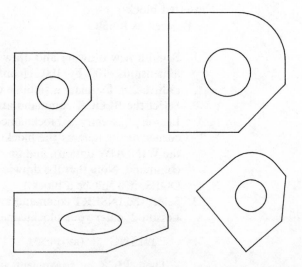

Figure L10.2.

Now select the EXPLODE command. (This 'unblocks' the individual items within an inserted block and makes them separate objects again.) PICK any item on the last block (i.e. that block with the rotation of 40). Then select the same edit command as before, and PICK the same item on this block as previously. Note that, this time, only the single object of the former block has been selected. Complete the edit command.

6. You may also 'unblock' a collection of items at the time of inserting, by placing an asterisk in front of the blockname entered.

Select the INSERT command again. Then, for the blockname, enter the prefixed name, for example:

*THING   (RETURN)

Now complete the INSERT command by PICKing a convenient insertion point and entering suitable values for X/Y scale and rotation. (*Note*: it is not possible to 'unblock' items to different X and Y scales via either EXPLODE, or our current routine.)

Then perform an edit routine as in step (5), PICKing one object in the inserted collection of entities. Note that only the single PICKed item has been selected. Complete the edit command.

7. Select the MINSERT command. (This will enable us to insert an ARRAY of blocks.) Proceed with an insert routine as in step (4), but with a scale factor of 0.4 in both X and Y, and zero rotation. AutoCAD then takes you through the same series of prompts as for a rectangular array (see Lesson 3). Respond by specifying the following parameters: number of rows: 2; Number of columns: 6; distance between rows: 65; distance between columns: 65.

Your completed array of blocks should be as in Fig. L10.3.

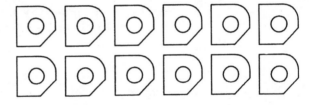

Figure L10.3.

8. We will now create some blocks with attributes. These are special entities which contain text to describe the parameters of inserted blocks. In this exercise we will make a simple block for a house plan, and describe each house via attributes.

Draw the house plan shown in Fig. L10.4 (overall size 200 by 100; estimate other sizes).

Select the ATTDEF command. AutoCAD then displays the prompt:

Attribute modes -- Invisible (N)
Constant(N) Verify (N) Preset (N)

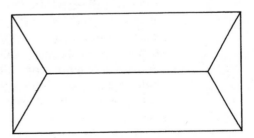

Figure L10.4.

Respond to this by entering:

I

(followed by RETURN if typed-in at the keyboard).

Note that the Invisible prompt is now reversed by being displayed as Invisible (Y). This means that we have specified a YES option to perform invisible attributes. The drawing will now remain in invisible attribute mode until such time as it is toggled back to Invisible (N) by entering I again. The other three attribute modes can be toggled to Y or N in the same way, but for now we will keep to the current settings, that is:

Invisible (Y) Constant (N) Verify (N)
Preset (N)

Now RETURN to leave the attribute modes prompt.

Then, in response to the Attribute tag prompt, enter:

NUMBER   (RETURN)

Then RETURN (to reject the option of Attribute prompt).

Then RETURN again (to reject the option of Default attribute value).

AutoCAD then prompts you for a start point for the attribute tag. Respond by PICKing a start point inside the house plan drawing, towards the top left. Then, for the text height, enter:

10   (RETURN)

Then, for rotation, enter:

0   (RETURN)

This completes the ATTDEF command, and your attribute tag ('NUMBER') should be displayed as in Fig. L10.5.

Note: If you are using AutoCAD Release 12 onwards, ATTDEF routines can also be achieved via a dialog box procedure. This is invoked by the DDATTDEF command.

9. Now repeat the ATTDEF routine three more times, keeping to the same attribute modes as previously (i.e. keep 'Invisible' toggled at 'Y' and the other modes at 'N'). On the successive occasions specify tags: NAME, OWNER and BEDROOMS. Specify 4 for the default attribute value of BEDROOMS. Otherwise enter the same values and responses as in step (8). PICK start points for the attribute tags approximately as shown in Fig. L10.5. Thus see these tags displayed.

10. Create a BLOCK called HOUSE, basepoint at lower left corner of the house plan, and selecting all drawn objects of the house and the attribute tags (e.g. by placing a window around the house and text).

INSERT this block using default scale factors and rotation.

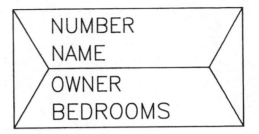

Figure L10.5.

AutoCAD then prompts you to enter values for the attributes on this block. If the ATTDIA system variable is set to a non-zero value (refer to later note), it does this by displaying the Enter Attributes dialog box (see Fig. L10.6). Note that the value for the tag BEDROOMS has automatically been entered at 4 (the default value we previously entered). Move your cursor to the empty box to the right of the OWNER tag, and PICK. Then enter:

SMITH   (RETURN)

Likewise, enter attribute values of SUNNEE and 3 for the tags NAME and NUMBER respectively. (If we wished, we could also change the BEDROOMS default value of 4 to another value by the same method, but in this case leave it as it is.)

Then move the cursor to the OK box and PICK. This completes the insert command.

You will see that the block has been inserted, but without any attribute text displayed. This is because we requested INVISIBLE attributes during the ATTDEF routines. Select the ATTDISP command. Then select the ON option. You will now see your attribute values displayed, as in Fig. L10.7.

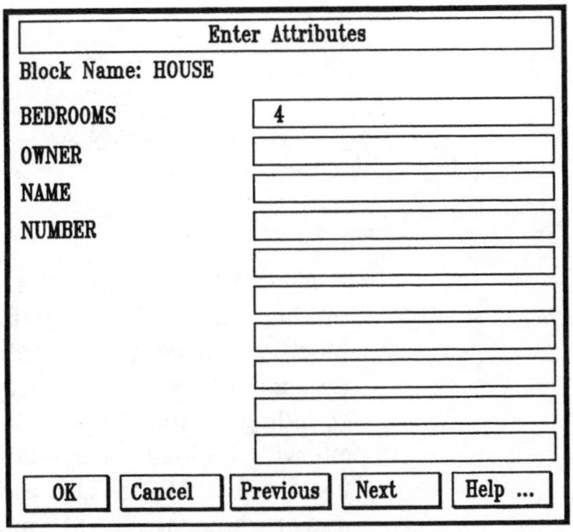

Figure L10.6.   The Enter Attributes dialog box.

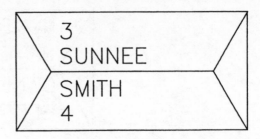

Figure L10.7.

Note: Use of the attribute dialog box is controlled by the ATTDIA system variable. The dialog box is displayed when ATTDIA is set to any non-zero number. If ATTDIA is set to zero, the dialog box is not displayed and AutoCAD prompts you to enter attribute values via the conventional lower screen area.

11. Select the ATTEDIT command. Then, in response to the `Edit attributes one at a time?` prompt, select the YES option, e.g. by typing: Y (RETURN). Then, accept defaults on the next three prompts via: RETURN RETURN RETURN.

    Now move the cursor to the attribute text SMITH, and PICK. Then RETURN.

    An options display then appears. Select the VALUE option, e.g. by typing: V (RETURN). Then select the REPLACE option, e.g. by typing: R (RETURN).

    Then, for the new attribute value, enter:

    BLOGGS   (RETURN)

    Thus see BLOGGS displayed as the new owner. RETURN to exit the ATTEDIT command.

12. Now use your block HOUSE to draw an avenue of houses with different attribute values on each (Fig. L10.8).

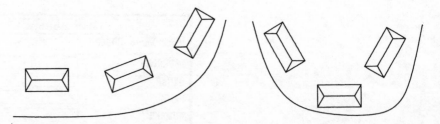

Figure L10.8.

Note: We have seen that blocks may be broken up into separate objects via the EXPLODE command. If you explode an inserted block which contains attributes, the attribute values will disappear (assuming they are currently displayed) and be replaced by their corresponding attribute tags.

13. We will now create a standards library from blocks, and use it. Create a block called RESISTOR, as in Fig. L10.9a, with rectangle size 3 by 10, and attribute tags NAME and VALUE (do not use INVISIBLE mode).

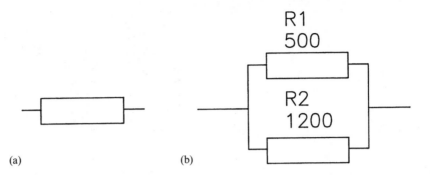

Figure L10.9.   (a)   (b)

Insert this block twice, and complete the simple circuit drawing shown in Fig. L10.9b.

Select the WBLOCK command. Note the prompt Filename:. Using the appropriate letter to specify your user floppy disk drive, enter a filename such as:

A:RESISTOR   (RETURN)

Now, in response to the Blockname: prompt, enter:

RESISTOR   (RETURN)

This has created a new drawing file on your floppy disk called RESISTOR, containing the data on your existing block of the same name. The new drawing can now be used as a standard which may be repeatedly inserted as a block onto other drawings. (Thus the WBLOCK command is a useful tool for exporting *part* of an existing drawing to a standards library.)

Now END your current drawing, and begin a new drawing called TRAN for storage on your floppy disk. Draw the item shown in Fig. L10.10. Use ATTDEF to give it a single attribute tag: NAME. Select the BASE command. PICK the basepoint at the circle centre. In this case, the complete drawing will be used as a standard in our library, so we will not need to use either the BLOCK command or the WBLOCK command. END your drawing.

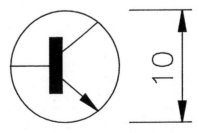

Figure L10.10.

We now have two drawings in our standards library, namely RESISTOR and TRAN. Study the circuit drawing in Fig. L10.11 and

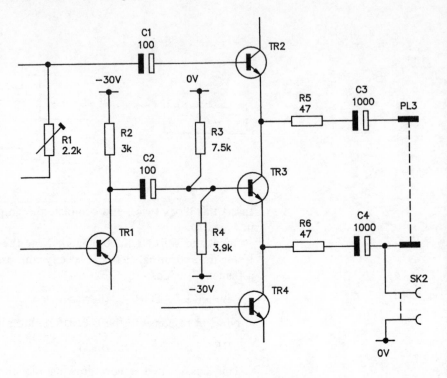

Figure L10.11.

produce some more new drawings for electrical symbols, using suitable names and attribute tags, thus further enlarging our standards library.

Begin a new drawing called CIRCUIT for storage on floppy disk. Draw the circuit shown in Fig. L10.11 by INSERTing the drawings from your standards library as external blocks (by the same method as for the NUT drawing in Lesson 2) and entering appropriate attribute values (e.g. your drawing standard TRAN could be inserted using the blockname: A:TRAN and with an attribute value such as: TR1. Complete the circuit drawing using the LINE command.

Part C

3D modelling on AutoCAD

This part of the book contains ten lessons (Lessons 11 to 20 inclusive) which cover the principles and techniques required to become proficient in the creation of three-dimensional designs using AutoCAD.

Note: Before attempting any of the lessons in Part C, it is essential that you complete all of the exercises in Part A. Most of the lessons in Part B also contain essential groundwork prior to beginning Part C.

Lesson 11

Simple 3D techniques

The basic principles of AutoCAD 3D have been described in Part A, with particular reference to the commands VPOINT and UCS, and the system variable THICKNESS. This lesson assumes that you have already worked through Part A, and thus have some knowledge of these principles. You may wish to refer back to Part A before you begin.

Suffice here to remind you that when you create any drawing using AutoCAD, you are always working in a 3D world. When you do 2D draughting work, however, you are only drawing on one plane (the XY plane) of this 3D world, only specifying points relative to two axes in it (the X and Y axes), and only viewing your objects as a 'bird's-eye' plan view (perpendicular to the XY plane). When you do 3D modelling, you make use of the third (Z) axis, enabling you to specify points three-dimensionally, and view objects from different directions to see the three-dimensional shapes formed. The XY plane can then be considered as 'ground level' from which you may specify 'heights' or 'depths' in the form of Z values.

All of the drawing commands we have used for 2D draughting may also be used to create 3D models, although some objects (such as ARCs) can only be drawn in a single plane and will not accept 3D (XYZ) coordinates.

The exercises in this lesson recall some of the groundwork in Part A as well as giving some more practice in 3D geometry routines and displays achieved from different 3D viewpoints.

Proceed as follows:

1. Begin a new drawing. Set LIMITS to 0, 0 (lower left corner) and 1000, 1000 (upper right corner). SNAP ON at 5 units. GRID ON at 10 units.
2. Select the SETVAR command. Then select the THICKNESS system variable. Then, for the thickness value, enter:

   20   (RETURN)

   This sets the current 3D thickness to 20 (i.e. future objects drawn will have an 'extruded' thickness of 20 units in the Z direction).
3. In a convenient area of the screen, draw the L-shape shown in Fig. L11.1, to size: 60 by 60 by 40. (At this stage, you may treat the exercise

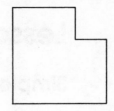

Figure L11.1.

purely as 2D draughting, using the LINE command to create the shape by exactly the same procedures adopted in the previous lessons.)

4. Once you have drawn Fig. L11.1, you may now consider this as the 'bird's eye' plan view of an L-shape box.

   Select the VPOINT command. Then, for the viewpoint position, enter:

   $$-8,-5,5 \quad \text{(RETURN)}$$

   You should now see the view shown in Fig. L11.2a. This displays the L-shape in 3D with a 'thickness' of 20 (as previously set). You can assume that the L-shape box is laid flat on the 'ground' (XY plane) and has a vertical 'height' of 20 (in the positive Z direction) from the ground.

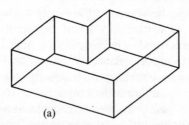 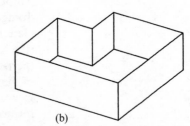

Figure L11.2.

(a)   (b)

Regarding the viewpoint, it is assumed that you, the viewer, are at an X, Y position of –8, –5 from zero datum, and at relative Z position of 5 (+Z is 'upwards' or 'above ground').

Note: The relative X, Y, Z figures are *ratios* only, i.e. you would achieve exactly the same display if you requested a viewpoint of, say, –16, –10, 10 or –32, –20, 20 or –4, –2.5, 2.5.

5. Select the HIDE command. Note how the appropriate lines are hidden (Fig. L11.2b), i.e. giving us a 'hollow box' instead of a 'solid slab'.

6. Now select the VPOINT command again, and enter:

   $$0,0,1 \quad \text{(RETURN)}$$

   This brings us back to our plan view again, i.e. you, the viewer, are assumed to be at an X, Y position of 0, 0 and thus looking exactly along the Z axis (which, in a plan view, comes perpendicularly out of the screen for positive). The Z value of 1, being positive, determines that we are above ground, looking down. For a plan view, the actual value entered for Z is irrelevant (for example, a VPOINT entry of 0, 0, 50 would give the same plan view).

Note: An alternative method of obtaining a plan view (in the current UCS) is to use the PLAN command.

7. Now determine the approximate VPOINT X, Y, Z ratios for the views shown in Fig. L11.3, and display each of these views in turn. (You will need to HIDE in each case.) Then go back to the original plan view.

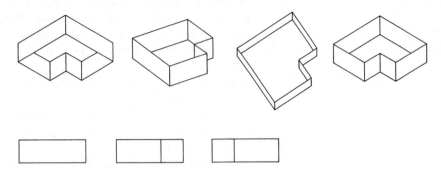

Figure L11.3.

8. Another way of selecting different viewpoint displays is via the 3D VIEW dialog box. This is displayed by PICKing the VIEW/VIEWPOINT/PRESETS option from pull-down menus. Once the icons are displayed, experiment with 3D views by adjusting rotational pointers on two diagrams in the dialog box (for x-axis and xy plane viewing positions respectively), followed by picking the OK box.

Then PICK VIEW/VIEWPOINT/AXES from pull-down menu, thus displaying the icon shown in Fig. L11.4. This gives dynamic VPOINT selection by moving an 'eye view' cross over a 'flattened globe' (assumed to be the Earth), whose North pole is in the centre. Selecting a viewpoint here would give a 'bird's eye' top plan view (0, 0, Z). The Equator is the inside circle. Selecting a viewpoint anywhere on the circumference of this circle would specify 'ground level' height

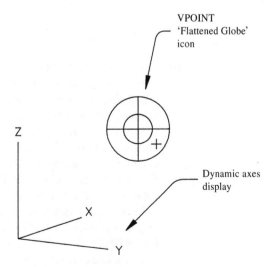

Figure L11.4.

and would thus result in a side view (X, Y, 0). The South pole is assumed to be the entire circumference of the outside circle. Selecting a viewpoint anywhere on this circumference would give a 'worm's eye' bottom plan view (0, 0, –Z). Move the cursor over the 'Earth' and meantime note also a dynamic display of rotating X, Y, Z axes. You can assume that the viewpoint is rotating with them. PICK a point on the flattened Earth and see the resulting 3D display. Then display a few more varying 3D views by this method until you have got a feel for it.

9. Now reset THICKNESS to a value of 40, by the same procedure as in step (2).

Get a 'bird's eye' plan view (either via VPOINT 0, 0, 1 or via the PLAN command).

Then draw a CIRCLE, radius 10, whose centre is at 20, 20 from the left-hand corner of the L-shape (Fig. L11.5a).

Select a VPOINT such as (–1, –1, 1). See the resulting 3D view (the circle being shown as a cylinder of thickness 40). Select the HIDE command. Note the different type of hidden display for the cylinder (Fig. L11.5b).

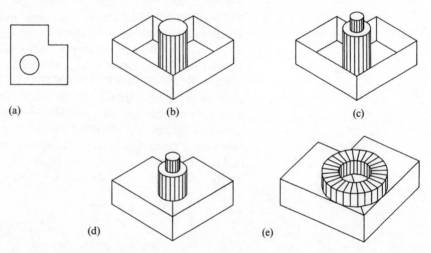

(a)   (b)   (c)

(d)   (e)

Figure L11.5.

10. Now select the UCS command. Select the ORIGIN option. Then select the CEN osnap and PICK the top circumference of the cylinder. Note the shifted UCS icon. (If you are unsure about this, refer back to the CAN exercise in Part A.)

Reset THICKNESS to a value of 10. Then select CIRCLE, and draw another cylinder, radius 5, thickness 10 (current value) on top of the existing cylinder. Select HIDE (Fig. L11.5c).

11. Select UCS. Select the ORIGIN option. Using the INT osnap, PICK a corner on the top edge of the L-shape box.

Select the CHANGE command. Move the cursor and PICK the larger cylinder. RETURN to complete the selection. Select the PROPERTIES option. Select the THICKNESS option. Then, for the new thickness value, enter:

20   (RETURN)

Then HIDE to see the larger cylinder with a changed thickness.

12. We will now convert our L-shape to look like a solid slab instead of a hollow box.

Select UCS. Select the WORLD option. Reset the current THICKNESS to a value of 20 via the SETVAR command. Get a 'bird's eye' plan view again (e.g. via VPOINT 0, 0, 1).

ERASE the L-shape and then redraw it to the same sizes and at the same position, but this time create it out of two trapezium-shaped SOLIDs (i.e. use the SOLID command twice), so that the L is bevelled at its corner. Select VPOINT −1, −1, 1. Then HIDE. See the 3D view with the new type of L-shape, as in Fig. L11.5d.

Do some more VPOINTs with HIDEs, to get the feel of the new shape.

13. ERASE the cylinders. Shift the ORIGIN of the UCS to the top edge of the L-shape again, as in step (11). Then draw a DOUGHNUT of 20 inner diameter, 40 outer diameter, and THICKNESS 10, resting on top of the L-shape where the cylinders were. (If you work from the VPOINT 0, 0, 1 plan view, you might find it useful to switch FILL to OFF temporarily—see Lesson 7.)

Get a VPOINT such as −1, −1, 1. Select HIDE. See a 3D view like Fig. L11.5e.

14. Now create a 3D model of the coffee table shown in Fig. L11.6. The top of the table can be modelled from a circular array of six solid equilateral triangles, each of side 30, thickness 5, and lower face 30 units above ground (i.e. the UCS should initially be set with its origin at, say, 0, 0, 30).

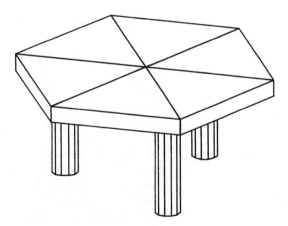

Figure L11.6.

There are three cylindrical legs, of radius 4, thickness 30, equi-spaced on a 25 radius circle.

Lesson 12

3DFACE, XYZ lines and 3D point filters

Introduction to 3DFACE

The 3DFACE command allows you to draw a face in any 3D plane, by specifying XYZ coordinates at three or four points. Whatever your current THICKNESS is set to, the thickness value of any 3DFACE is always zero.

Proceed as follows:

1. Begin a new drawing and set your drawing limits to −3000, −3000 (lower left corner), 8000, 8000 (upper right corner).
2. Set the current THICKNESS to a value of 5200.
3. Working from the default plan viewpoint (0, 0, 1), use the LINE command to draw a rectangle 5000 units long (X direction), 3000 units high (Y direction), with the lower left corner at point (0, 0).

   Select the VPOINT and get a viewpoint such as −1, −1, 1. Thus see a 3D box of sides 5200, 3000 and 5200 in the X, Y and Z directions respectively, with a base corner at point (0, 0, 0), as shown in Fig. L12.1a.

   Set THICKNESS back to zero.
4. Select the 3DFACE command. Then use the END osnap, e.g. by typing: END (RETURN), to PICK point a (Fig. L12.1b) as the first point. Then for the second point, enter:

   0,1500,7200   (RETURN)

   Thus point b in Fig. L12.1b has been specified. Now, using the END osnap, PICK point c in Fig. L12.1b. Then RETURN and RETURN again to complete the 3DFACE command.

   See the triangular 3DFACE abc as in Fig. L12.1b.
5. Select the COPY command to create an identical triangular 3DFACE def, by PICKing face abc and using END osnap to PICK point a as the base point and point d as the second point of displacement. Then select HIDE to see the 3D view in Fig. L12.1b.
6. Reselect the 3DFACE command. Create a rectangular 3D face, using the END osnap to PICK points a, d, e and b, as first, second, third and

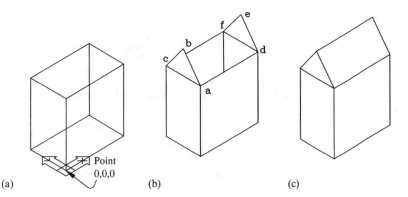

(a)   (b)   (c)

fourth points respectively, before exiting the 3DFACE command with a single RETURN.

Similarly, create a rectangular 3D face befc. Then select HIDE. See the 3D 'house' shape as in Fig. L12.1c.

7. Now create a trapezium-shaped 3D face, using the END osnap to specify the first point at e, and keyboard input to specify the other three corners at points (5000, 1500, 8200), (5000, 600, 8200) and (5000, 600, 6000), as in Fig. L12.2a.

8. COPY the trapezium-shaped 3D face, using the END osnap to PICK any of its four corners as the base point, and in response to the Second point of displacement prompt, entering:

$$@-900,0,0 \quad \text{(RETURN)}$$

Thus see the display shown in Fig. L12.2b.

9. Use the 3DFACE command and END osnap to create two more rectangular 3D faces which complete a 'chimney' shape, then HIDE to see this chimney, as in Fig. L12.2c.

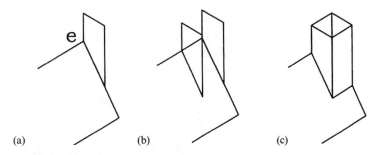

(a)   (b)   (c)

XYZ lines and 3D point filters

1. Reset THICKNESS to 200.
2. Use VPOINT (or PLAN) to get a viewpoint of 0, 0, 1.
3. Select the LINE command and, in response to the From point: prompt, enter:

3800,-1200,0   (RETURN)

Then, in response to the To point: prompt, enter:

@1200<0   (RETURN)

Complete the LINE command with another RETURN.

We have thus drawn a LINE starting from the 3D XYZ coordinate point (3800, −1200, 0), and ending at 1200 units from the start point in the direction of 'angle 0' (i.e. 'eastwards') in the current XY plane.

4. XY point filters were previously used for 2D work in Lesson 6, to which you should refer if necessary. In this lesson we will use XYZ point filters for our 3D work.

Reselect the LINE command. In response to the From point: prompt, enter:

.XY

(followed by RETURN if typed-in at the keyboard).

Then use the END osnap to PICK the same XY start point as for your previous line. Note the Need Z: prompt. Respond to this by entering:

0,0,200   (RETURN)

Thus we have specified the start point of our line to be at the same XY value as the previous line, and at a Z value of 200 (the 0, 0 XY values being ignored due to the point filter operation).

In response to the To point: prompt, enter:

@1200<30   (RETURN)

Complete the LINE command with another RETURN.

The endpoint of our LINE is thus 1200 units from its start point, in a direction of 30 degrees in the current XY plane. (In this case, the Z value of the endpoint is assumed to be 200, as for the start point.)

5. Now continue as in (4), until you have drawn a total of thirteen lines (including the two already drawn), radiating from the same XY starting position, but successively increasing by 200 units in Z, and increasing by angular increments of 30 degrees. (The thirteenth line will thus have a Z value of 0, 0, 2400, and an endpoint of @1200 < 360.)

In VPOINT 0, 0, 1 (plan), your drawing should then appear as in Fig. L12.3 (with the first and thirteenth radial lines appearing to be coincident).

Now set VPOINT to a value such as −1, −1, 1 and then HIDE, to see the 3D effect of the thirteen lines (Fig. L12.4).

6. Reset VPOINT to 0, 0, 1 and THICKNESS to 0.

7. Select the LINE command. Use point filter .XY and the END osnap to PICK point g (Fig. L12.3) as start point. Then, in response to Need Z: enter:

0,0,1000   (RETURN)

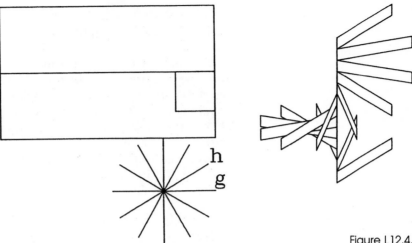

Figure L12.3.   Figure L12.4.

Similarly, PICK point h as the end point, with a Z value of 0, 0, 1200.

Continue thus until you have twelve chord line segments, as in Fig. L12.5, with Z values successively increasing at 200 intervals. (The end-point of the twelfth line will thus be at point g in XY, and have a Z value of 0, 0, 3400.)

Now get a VPOINT such as –1, –1, 1 to see the 3D effect, with the twelve chord line segments lying on a helix path, as in Fig. L12.6. As may now be apparent, we have constructed the skeleton structure of a spiral staircase, with the helix path of the twelve line segments forming the handrail.

8. Reset **VPOINT** to 0, 0, 1 (plan). Create a triangular 3DFACE with XY locations (3800, –1200), point g, point h; and with Z value of 200. (Make use of appropriate combinations of numeric XYZ coordinate input, point filters, and END osnap to specify each of the three corners.)

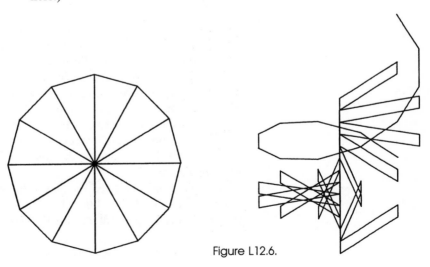

Figure L12.5.   Figure L12.6.

Get a VPOINT such as –1, –1, 1 to see the 3D effect. (The triangular 3DFACE should be displayed as the first step of the emerging spiral staircase.)

Reset 3DFACE to 0, 0, 1 (plan).

9. Here, we will make the triangular 3dface into a block, which we will insert eleven times in order to complete a total of twelve steps for our spiral staircase. (Blocks have been discussed in Lessons 2 and 10 in Part B. You may wish to refer back to the associated exercises in order to refresh your memory.)

Select the BLOCK command. Enter any appropriate block name (e.g. TRISTEP). Then, in response to the `Insertion base point:` prompt, enter:

`3800,-1200,200`   (RETURN)

Then, in response to the `Select objects:` prompt, select the LAST option, e.g. by typing: L (RETURN), thus selecting the last triangular 3dface. Complete the BLOCK command with another RETURN.

Retrieve the triangular 3dface via the OOPS command. (As seen in Lessons 2 and 10, items selected for a block are automatically erased after the BLOCK command.)

10. Select the INSERT command. Enter the block name you chose in (9). Then, in response to the `Insertion point:` prompt, specify an XY location of (3800, –1200) and a Z value of 400. This may be achieved either by entering the numeric XYZ value (3800, –1200, 400) or via a combination of point filter and END osnap.

Then, in response to the `X scale factor:` prompt, do a RETURN, for a scale of 1. In response to the `Y scale factor:` prompt, do another RETURN. In response to the `Rotation angle:` prompt, enter:

`30`   (RETURN)

11. Continue as in (10) until you have inserted eleven blocks, whose insertion points are all at XY location (3800, –1200) but with Z values successively increasing at 200 increments, and rotation angles successively increasing by 30 degree increments. (During this operation you are advised to perform the insertions while in the 0, 0, 1 plan viewpoint. However, you may wish to periodically get 3D viewpoints to check your emerging structure of steps in 3D, before resetting to 0, 0, 1 plan viewpoint for continuing the insertions. Alternatively, you could use multiple viewport display, as was discussed in Part A and will be enlarged upon in Lesson 15.)

12. When you have completed the eleven block insertions, get a 3D viewpoint such as –1, –1, 1 and then HIDE, to see the twelve spiral steps (i.e. the original triangular 3dface plus the eleven inserted blocks), as in Fig. L12.7a.

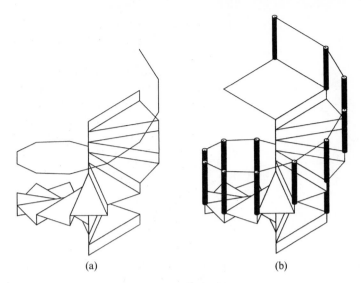

Figure L12.7.   (a)   (b)

13. Complete the spiral staircase as in Fig. L12.7b, with fourteen circles of radius 40, thickness 800, using appropriate .XY point filters and Z values. (The top step is a 1200 square 3D face with LINE side rail.)

Completing the house drawing

Now modify and add items to complete the 3D house shown in Figs L12.8 and L12.9. (Assume that the grid dots shown are at intervals of 200.)

Execute regular VPOINT changes and HIDEs to ensure that your 3D drawing is correct in all planes. (If you feel competent with the use of multiple viewports at this stage, then this would also be a useful facility.)

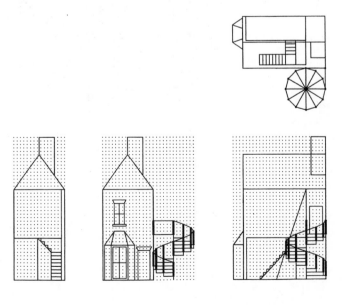

Figure L12.8.

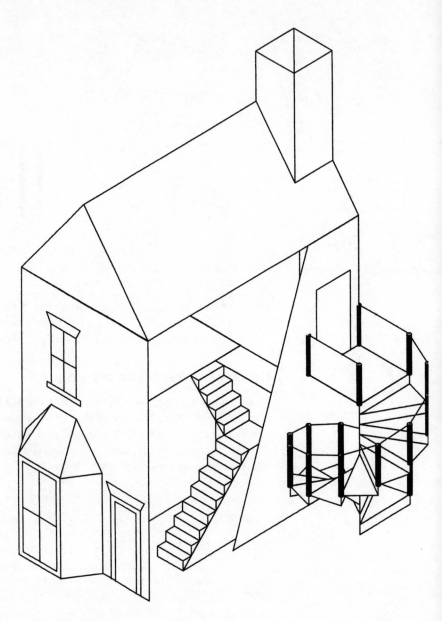

Figure L12.9.

Lesson 13

UCS and WCS

The purpose of this lesson is to revise the principles and procedures of UCS techniques applied to 3D modelling, which were extensively used during the CAN exercise in Part A, and to introduce some more UCS facilities. If you feel that you are out of practice with UCS techniques, then you are strongly recommended to work through the CAN exercise of Part A again. Assuming that you have already done that exercise, it should not take long to go through it again, and will remind you of procedures which are essential tools in the successful completion of the exercises in this lesson.

Principle of the User Coordinate System (UCS)

As stated in Part A, prior to Release 10 of AutoCAD the creation and editing of drawings was done within a single, fixed coordinate system. Points in this system were defined from an absolute zero datum which could not be moved.

After Release 10, this fixed absolute datum still exists, and is called the World Coordinate System (WCS). However, you may now also define your own User Coordinate System (UCS). Unlike the WCS, the UCS may be repositioned at any time, and its XYZ framework may be rotated in 3D to any direction required (although the three axes retain the same perpendicular directions relative to each other). All coordinate values for drawing entities (and object thicknesses) are understood by AutoCAD to be relative to the current UCS, whatever its current position and orientation.

The UCS icon

The position and orientation of your current UCS is indicated by the UCS icon. Additional information is also conveyed via the following variations of the UCS icon display:

- A 'W' is displayed in the 'Y' arm of the UCS icon if the current UCS is the same as the World Coordinate System (Fig. L13.1a).

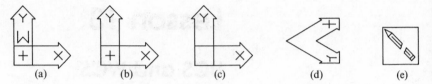

Figure L13.1.

- The 'W' is omitted from the icon if the current UCS is anything other than the WCS (e.g. as in Fig. L13.1b).
- In the previous two cases, a '+' was shown at the base of the icon. This signifies that the icon is located at the origin of the current UCS, which will always be the case if that origin is clearly visible on the screen, with enough space to show the icon at the origin point. However, there may be instances when you have zoomed or panned to an area which does not contain the current UCS origin, in which case the '+' is omitted from the icon (e.g. as in Fig. L13.1c).
- A box is formed at the base of the icon if you are viewing the current UCS from above (i.e. towards its positive Z direction). If you view your current UCS from below (i.e. towards its negative Z direction), the box is omitted from the icon (e.g. as in Fig. L13.1d).
- If you view the current UCS 'edge on' (i.e. you, the viewer, are positioned at the 'ground level' XY plane of the current UCS), the UCS icon is replaced by a 'broken pencil' icon, as shown in Fig. L13.1e.

The UCS command—options

In the CAN exercise of Part A, a number of different options were selected during the use of the UCS command. These options were:

- ORIGIN (O)   This allows you to define a new UCS by shifting the origin of the current UCS to another point in 3D space, while leaving the direction of its X, Y and Z axes unchanged (Fig. L13.2).
- ZAXIS (ZA)   This allows you to define a new UCS by specifying a new direction for your positive Z axis, with the new X and Y axes then being automatically adjusted (Fig. L13.3).
- 3POINT (3)   This is perhaps the most useful option, which allows you to define a new UCS by specifying: the new origin point; any point on the positive portion of the new X axis; any point on the positive Y portion of the new XY plane (Fig. L13.4).
- WORLD (W)   This is the default option, which allows you to set the current UCS to be the same as the World Coordinate System (WCS).

Apart from the foregoing UCS options, there are several others, from which you may find the following of use in tackling the exercises contained in this lesson:

- X or Y or Z (shown as 'X/Y/Z' in the screen prompt)   By choosing one of these three options, you may define a new UCS by specifying an angle of rotation about the particular axis chosen. The specified direction of

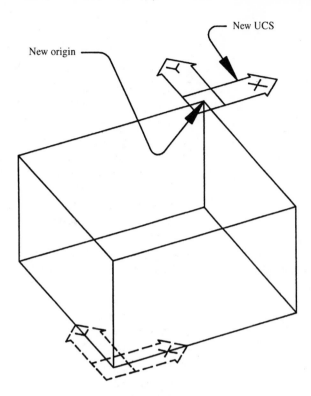

Figure L13.2.   UCS Origin.

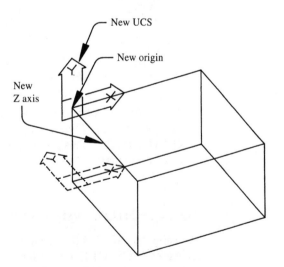

Figure L13.3.   UCS ZAXIS.

rotation (by default, positive is anticlockwise) assumes that you are looking towards the positive direction of the chosen axis (Fig. L13.5).

- PREVIOUS (P)   This restores the previous UCS defined.
- SAVE (S)   This allows you to name and save the current UCS. The
  name can be up to 31 characters long and may contain letters, numbers
  and/or characters: '$' (dollar); '-' (hyphen); '_' (underscore).

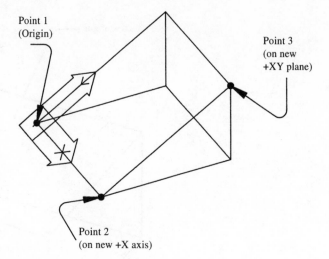

Figure L13.4.   UCS 3POINT.

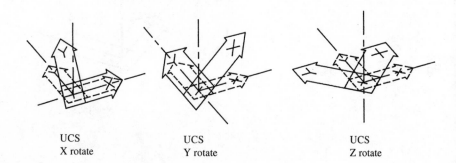

Figure L13.5.

	UCS	UCS	UCS
	X rotate	Y rotate	Z rotate

You may thus build up a library of saved UCSs for later repeated use on your drawing. (These may be listed via the ? option.)

- RESTORE (R)   This allows you to specify a previously saved UCS and make it current.

The UCSFOLLOW system variable

By using the SETVAR command, or directly after Release 12, you may access the UCSFOLLOW system variable, which enables you to get automatic plan views (VPOINT 0, 0, 1) relative to every new current UCS.

If you wish to use this facility, you may do so at any stage of your drawing by setting UCSFOLLOW to a value of 1. When you no longer wish to retain this facility, you may switch off UCSFOLLOW by resetting it to its default value of 0 at any stage of your drawing.

When using multiple viewports, UCSFOLLOW may be set separately for each viewport.

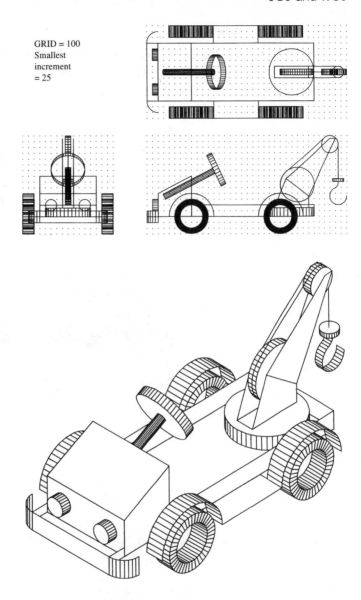

GRID = 100
Smallest
increment
= 25

Figure L13.6.

The UCSICON and WORLDVIEW system variables

These variables also effect screen displays according to UCS settings.

The UCSICON system variable effects the display of the UCS icon. In all subsequent exercises, it is assumed that UCSICON is set to the options: ON and ORIGIN(ON). This means that the UCS icon will always be displayed and will be positioned at the origin of the current UCS.

The WORLDVIEW system variable automatically reverts to WCS display when a new viewpoint is set, if WORLDVIEW is set to a value of 1. In subsequent exercises it is assumed that WORLDVIEW is not required and is thus switched off by setting it to a value of 0.

Exercises

Create the 3D drawings shown in Figs L13.6 and L13.7, using your current knowledge and acquired 3D modelling skills. Obtain sizes by noting the

GRID = 100
Smallest
increment
= 12.5

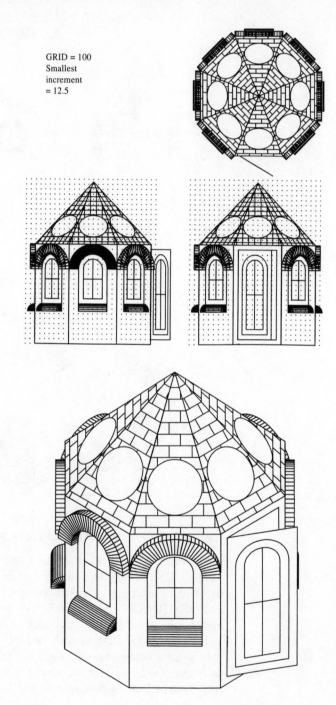

Figure L13.7.

spacings of the grid dots shown and the smallest increments of the constituent items in the drawings.

Note: To successfully complete these 3D drawings, it is essential that you have already completed (and preferably recently revised) the CAN exercise in Part A (Chapter 6), as well as Lessons 11 and 12.

Lesson 14

Continued 3DFACE and invisible edges

Start

1. Begin a new drawing. Set LIMITS to corners 0, 0 (lower left) and 15000, 15000 (upper right). Set SNAP to a suitable value, such as 500.
2. Set THICKNESS to 6000.
3. Working in the World Coordinate System (WCS), use the LINE command to draw a rectangle 6000 wide (i.e. in the X direction) and 5000 high (i.e. in the Y direction).
4. Set VPOINT to –1, –1, 1. Then HIDE. Thus see the 3D box as in Fig. L14.1a.
5. Change the UCS as in Fig. L14.1b. Set VPOINT to 0, 0, 1 (plan). Set THICKNESS to –6000.
6. Draw an 'SER' ARC (Start, End, Radius), as follows.
   Select the ARC command. Then, as the START POINT, enter:

   > 2500,10000   (RETURN)

   Then, select the END option, and with SNAP ON, PICK point A in Fig. L14.2a as the endpoint of the arc. Then, select the RADIUS option and, for the radius value, enter:

   > 4500   (RETURN)

7. Your drawing should now appear as in Fig. L14.2a.
   MIRROR the arc as in Fig. L14.2b. Then set VPOINT to –1, –1, 1. Then HIDE.
   See the 3D construction, as in Fig. L14.2c.
8. Reset VPOINT to 0, 0, 1.
9. Set THICKNESS to 0, and PDMODE to 3.
10. Select the DIVIDE command. Then, in response to the Select object to divide: prompt, PICK the left arc. Then, in response to the Number of segments: prompt, enter:

    > 5   (RETURN)

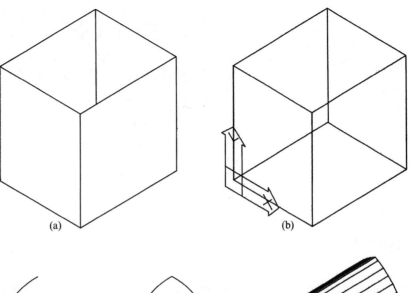

Figure L14.1.
(a)   (b)

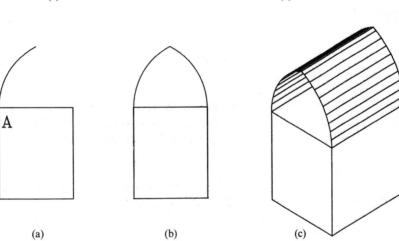

Figure L14.2.
(a)   (b)   (c)

11. Repeat (10) exactly for the right arc. Thus see the two arcs divided into segments with '×' nodes displayed, as in Fig. L14.3. (Perform a regeneration via the REGEN command if the nodes are not immediately visible.)

Continued faces/invisible edges

1. Select the 3DFACE command. Then, in response to the First point: prompt, select the XY point filter by entering:

    .XY

(followed by RETURN if typed-in at the keyboard).

   Then use the END osnap, e.g. by typing: End (RETURN), to PICK point 1 in Fig. L14.4. Then, in response to the Need Z: prompt, enter:

    0,0,0   (RETURN)

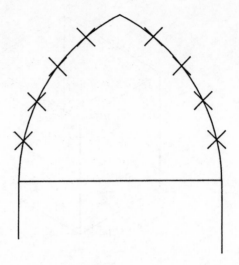

Figure L14.3.

Then, in response to the Second point: prompt, enter:

.XY

(followed by RETURN if typed-in at the keyboard).

Then use the END osnap to PICK point 2 in Fig. L14.4. In response to the Need Z: prompt, enter:

0,0,0   (RETURN)

Now, in response to the Third point: prompt, request an *invisible edge*, by entering:

I

(followed by RETURN if typed-in at the keyboard).

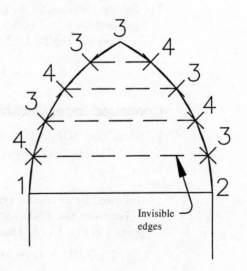

Figure L14.4.

Then, enter:

.XY

(followed by RETURN if typed-in at the keyboard).

Then use the NODE osnap, e.g. by typing: NODE (RETURN), to PICK the lowest node point 3 in Fig. L14.4. Then, in response to the Need Z: prompt, enter:

0,0,-200   (RETURN)

Now, in response to the Fourth point: prompt, move your pointing device leftwards and use the point filter .XY and NODE osnap again to PICK the lowest node point 4 in Fig. L14.4. Then, in response to the Need Z: prompt, enter:

0,0,-200   (RETURN)

Note: Do not exit the 3DFACE command. Stay in this command for the next part of the exercise.

2. We have thus done our construction of the lowest 'Edge 3–4' in Fig. L14.4, but you will note that, due to the INVISIBLE request prior to PICKing point 3, this edge does not appear on the screen.

Staying in the 3DFACE command, note the Third point: prompt, and respond to this by entering:

I

(followed by RETURN if typed-in at the keyboard).

Then move your pointing device upwards from the last node point 4, and use the .XY point filter and NODE osnap again to PICK the next node point 3. Then, in response to the Need Z: prompt, enter:

0,0,-400   (RETURN)

Now, in response to the Fourth point: prompt, move your pointing device rightwards from the last node point 3, and use the .XY point filter and NODE osnap again to PICK the next node point 4. Then, in response to the Need Z: prompt, enter:

0,0,-400   (RETURN)

Note: Do not exit the 3DFACE command. Stay in this command for the next part of the exercise.

3. While still in the 3DFACE command, note that the Third point: prompt has appeared once more.

Remaining in the 3DFACE command, continue as in (2), using appropriate I requests for invisible horizontal edges, .XY point filters, NODE osnaps, and Z values in increments of –200 for each successive horizontal edge, until you have reached the top node point 3 of Fig. L14.4 (which will thus have a Z value specified as 0, 0, –1000).

Note: The I entry should always precede any point filter or osnap entry, and should be actioned before specifying the start point of the edge which you wish to be invisible.

When you have completed the specification for the top node point 3, respond to the next `Fourth point:` prompt by entering RETURN, then RETURN again, to exit the 3DFACE command.

4. Set VPOINT to –1, –1, 1. See the profile of visible 3D face edges across the 3D thickness extrusion of the two arcs (Fig. L14.5).
5. ERASE the two arcs and HIDE. See Fig. L14.6.

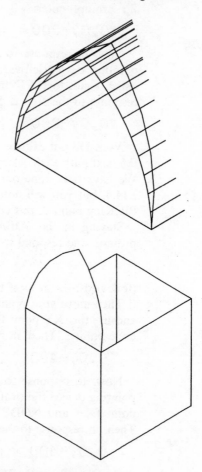

Figure L14.5.

Figure L14.6.

The SPLFRAME system variable

The SPLFRAME system variable has previously been used in Lesson 9 during spline curve procedures. It is also relevant to invisible edges on 3D faces. Proceed as follows:

1. Select SPLFRAME e.g. via SETVAR. Set SPLFRAME to a value of 1.
2. Regenerate the drawing via the REGEN command. Note that the 'invisible' edges are now displayed (Fig. L14.7a).
3. Using any suitable procedure, set to any UCS whose XY plane is parallel to that of the WCS, and whose origin has a Z value of 6000 relative to the WCS.

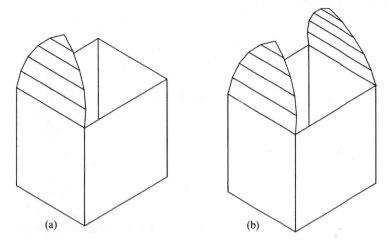

Figure L14.7.   (a)   (b)

4. Now MIRROR the created 3D faces to achieve the construction shown in Fig. L14.7b. (You may find it useful to invoke the MID osnap, from within the MIRROR command, for defining each of the two points of the mirror line.)
5. Now create the additional continued 3DFACEs shown in Fig. L14.8a. (These contain no invisible edges.)
6. Reset SPLFRAME back to 0. Regenerate the drawing via the REGEN command. Then HIDE. Thus see Fig. L14.8b.

Windmill exercise

Add/edit items to the existing drawing in order to complete a 3D construction of the windmill shown in the remaining figures of this lesson. Obtain sizes via the information given about grid dot spacings and smallest increments, against the figures.

The exercise will test all your current knowledge and acquired skills in 3D modelling. There is particular emphasis on 3D faces, some of which require

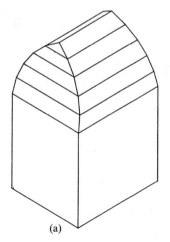
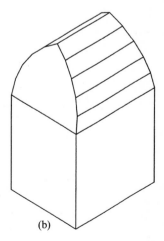

Figure L14.8.   (a)   (b)

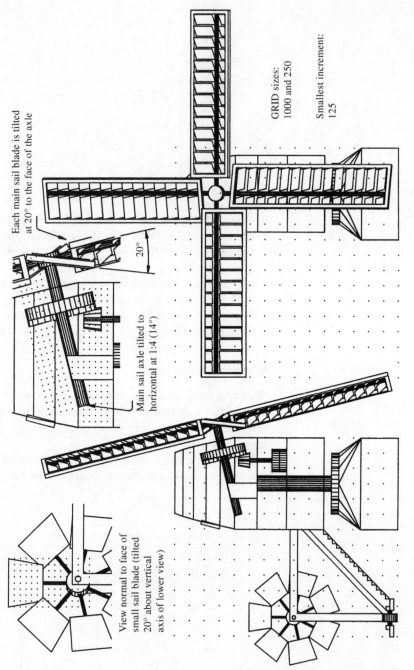

Each main sail blade is tilted at 20° to the face of the axle

20°

Main sail axle tilted to horizontal at 1:4 (14°)

View normal to face of small sail blade (tilted 20° about vertical axis of lower view)

GRID sizes:
1000 and 250

Smallest increment:
125

Figure L14.9.

244

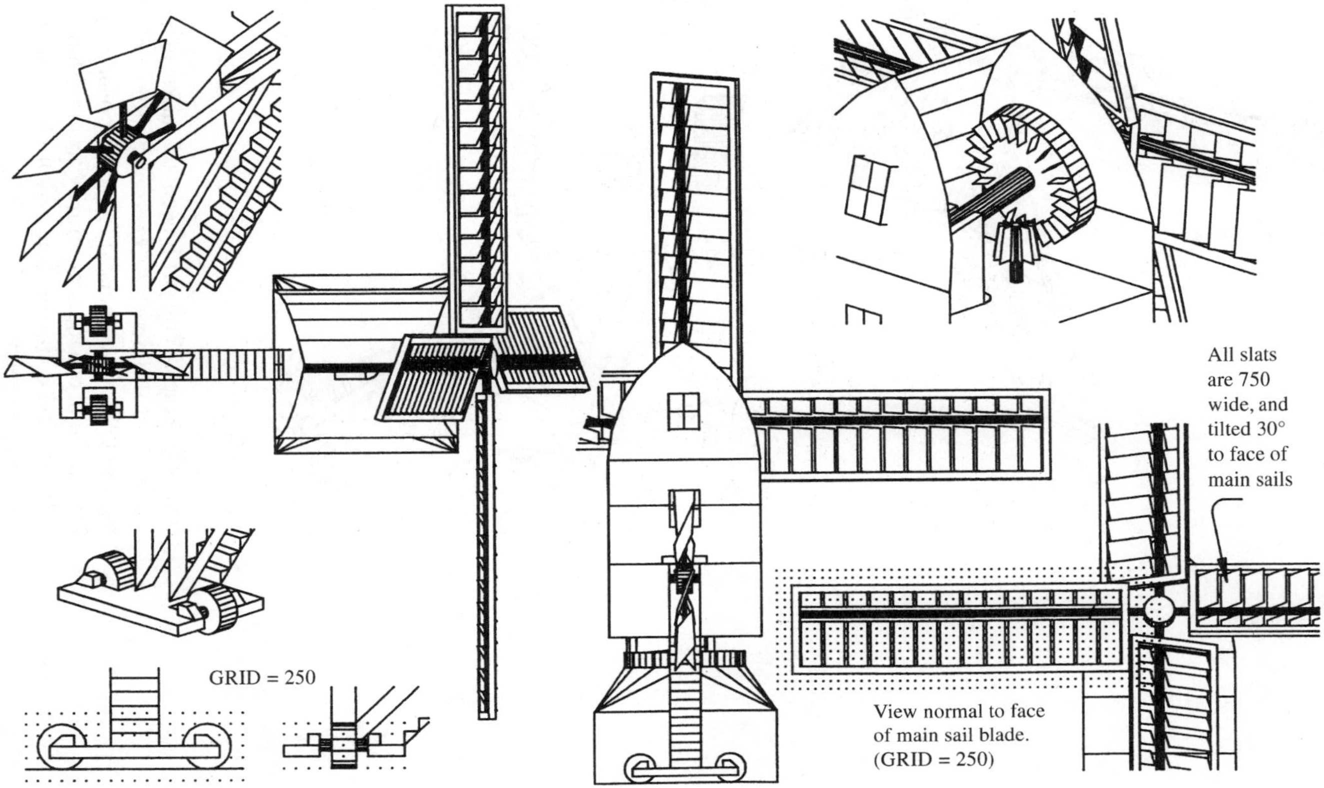

All slats are 750 wide, and tilted 30° to face of main sails

View normal to face of main sail blade. (GRID = 250)

GRID = 250

Figure L14.10.

Figure L14.11.

VPOINT = –2, –2, 1

invisible edges. You will need to make extensive use of point filtering, osnaps and different UCS settings. (Remember, it is not a good policy to use the OSNAP command for setting osnaps when you are doing 3D work. Invoke your osnaps temporarily from within other commands.)

If you feel confident using multiple viewports, these can also be a useful tool in this exercise.

Lesson 15

3D display techniques

Multiple views (VIEWPORTS)

During the CAN exercise in Part A (Chapter 6), we saw that you may obtain multiple views of your drawing on a single screen via the VIEWPORTS (or VPORTS) command.

Refer back to that section of Part A, and revise the principles and procedures involved in the VIEWPORTS command.

Then proceed as follows:

1. Retrieve your CAN drawing which you created in Part A (and perhaps redrew as a prelude to Lesson 13), using either the Edit an Existing Drawing option (pre-AutoCAD Release 12) or the OPEN command (Release 12 onwards).
2. The CAN exercise of Part A concluded with a display containing four viewports, each showing a different view of the completed CAN drawing. This display was shown in Fig. A6.54 (page 79) and is now shown simplified in Fig. L15.1. In both of these figures, the CURRENT VIEWPORT is at top left of screen.

   If you have already edited your CAN drawing since it was created in Part A, run through that VIEWPORTS exercise again until your display is again as Fig. A6.54 or Fig. L15.1.
3. Working from the display in Fig. L15.1, move your pointing device until the cursor enters the lower right viewport. Then PICK. This viewport is thus now the CURRENT one.
4. Select the VIEWPORTS command. Then select the SINGLE option, e.g. by typing: SI (RETURN). Note that the screen now displays only a single view conforming to that which was contained in the current viewport.
5. Select the VIEWPORTS command again. Then select the 3 option. Then RETURN to accept the default RIGHT option. Thus see a display with three viewports, the largest being at the right of the screen.
6. Adjust the viewpoint in each viewport (making each viewport current in turn). Then perform appropriate ZOOMs or PANs until you have a display similar to Fig. L15.2.

Current viewport

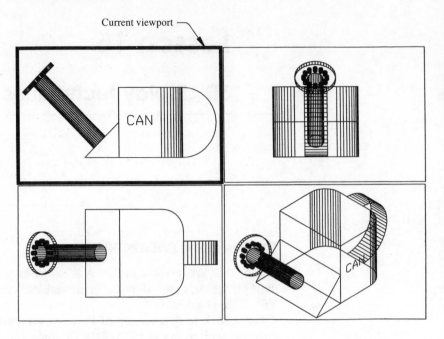

Figure L15.1.

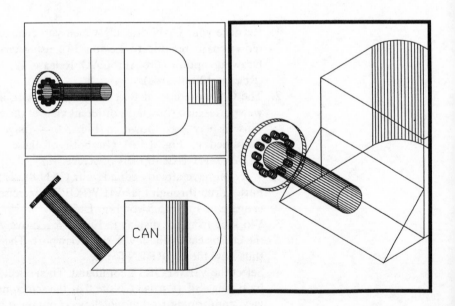

Figure L15.2.

7. Now PICK the largest viewport to make it current, and then select the SINGLE (SI) option of the VIEWPORTS command to go back to a single 3D display. ZOOM/PAN to get a full 3D view of the complete CAN.

Paper space mode

Since AutoCAD Release 11, it is possible to edit viewport boxes as though they were ordinary drawing entities by switching from *model space* mode to *paper space* mode.

When you are in model space mode, you may model your component in each viewport, which is treated as a separate 3D world. The viewport boxes are of a fixed size governed by the TILEMODE system variable, when this is set to a value of 1.

If you set TILEMODE to 0, AutoCAD takes you into paper space mode. Your former 3D display is then considered as a flat 'paper' drawing, which may be edited accordingly.

Proceed as follows:

1. Ensuring that SNAP is set to OFF, access the TILEMODE system variable (e.g. via the SETVAR command). Then set TILEMODE to a value of 0. AutoCAD will thus take you into paper space mode, and the appropriate Paper Space icon will be displayed at the corner of the blank screen (see Fig. L15.3).

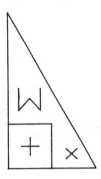

Figure L15.3.   The Paper Space icon.

2. Select the MVIEW command. This allows us to create our own viewports to any size we wish on our 'flat sheet of paper' in paper space mode.

   In response to the `First point:` prompt, move your cursor near to lower left of screen and PICK. Now move the cursor towards upper right of screen, noting the emerging window which will define the size of your first created viewport in paper space mode. When your cursor is close to top right of screen, PICK. Your first viewport in paper space is thus defined, and you will see the 3D view of the CAN shown.

3. Repeat the MVIEW command three more times, PICKing appropriate points in turn, to create the total of four viewports of the approximate sizes and locations shown in Fig. L15.4.

4. Select the MSPACE command. This converts your created viewports back into model space mode while TILEMODE is still set to 0. You may specify which viewport you wish to be current by PICKing (as we have done previously). However, since we have some small viewports

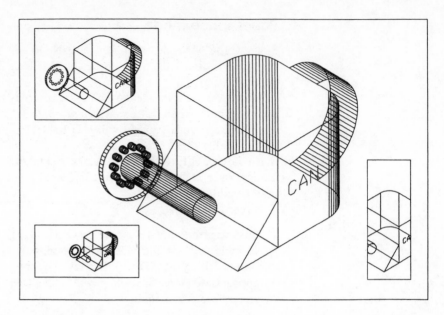

Figure L15.4.

inside a larger one, you may experience difficulty in picking the smaller ones to be current. In this case CTRL-V may be used as a 'circular toggle' to make each viewport current in turn. Thus, if you repeatedly press CTRL-V at the keyboard, you can successively change current viewports until you get the one you want.

Use the VPOINT command to get different viewpoints of the CAN in each of the smaller viewports, as shown in Fig. L15.5.

5. Select the PSPACE command. This takes us back to paper space mode. Remember, the display is now considered as one piece of flat paper with

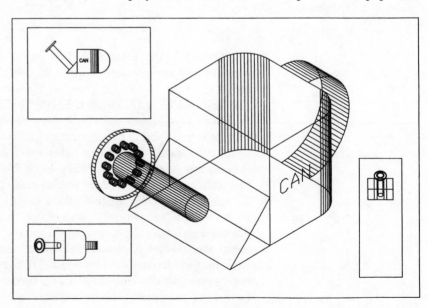

Figure L15.5.

a single 2D cursor, and all of its contents, including the viewports borders, may be edited as ordinary drawing entities. Thus use the STRETCH command to change the shape of the viewport borders as in Fig. L15.6. (You may also wish to use the MOVE command, placing a WINDOW around chosen viewports, and shift the viewports to different positions on the screen.)

6. If you wish to tidy up your viewport displays in model space, you may do so by selecting MSPACE again. (For example, you might want to make some adjustments via ZOOM or PAN in selected viewports, as in Fig. L15.7.)

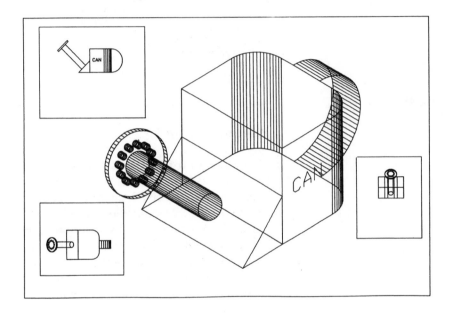

Figure L15.6.

7. While in paper space mode you can also PLOT your drawing at this stage, with the complete screen display being plotted on one hard copy (including different viewports) exactly as shown on screen.

The DVIEW command (CAMERA option)

The DVIEW command is the most versatile display command available for advanced 3D modelling, and has particular significance to perspective work, which will be discussed in Lesson 16.

The CAMERA (CA) option of the DVIEW command assumes that you are a photographer who can move around your drawing while keeping your camera lens projected towards a constant 'target sight' (this is the object you are looking at). As you 'walk with your camera' around the target you can see the object change in appearance (with dynamic display option).

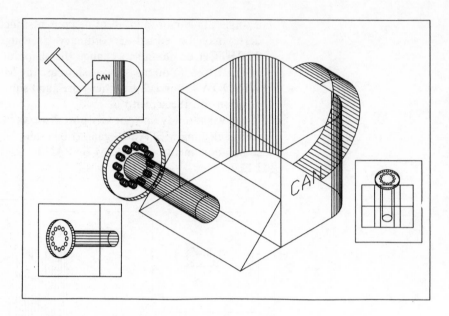

Figure L15.7.

Proceed as follows:

1. Ensure that **TILEMODE** is set to 1 (e.g. via **SETVAR**) and that you are thus in model space mode. Get a single viewport (if you have not already done so) via the **SINGLE (SI)** option of the **VIEWPORTS** command.
2. Set to the WCS (via the W option of UCS). Set VPOINT to 0, 0, 1 (plan). ZOOM/PAN to get a full view of the complete CAN.
3. Select the **DVIEW** command. Then, in response to the `Select objects:` prompt, select all the items of your CAN drawing (e.g. by placing a **WINDOW** around them). When you have completed the selection, RETURN, and note the following options prompt:

   ```
   CAmera/TArget/Distance/POints/PAn/
   Zoom/TWist/CLip/Hide/Hide/Undo/<exit>:
   ```

   Select the CAMERA (CA) option, and note that an 'angle' prompt has appeared on the screen. This initially defaults to a value of 90 degrees (complying with our 'bird's eye' plan view of the can).
   Move your pointing device. See the CAN display dynamically changing as you move. Continue to move up and down the full screen, thus moving the camera through the full rotational path normal to the XY plane. (For example, 0 camera angle will give a 'front view' as seen from the 'ground level' XY plane; −90 camera angle will give a 'worm's eye' plan view as seen from beneath the can.) The principle is illustrated in Fig. L15.8.
   Finally, move your pointing device to see a view similar to Fig. L15.9, then PICK. Select CAMERA again, then RETURN. Move your pointing device leftwards, noting the dynamically changing 3D display. This is like walking with your camera on the XY plane ('ground level') in a

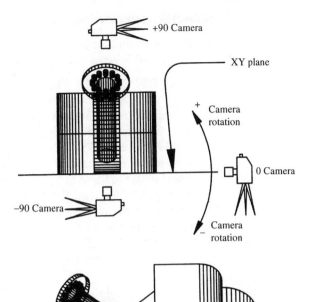

Figure L15.8.

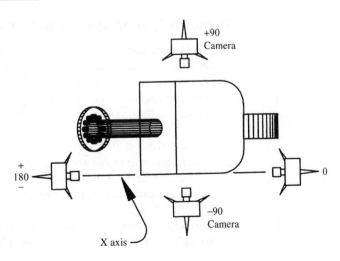

Figure L15.9.

clockwise circular path (relative to the X axis) around the can while
keeping the lens projected towards the target. Thus see the dynamically
changing 3D views from 0 to −180 degrees rotation. (The principle is
shown in Fig. L15.10.) Now slide rightwards to +180 degrees, to get
dynamic views via the anticlockwise path. Slide back and PICK a 3D
view of your choosing. Then select the EXIT option of the DVIEW
command.

Figure L15.10.

Selected preview items

To improve computer performance, you may restrict the dynamic display to selected preview items during DVIEW routines. Proceed as follows:

1. Select DVIEW again. Then select only the items shown in Fig. L15.11 (e.g. by PICKing them). RETURN after you have selected your items.
2. Now select the CAMERA option and adjust to about 45 degrees (noting only the selected items being dynamically displayed). PICK. The reselect CAMERA and RETURN.
3. Now adjust across the full range and thus see a series of dynamic 3D views similar to those in Fig. L15.11. Finally bring the slider to see a view like Fig. L15.11e, and then PICK.
4. Now select the HIDE option of DVIEW to see the selected items with hidden lines removed.
5. Finally, select the EXIT option of DVIEW, to see the complete CAN at the specified camera view.

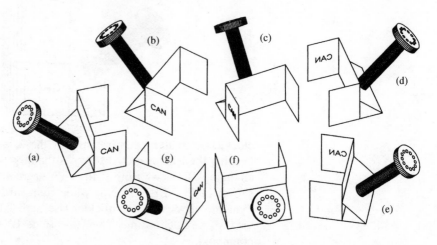

Figure L15.11.

Further DVIEW options: TARGET, TWIST, ZOOM and PAN

As previously stated, the TARGET is what you are looking at from the camera. If you rotate to a new target point, this is like staying with your camera at the same vantage point, but swinging the camera around to see something else.

Proceed as follows:

1. Get VPOINT 0, 0, 1 (plan).
2. Check that you are in the WCS and set THICKNESS to a value of 150 via e.g. the SETVAR command.
3. Draw an equilateral triangle of sides 150 at the position shown in Fig. L15.12.
4. We will now rotate the target through 50 degrees. The principle is illustrated in Fig. L15.13. (*Note*: The value of the actual distance between

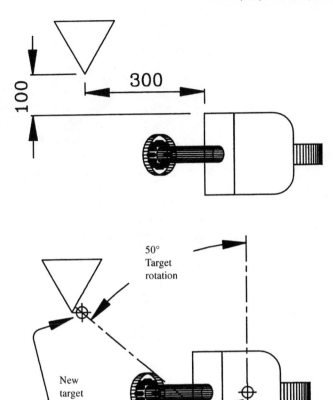

Figure L15.12.

Figure L15.13.

camera and target is unimportant until we do perspective work in Lesson 16.)

Select DVIEW. Select the whole CAN and the triangle. RETURN when you have selected all the items. Select the CAMERA option. Adjust to about 30 degrees. PICK. Reselect CAMERA, RETURN and adjust to about −90 degrees. PICK. Your new view should appear like Fig. L15.14a.

Select the TARGET option. Then RETURN to accept the current angle from the XY plane. Now adjust the angle in the XY plane from 90 degrees (the current value) to 140 degrees. PICK.

Now select the EXIT option of DVIEW, and then select the HIDE command. Your view should be as Fig. L15.14b.

5. Select DVIEW again. Select the CAN items only. RETURN to complete the object selection.

Now select the TWIST option (this rotates the current view of selected items about midscreen). Move your pointing device and, noting the dynamically-changing angle display at the top of the screen, adjust the dynamic screen display to about 160 degrees twist. PICK.

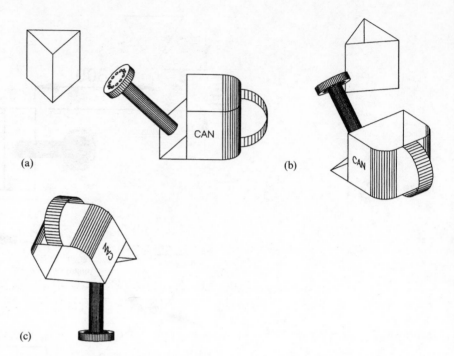

(a)

(b)

Figure L15.14.   (c)

Now select the HIDE option of the DVIEW command. Your view should be like Fig. L15.14c.

6. Select the PAN option of DVIEW. Then PICK two suitable points in turn (as you would do for the PAN command) to bring your view closer to midscreen.

7. Now select the ZOOM option of DVIEW and, noting the resulting top horizontal slider bar, adjust to a value of about 2×. Then PICK. Thus see the resulting zoomed display.

8. Select the EXIT option of DVIEW.

Lesson 16

Perspective display techniques

Garden exercise—start

In this exercise, we will be using some of the drawings already created in previous lessons. However, in order to maintain efficiency of computer performance, you should now edit these drawings for simplicity, as shown in Figs L16.1–L16.4.

Then begin a new AutoCAD drawing and proceed as follows:

1. Create a rectangular 3dface on layer 0; in the WCS; with VPOINT 0, 0, 1; at 'ground level' (zero Z); and of sides 5600 in X and 16 800 in Y (use suitable LIMITS and SNAP settings). This rectangular 3dface will form the garden plot shown in Fig. L16.5.

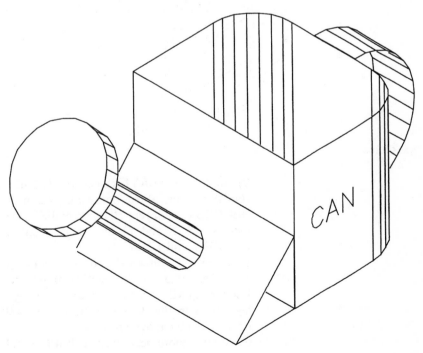

Figure L16.1.

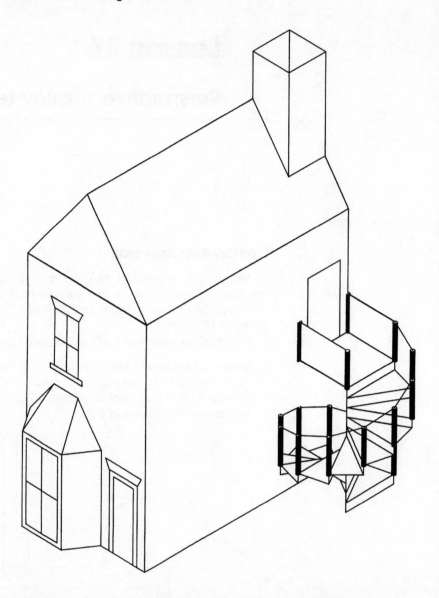

Figure L16.2.

2. Create two new LAYERS called HOUSE and SUMHOUSE.
3. INSERT your edited house and summerhouse drawings as external BLOCKS onto layers HOUSE and SUMHOUSE respectively, at scale factors of 1 (X and Y), and at the positions and orientations shown in Figs L16.5 and L16.6.
4. Use the LINE command to draw a garden path on layer 0 and at zero Z, as in Fig. L16.5 (13 tiles, each 1000 square, and with 200 inside border).
5. Use the LINE command to draw railings around the garden plot on layer 0, as in Fig. L16.6 (verticals are 2000 high, at 800 spacings; horizontal is 1600 above ground).
6. Create two more new layers, called CRANE and CAN.

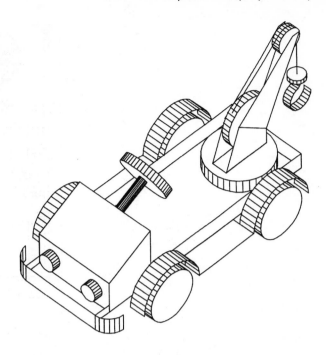

Figure L16.3.

Figure L16.4.

7. Keeping bases at ground level, INSERT your edited toy crane drawing (X/Y scale factor 0.5) and edited CAN drawing (X/Y scale factor 2.5) as external BLOCKS on layers CRANE and CAN respectively, at the approximate positions and orientations shown in Figs L16.5 and L16.6.

Perspective DVIEW work (DISTANCE option)

Here, we will use the DISTANCE option of DVIEW to get perspective displays. We will also make use of the POINTS option of DVIEW, which

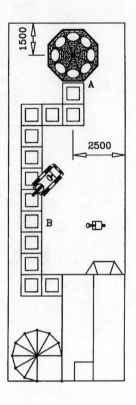

Figure L16.5.

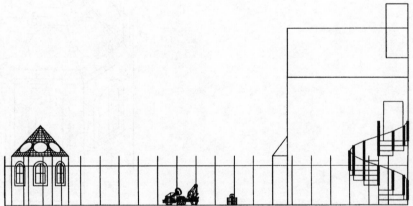

Figure L16.6.

allows us to define **TARGET** and **CAMERA** at two specified points in 3D space.

Proceed as follows:

1. Use the **FREEZE** option of the **LAYER** command to freeze the layer **HOUSE** (thus making the house invisible).
2. While in **VPOINT** 0, 0, 1 (plan), select the **DVIEW** command. Then, in response to the Select objects: prompt, select objects by pla-

cing a window enclosing the summer house and the toy crane. Then RETURN to complete the selection procedure.

3. Now select the POINTS option of DVIEW, e.g. by typing: PO (RETURN). Then, in response to the `Enter target point:` prompt, use the .XY point filter to PICK a point approximately at A in Fig. L16.5. In response to the resulting `Need Z:` prompt, enter:

   0,0,400   (RETURN)

   AutoCAD then prompts you to `Enter camera point:`. Respond to this by using the .XY point filter to PICK a point approximately at B in Fig. L16.5. In response to the resulting `Need Z:` prompt, enter:

   0,0,800   (RETURN)

   See the resulting 3D display.

4. While still in the DVIEW command, select the DISTANCE option, e.g. by typing: D (RETURN). Note the horizontal slider bar which has appeared at the top of the screen. Move the slider via your pointing device, noting the simultaneously changing 3D display, until you get a perspective view like Fig. L16.7. PICK. Note the Perspective icon which has appeared at lower left of the screen.

5. Select the EXIT option of DVIEW. Select HIDE. Thus see the complete perspective view, as in Fig. L16.7.

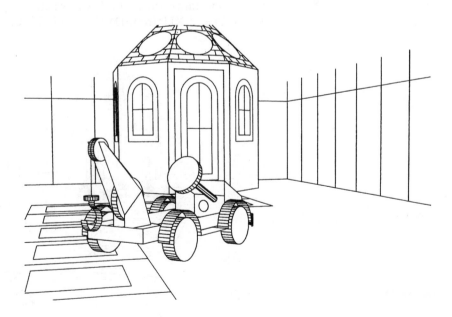

Figure L16.7.

6. Select DVIEW again. In response to the `Select objects:` prompt, specify PREVIOUS, then RETURN to complete the selection routine.

Figure L16.8.

    Now select the DISTANCE option. Move the slider bar leftwards of the 1× mark (this moves the camera closer to the target from the current distance). PICK when you get a view similar to Fig. L16.8. Then EXIT from DVIEW and HIDE.

7. Repeat the DVIEW/DISTANCE procedure, this time moving the slider bar rightwards of the 1× mark (thus moving the camera further out from the current target distance). PICK when you get a view similar to Fig. L16.9. Then EXIT from DVIEW and HIDE.

Figure L16.9.

Clipping planes

Front and back *clipping planes* allow you to create cutaway or section views in 3D. They are like invisible walls perpendicular to the line of sight between camera and target. Anything 'outside' these two walls becomes invisible, and items crossing them are sectioned through and cut away. Clipping planes are positioned at a specified distance from the target. Fig. L16.10 shows the principle of clipping planes.

Proceed as follows:

1. Select DVIEW. Select PREVIOUS objects. RETURN to complete selection procedure.
2. Now select the CLIP option of DVIEW, e.g. by typing: CL (RETURN). Then select the BACK option. Thus see the horizontal slider bar which has appeared at the top of the screen. Adjust this target sight slider bar until the summer house is partly cut away, as in Fig. L16.11. PICK. Then, remaining in the DVIEW command, select the CLIP option again. Now select the FRONT option. Adjust the slider bar until the toy crane is partly cut away, as in Fig. L16.11. PICK.

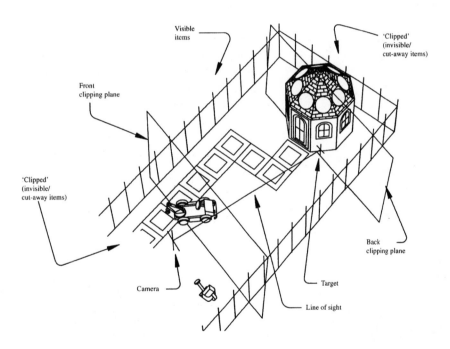

Figure L16.10.

3. EXIT from DVIEW and HIDE. See the clipped perspective display, as in Fig. L16.11.

Other perspective effects

Once perspective mode has been invoked via the DISTANCE option of DVIEW, the other DVIEW options, CAMERA, TARGET, ZOOM, PAN and TWIST, can give different effects from that expected in non-perspective mode.

Figure L16.11.

Proceed as follows:

1. Select DVIEW again. Select PREVIOUS objects. RETURN to complete the selection procedure.
2. Now select the ZOOM option of DVIEW. In perspective mode, this option allows you to increase a camera lens length (simulating a tele-photo lens) or decrease (simulating a wide-angle lens). Use the slider bar to increase the lens length for a view similar to Fig. L16.12.

Figure L16.12.

3. Now select the UNDO option of DVIEW. Then select the CLIP option. Select OFF (thus cancelling the clipping effect). We should thus now be back to Fig. L16.9.
4. While still in the DVIEW command, select the DISTANCE option, and get a view similar to Fig. L16.7 again. Remain in the DVIEW command.
5. While still in DVIEW, select the PAN option. Then, in response to the `Displacement base point:` prompt, PICK a point at about midscreen. Now, in response to the `Second point:` prompt, move your cursor rightwards until you get a view similar to Fig. L16.13. Note

Figure L16.13.

that the nearest objects have been panned rightwards in perspective (like shifting the camera leftwards). PICK.

6. While still in DVIEW, select the UNDO option, to go back to the previous view. Then select the TARGET option. In response to the `Enter angle from X-Y plane:` prompt, enter a RETURN to retain the current target rotation relative to the XY plane. Now move the top slider bar rightwards (thus rotating the camera rightwards to a new target point) until you get a view similar to Fig. L16.14. PICK.

7. While still in DVIEW, select UNDO again, and then select the CAMERA option. Adjust your pointing device upwards (thus moving with your camera to a steeper angle relative to the XY plane), until you get a view similar to Fig. L16.15. PICK.

Figure L16.14.

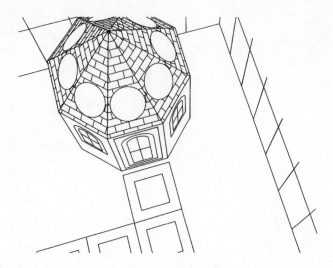

Figure L16.15.

8. While still in DVIEW, select the TWIST option. Then adjust the cross-hair cursor via your pointing device, until you get a view like Fig. L16.16. PICK. Then EXIT the DVIEW command.

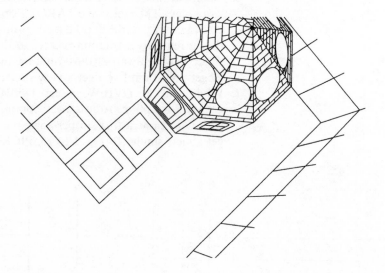

Figure L16.16.

Further exercises

1. Use the THAW option of the LAYER command to thaw the layer HOUSE. Use the FREEZE option of the LAYER command to freeze the layer SUMHOUSE. Then use the POINTS and DISTANCE options of DVIEW to obtain a view similar to Fig. L16.17.
2. Use perspective DVIEW techniques to create views like Figs L16.18–L16.22.

   FREEZE/THAW appropriate layers as and when required.

Figure L16.17.

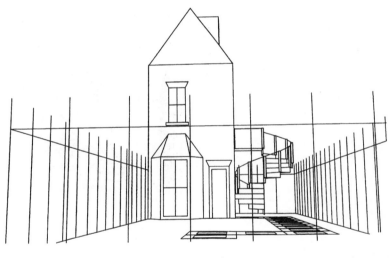

Figure L16.18.

Figure L16.19.

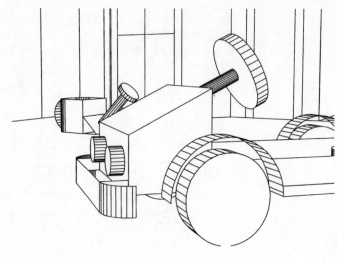

Figure L16.20.

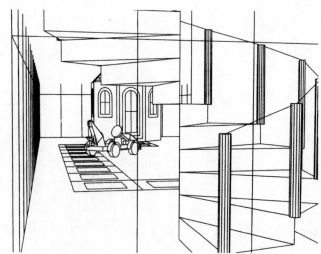

Figure L16.21.

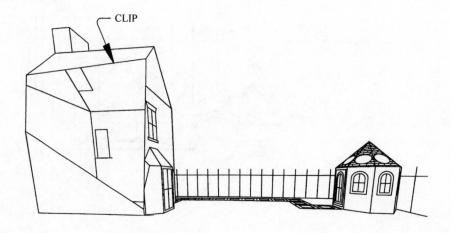

Figure L16.22.   Wide-angled lens effect via DVIEW ZOOM.

3. Create perspective views of your WINDMILL drawing (Lesson 14) on three viewports.
4. Model your computer room in 3D and display perspective views of its layout.

Lesson 17

3D surface modelling—MESH commands

Introduction to mesh surfaces

An important tool in advanced 3D modelling work is the creation of curved surfaces which are approximated to a complex of 3D faces in the form of a *mesh*.

In this lesson we will use four of the AutoCAD commands which create different types of 3D surface meshes, namely: RULESURF, TABSURF, EDGESURF and REVSURF.

In doing so, we will redesign our CAN drawing which we created in Part A (Chapter 6), and have used again in Lessons 15 and 16.

Use of layers in surface modelling

Intricate surface models with meshes can become extremely difficult to visualize and develop if your drawing is not structured in an organized fashion. An important tool in achieving this is the use of separate layers for each surface mesh, and also for the initial geometric construction required for the creation of those meshes.

Proceed as follows:

1. Begin a new drawing on AutoCAD. Then select the LAYER command, and create ten new layers called CONS, SIDES, TOPHANDLE, SPOUT, SPRINKLER, BACKHANDLE, TOPFACE, FRONTFACE, BACKFACE and BASEFACE.
2. Use the COLOR option of the LAYER command to specify the following colours to your created layers:

RED:	Layers SIDES, FRONTFACE, BACKFACE, and BASEFACE
BLUE:	Layer SPOUT
CYAN:	Layer SPRINKLER
MAGENTA:	Layer TOPHANDLE

> GREEN: Layer TOPFACE
> YELLOW: Layer BACKHANDLE

(Keep layer CONS at the default colour: WHITE.)

3. Use the SET option of the LAYER command to set layer CONS as the current layer.

Initial geometric construction

We will create all our basic geometric construction on layer CONS. Proceed as follows:

1. While in the WCS and VPOINT 0, 0, 1 (plan), use the LINE command to draw ten lines in 3D space, enclosing the areas shown as A, B and C in Fig. L17.1. (Use keyboard input to specify the XYZ coordinates shown in the figure.)
2. Use the VPOINT command to get a 3D view such as –1, –1, 1 (Fig. L17.2a).

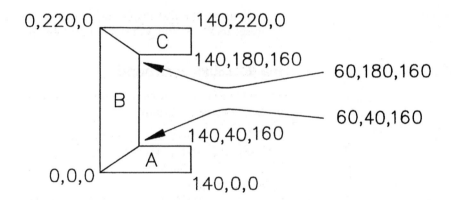

Figure L17.1.

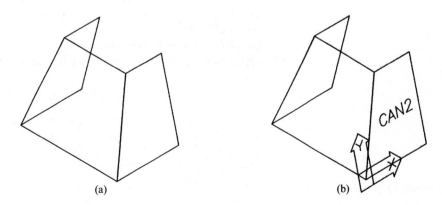

Figure L17.2.   (a)   (b)

Side faces

1. SET layer SIDES as the current layer (keeping layer CONS set to ON).
2. Select the 3DFACE command. Then, working in rotational order, use the END osnap to PICK the four existing line corners of the area which was initially specified as A in Fig. L17.1. (The resulting quadrilateral 3D face thus becomes the right-hand side face of the 3D view in Fig. L17.2a.) RETURN to complete the 3DFACE command.

   Similarly, create a left-hand side face on your 3D view in Fig. L17.2a, via a quadrilateral 3DFACE enclosing the area which was initially specified as C in Fig. L17.1.
3. Select the UCS command, then the 3POINT option. Use suitable osnaps to set the UCS to the slanted plane of the right-hand side face, as in Fig. L17.2b.
4. Use either the TEXT or the DTEXT command to create text on the right-hand side face, specifying these parameters:

Text height:	20
Start point:	50, 70 (relative to current UCS)
Rotation:	0
Text:	CAN2

   Thus see the text displayed, as in Fig. L17.2b.
5. Reset to WCS, and VPOINT 0, 0, 1 (plan).

The RULESURF command

The RULESURF command draws a ruled surface between two existing profiles. Proceed as follows:

1. SET layer CONS as the current layer.
2. Use the PLINE command to draw the polyline shown as 'PLINE1' in Fig. L17.3a. (Thus the polyline is made up of: 80R ARC, then LINE, then 80R ARC.)
3. Use the ORIGIN option of the UCS command to shift the UCS to point: 140, 80, 160.
4. Use the PLINE command to draw the polyline shown as 'PLINE2' in Fig. L17.3a. (Thus the polyline is made up of: 40R ARC, then LINE, then 40R ARC.)
5. Get a 3D viewpoint such as −1, −1, 1 (Fig. L17.3b).
6. SET layer BACKFACE as the current layer.

Figure L17.3.

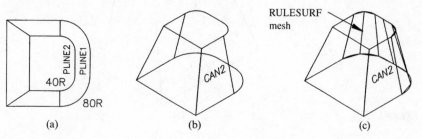

(a)   (b)   (c)

7. Select the RULESURF command. Then PICK each of the two PLINEs in turn. Thus see the created RULESURF surface, as in Fig. L17.3c. HIDE.

The TABSURF command

The TABSURF command extrudes a profile the length and direction of a specified *direction vector*.

Proceed as follows:

1. SET layer CONS as the current layer. Then use the FREEZE option of the LAYER command to freeze layer BACKFACE (thus making the back face ruled surface invisible).
2. Set UCS at centre base and in line with the front slope, as shown in Fig. L17.4a, via the 3POINT option of UCS and appropriate MID and INT osnaps. Then set VPOINT to 0, 0, 1.
3. Create a curved PLINE profile as in Fig. L17.4b, via the PLINE, and PEDIT (option FIT), commands. (Note the required start and end points shown. Estimate suitable vertex positions during the PLINE command, to achieve the desired shape of curve after the PEDIT FIT routine. If necessary, use the EDIT VERTEX option of PEDIT to improve your created curve.)
4. MIRROR the PLINE curve about the current Y axis. Then, use the SAVE option of the UCS command to save the current UCS under the name of : FFACE. Now set to the WCS, and get VPOINT –1, –1, 1 (Fig. L17.4c).
5. Draw any LINE of length 40 in the direction + X, 0, 0, e.g. as shown in Fig. L17.4c. We will use this as our direction vector.
6. SET layer TOPHANDLE as the current layer.
7. Select the TABSURF command. Then, in response to the Select path curve: prompt, PICK the first PLINE curve you created. Then, in response to the Select direction vector: prompt, PICK the 40 length line at point 1 (Fig. L17.4c).

    Repeat this procedure for the second PLINE curve. The resulting TABSURF extrusions should appear as in Fig. L17.4d.

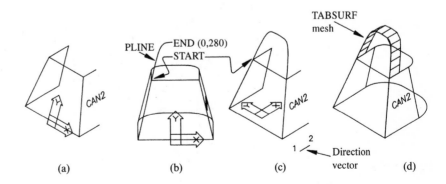

Figure L17.4. (a) (b) (c) (d)

The EDGESURF command

The EDGESURF command creates a blended curved surface to four existing edges.

Proceed as follows:

1. Select the RESTORE option of the UCS command to reset the UCS to FFACE. SET layer CONS as the current layer. Then get VPOINT 0, 0, 1.

2. Select the ELLIPSE command, and draw an ellipse to the following parameters (all relative to the current UCS):

    Axis endpoint 1:   0, 0
    Axis endpoint 2:   0, 150
    Other distance: 40

3. Draw two LINES to the following parameters (relative to the current UCS):

    From point: 0, 0
    To point: 0, 150

    From point: 0, 0, 0
    To point: 0, 0, 250

4. TRIM the ellipse to the first line, then go back to the previous 3D view, e.g. via ZOOM PREVIOUS. Thus see the trimmed ellipse in 3D, as in Fig. L17.5a.

5. Select the UCS command. Select the ORIGIN option. Then, in response to the `Origin:` prompt, enter:

    `0,0,250`   (RETURN)

6. Now, assuming data is relative to the current UCS, draw a 3P ARC to the following parameters:

    Start point: 0, 0
    Second point: 12.5, 12.5
    End point: 0, 25

You should thus see the completed arc in 3D, as shown in Fig. L17.5a.

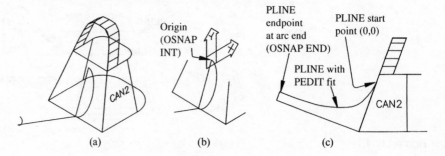

Figure L17.5.

(a)   (b)   (c)

7. Get the WCS. Then reset the UCS again, as shown in Fig. L17.5b.
8. Set VPOINT to 0, 0, 1. Then use the PLINE and PEDIT commands to create a polyline curve approximately the same as that in Fig. L17.5c, starting at the current 0, 0 point and, via the END osnap, ending at the endpoint of the arc. (Estimate suitable positions for the intermediate vertices during the PLINE command. Use the FIT option of PEDIT to create the curve. Improve the curve shape via the EDIT VERTEX option of PEDIT if necessary.)
9. SET layer SPOUT as the current layer. Go back to the previous 3D view, e.g. via ZOOM PREVIOUS (Fig. L17.6a).

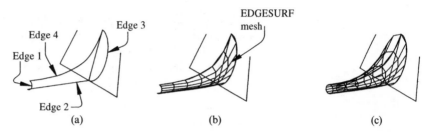

Figure L17.6.

10. Select the EDGESURF command. AutoCAD then asks you to select four edges in turn. Respond by successively PICKing the arc, last line, half-ellipse and last pline curve as edges 1, 2, 3 and 4 respectively (Fig. L17.6a). Thus see the resulting EDGESURF mesh (Fig. L17.6b).
11. Use the RESTORE option of the UCS command to reset the UCS to FFACE.
12. Select the MIRROR command, select the created EDGESURF mesh (which AutoCAD assumes is a single BLOCK object) and mirror this mesh about the current Y axis (Fig. 17.6c).

The REVSURF command

The REVSURF command creates a surface of revolution about an existing axis.

Proceed as follows:

1. SET layer CONS as the current layer. Then FREEZE layer SPOUT (thus making the EDGESURF meshes invisible).
2. Draw a LINE to the following parameters:

   From point: 0, 12.5, 200
   To point: 0, 12.5, 400

3. Select the UCS command. Then select the Y option. Then, in response to the Rotation angle about Y axis: prompt, enter:

   90   (RETURN)

   Thus see the new UCS rotated through 90 degrees about the current Y axis, as shown in Fig. L17.7a.

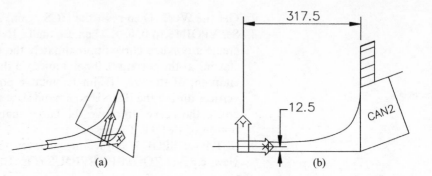

Figure L17.7.

(a)   (b)

4. Get VPOINT 0, 0, 1. Then use the ORIGIN option of the UCS command to shift the UCS to the position shown in Fig. L17.7b.
5. Draw a PLINE containing line and arc segments which conform to the parameters shown in Fig. L17.8. (Assume the coordinates shown are relative to the current UCS.)

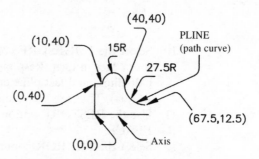

Figure L17.8.

6. SET layer SPRINKLER as the current layer.
7. Select the REVSURF command. Then, in response to the Select path curve: prompt, PICK the PLINE you drew in (5). Then, in response to the Select axis of revolution: prompt, PICK the LINE you drew in (2) (currently displayed horizontally, as in Fig. L17.8). Now RETURN to accept the default 0 for the start angle. Then RETURN again, to accept the default Full circle for the included angle. This completes the REVSURF command, and your created REVSURF mesh should be displayed as in Fig. L17.9.
8. Now retrieve your previous 3D vpoint (e.g. via ZOOM PREVIOUS), to see your REVSURF mesh in 3D (Fig. L17.10a). This represents the sprinkler of the evolving design of CAN2.
   Note: It is also possible to perform REVSURF for an axis outside the path curve, and with included angles less than 360 degrees, as shown on the example in Fig. L17.10b.
9. Complete the sprinkler by setting to a suitable UCS, and then drawing a polar ARRAY of twelve circles on the front face of the sprinkler, as shown in Fig. L17.11. (You may find it helpful to refer back to the corresponding stage in the creation of the original CAN drawing in Part A.)

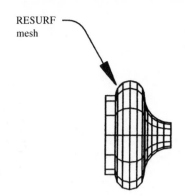

RESURF
mesh

Figure L17.9.

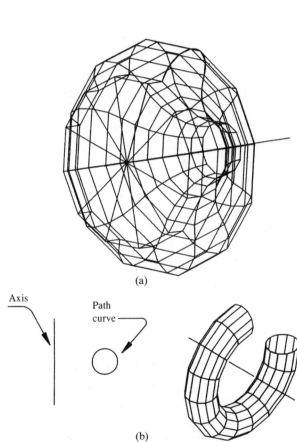

(a)

Axis

Path
curve

(b)

Figure L17.10.   (a)
Previous REVSURF mesh in
3D; (b) further example of
REVSURF (270° included
angle).

Base face

1. Set layer **BASEFACE** as the current layer.
2. Select the **3DFACE** command and use appropriate intermediate osnaps (e.g. MID, NEAR, END) to produce a continued flat mesh with invisible (I) edges, as indicated in Fig. L17.12. (The relevant procedures have been fully described in Lesson 14.)

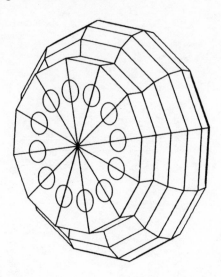

Figure L17.11.

3. Set to WCS. Set the SPLFRAME system variable to a value of 1, and REGEN to see the invisible edges. Then MIRROR the 3dface mesh, as indicated in Fig. L17.12.

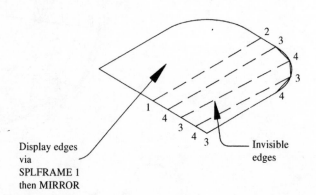

Figure L17.12.

Final design of CAN2

Complete the design of CAN2 via the additional 3D mesh surfaces shown in Figs L17.13 and L17.14. (SET and FREEZE appropriate layers as required.)

Finally, use the THAW option of the LAYER command to thaw all frozen layers, switch layer CONS OFF, get a 3D vpoint, and HIDE to see the completed design.

Further exercises

1. Create the 3D surface mesh of the tubular frame chair shown in Figs L17.15 and L17.16. Note the construction details provided. (As for the

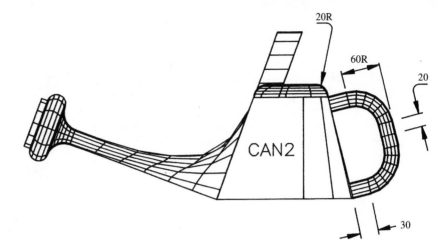

20R

60R

20

CAN2

30

Figure L17.13.

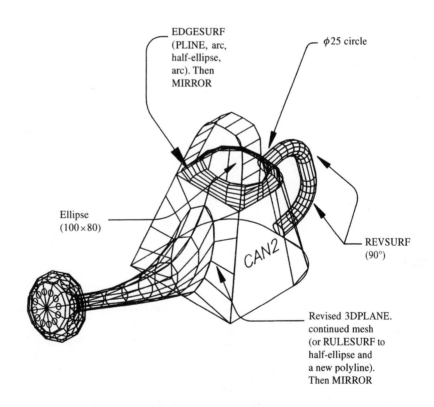

EDGESURF
(PLINE, arc,
half-ellipse,
arc). Then
MIRROR

ϕ25 circle

Ellipse
(100×80)

CAN2

REVSURF
(90°)

Revised 3DPLANE.
continued mesh
(or RULESURF to
half-ellipse and
a new polyline).
Then MIRROR

Figure L17.14.

CAN2 exercise, the initial construction items for each exercise should be drawn on a separate layer with an appropriate name such as CONS.)

2. Create a 3D surface mesh of the component initially drawn in Lesson 4 as a dimensioning exercise (Fig. L4.8). Choose suitable mesh types and densities in order to achieve a solution similar to that shown in Fig. L17.17.

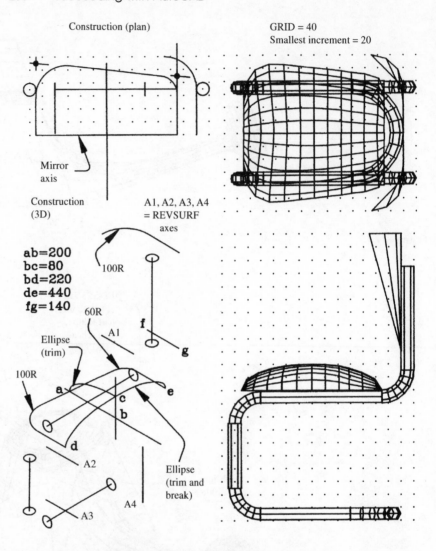

Construction (plan)

GRID = 40
Smallest increment = 20

Mirror
axis

Construction
(3D)

A1, A2, A3, A4
= REVSURF
axes

ab=200
bc=80
bd=220
de=440
fg=140

100R

60R

Ellipse
(trim)

100R

a

A1

f

g

c

b

e

d

A2

A3

A4

Ellipse
(trim and
break)

Figure L17.15.

Note: It is sometimes useful to enhance the quality of your 3D meshes by controlling their density in either one or two directions (called the M direction and N direction).

The density of a RULESURF mesh or a TABSURF mesh may be controlled in one direction only via the SURFTAB1 system variable (higher values giving denser meshes).

The density of a EDGESURF mesh or REVSURF mesh may be controlled in both M direction and N direction via the system variables SURFTAB1 and SURFTAB2.

When using EDGESURF, the M direction is defined as the direction of the first edge selected. When using REVSURF, the M direction is defined as the circmferential direction of the revolved surface.

The values of SURFTAB1 and SURFTAB2 may be set via the SETVAR command.

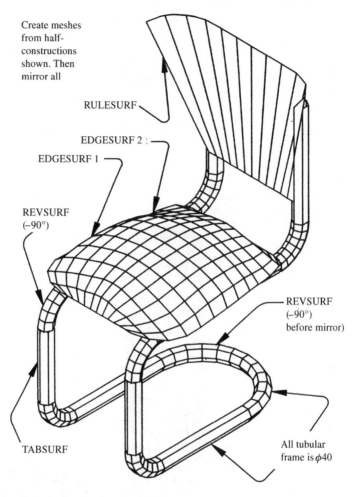

Create meshes
from half-
constructions
shown. Then
mirror all

RULESURF

EDGESURF 2

EDGESURF 1

REVSURF
(−90°)

REVSURF
(−90°)
before mirror)

TABSURF

All tubular
frame is $\phi 40$

Figure L17.16.

Rendering your surface meshes

Since Release 12, it is possible to create superior shaded and rendered
images of your 3D surface models. This facility was further enhanced
with Release 13. A number of techniques exist for doing this, but in most
cases the best results can be achieved by using the RENDER command.
This is an AutoLISP program which is normally invoked via screen menu or
toolbar selection.

On most systems, by applying this capability to the completed 3D models
in Figs L17.16 and L17.17 you could achieve 3D images similar to those
shown in Figs L17.18 and L17.19.

The RENDER command also has options for controlling the rendered
effect by simulating movable light sources and light intensities. In the
Windows environment you can get a cascaded stack of all the rendered
images produced on your drawing.

You may obtain a hard copy of the rendered image if you have a raster
device such as an ink jet, laser or electrostatic plotter.

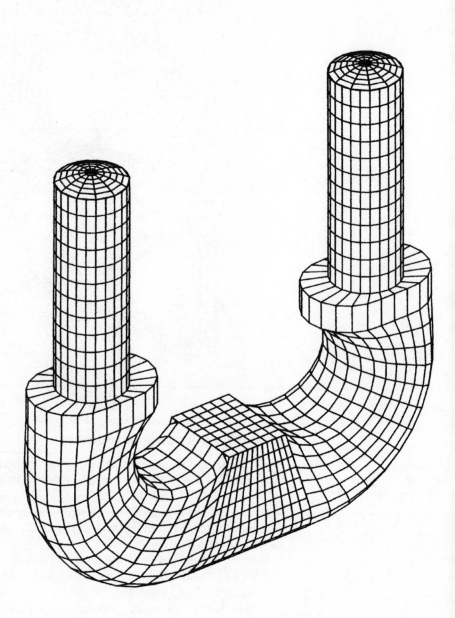

Figure L17.17.

Figure L17.18. Supplied by kind permission of the University of Greenwich.

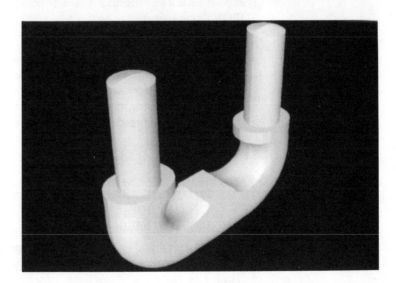

Figure L17.19. Supplied by kind permission of the University of Greenwich.

Lesson 18

3D polylines

The 3DPOLY command

The PLINE command will not allow you to draw a polyline with specified points outside the current UCS XY plane. To do this you must use the 3DPOLY command.

Proceed as follows:

1. Begin a new drawing and, working from VPOINT 0, 0, 1 of the WCS, select the 3DPOLY command. Then, in response to the From point: and successive To point: prompts, draw the 3D polyline ABCDEF shown in Fig. L18.1a, by entering the following XYZ coordinate data for the respective points:

    A: 20, 30, 5
    B: 300, 100, 50
    C: 210, 290, 200
    D: 40, 210, 300
    E: 150, 100, 500
    F: 250, 160, 400

    Then RETURN to complete the 3DPOLY command.
2. Now set VPOINT to, say, 0, −1, 1. Thus see a 3D view of the polyline (Fig. L18.1b).

PEDIT in 3D

You may use the PEDIT command to edit a 3D polyline, but there are fewer options than for a 2D PLINE.

Proceed as follows:

1. Select the PEDIT command. Then, in response to the Select polyline: prompt, PICK any point on your 3D polyline.
2. Select the SPLINE (S) option. Then select the EXIT (X) option, to complete the PEDIT command.

    Thus see the 3D view of a 3D spline curve (Fig. L18.2a).

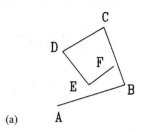

(a)

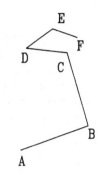

(b)

Figure L18.1.

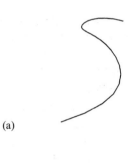

(a)

Figure L18.2.

(b)

3. Now reset to VPOINT 0, 0, 1. Thus see the plan view of the 3D spline curve (Fig. L18.2b).

Associated system variables

As in 2D, the system variables SPLFRAME and SPLINETYPE may be applied to 3D splines.

Proceed as follows:

1. Reset to your 3D viewpoint (e.g. 0, −1, 1).
2. Specify SPLFRAME as the system variable, and enter a value of 1 for its setting.

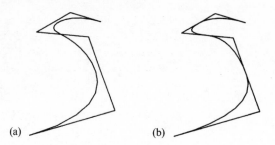

Figure L18.3.   (a)   (b)

3. Select the REGEN command. Thus see the frame displayed around the 3D spline (Fig. L18.3a).
4. Specify SPLINETYPE as the system variable, and enter a value of 5 for its setting. This changes SPLINETYPE from its default setting of 6 (giving a 'cubic B-spline' curve), to a setting of 5 (giving a 'quadratic B-spine' curve).
5. Select PEDIT. PICK 3D spline. Then select the DECURVE option. Now select the SPLINE option. EXIT the PEDIT command.
   See the modified spline shape (Fig. L18.3b).

Exercise—3D spiral (helix)

Proceed as follows:

1. Ensure that the following settings are current:

> WCS
> VPOINT: 0, 0, 1 (plan)
> SPLFRAME: 0
> SPLINETYPE: 5
> LIMITS: −500, −500 (lower left); 500, 500 (upper right)

2. ERASE the last spline curve.
3. Draw a POLYGON with twelve sides, centre 0, 0 and CIR-CUMSCRIBING a circle of radius 100 (Fig. L18.4).

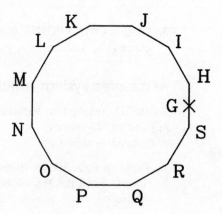

Figure L18.4.

4. Select the 3DPOLY command. Then, in response to the From point: prompt, use the MID osnap to PICK point G (Fig. L18.4) on the polygon right edge. Then, in response to the To point: prompt, invoke point filtering by entering:

   .XY

followed by RETURN if typed-in at the keyboard.
   Then use the END osnap to PICK point H. Note the Need Z: prompt. Respond to this by entering:

   0,0,5   (RETURN)

Now, in response to the To point: prompt, enter:

   .XY

followed by RETURN if typed-in at the keyboard.
   Then use the END osnap to PICK point I. Note the Need Z: prompt. Respond to this by entering:

   0,0,15   (RETURN)

Continue thus at each successive corner, increasing the Z value by 10 each time, until you enter a value of: 0,0,115 at point S. Then, use the .XY point filter again, followed by the MID osnap, and PICK point G. In response to the Need Z: prompt, enter:

   0,0,120   (RETURN)

Then RETURN again to complete the 3DPOLY command.
5. Set VPOINT to 0, −1, 1 . Thus see the polyline and polygon in 3D (Fig. L18.5a).
6. Use the PEDIT command to create a SPLINE curve from the 3D polyline (Fig. L18.5b).
7. ERASE the polygon (Fig. L18.5c). Then COPY the spline curve from point G1 to point G2. Now COPY the two spline curves again, to achieve the 'spring' helix shown in Fig. L18.6.
8. Check that the helix curve is correct in all planes by setting to the VPOINT values shown in Fig. L18.7.

Exercise—Square section helical spring

Proceed as follows:

1. Go back to stage (6) of the previous exercise by erasing three splines (thus leaving the single 3D spline curve of Fig. L18.5b).
2. Draw a POLYGON, with twelve sides, centre 0, 0, and CIRCUMSCRIBING a circle of radius 70. Then repeat the same steps as in the previous exercise, to produce a 3D spline using the new polygon and with an overall Z height of 120, as before. The new 3D spline curve should thus be concentric within the previous one (Fig. L18.8).

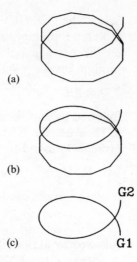

(a)

(b)

G2

Figure L18.5.   (c)   G1

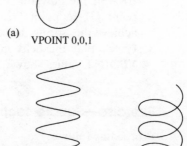

Figure L18.6.

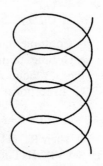

(a)
VPOINT 0,0,1

Figure L18.7.

(b)   (c)
VPOINT 0,-1,0   VPOINT -1,-1,1

3. Now, set the system variable SURFTAB1 to a value of 24, and, on a new layer, create a RULESURF mesh between the two 3D splines (Fig. L18.9a).

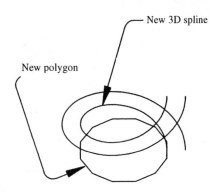

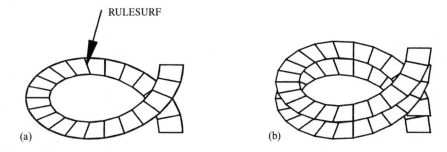

Figure L18.8.   Concentric
3D splines (VPOINT 0, −1,
1).

Figure L18.9.   (a)   (b)

4. COPY the RULESURF mesh 'upwards' in Z by 30 units (Fig. L18.9b).
5. FREEZE the layer created in (3) and create another new layer and make
    this current. Then use the TABSURF command with an appropriately
    created direction vector of length 30 units, to produce the two meshes
    (one from each spline curve) shown in Fig. L18.10.

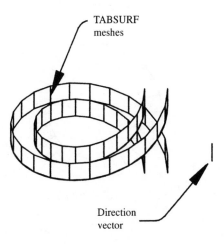

Figure L18.10.

6. THAW the frozen layer. Turn your first layer OFF, to make the spline
    curves invisible. Thus see Fig. L18.11.

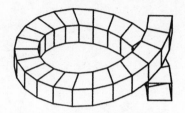

Figure L18.11.

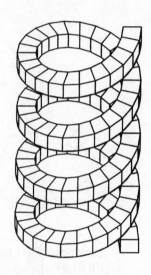

Figure L18.12.
Completed spring
(VPOINT 0, –1, 1).

7. Perform appropriate COPY routines, add two square 3D faces, and
   HIDE. Thus see the square section spring (Fig. L18.12). Finally, check
   that the 3D geometry of the spring is correct by obtaining successive
   viewpoints as shown in Fig. L18.13.

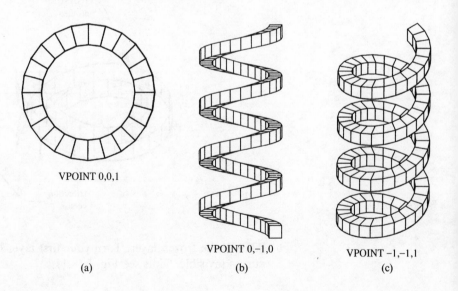

Figure L18.13.   (a)   (b)   (c)

Further exercises

Model the 3D item shown in Fig. L18.14 according to the instructions given in Fig. L18.15. Take all grid spacings as 100 units. Pay particular attention to the 3DPOLY routines involved.

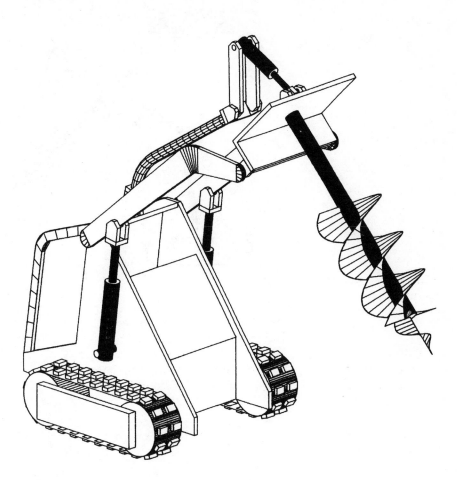

Figure L18.14.

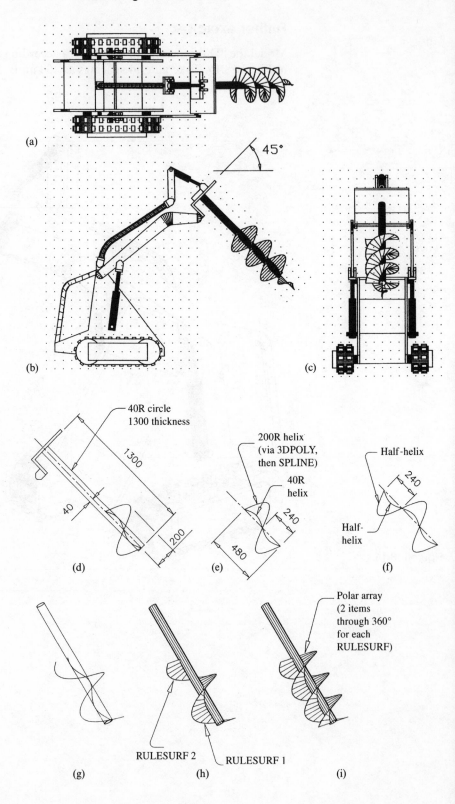

Figure L18.15.

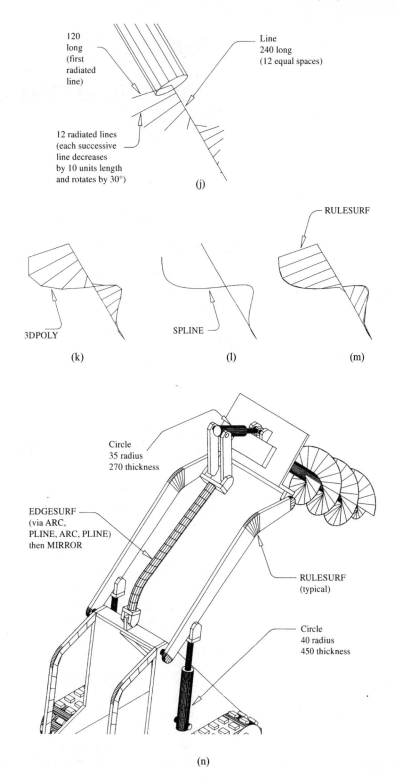

120 long (first radiated line)

Line 240 long (12 equal spaces)

12 radiated lines (each successive line decreases by 10 units length and rotates by 30°)

(j)

RULESURF

3DPOLY

SPLINE

(k)

(l)

(m)

Circle 35 radius 270 thickness

EDGESURF (via ARC, PLINE, ARC, PLINE) then MIRROR

RULESURF (typical)

Circle 40 radius 450 thickness

Figure L18.15.

(n)

Lesson 19

3DMESH and mesh editing

The 3DMESH command

The 3DMESH command allows you to create a mesh via the location of each vertex, and the number of vertices in the mesh.

Proceed as follows:

1. Begin a new drawing. Ensure you are in the WCS, with VPOINT at 0, 0, 1 (plan).
2. Select the 3DMESH command. Then, in response to the Mesh M size: prompt, enter a value of 5. Now, in response to the Mesh N size: prompt, enter a value of 4. (We have thus specified a mesh with 5 vertices in the M direction and 4 vertices in the N direction, as indicated in Fig. L19.1.)

   AutoCAD now displays the prompt: Vertex (0,0):. Respond by entering:

   > 200,100,30   (RETURN)

   AutoCAD then displays the prompt: Vertex (0,1):. Respond by entering:

   > 200,150,40   (RETURN)

   We have thus specified XYZ coordinate values for vertices (0, 0) and (0, 1). These are shown in Fig. L19.1.

   Now specify the coordinate values for the remaining 18 vertices of the mesh, by entering the following data:

Vertex (0, 2):	200, 200, 30
Vertex (0, 3):	200, 250, 60
Vertex (1, 0):	250, 100, 0
Vertex (1, 1):	250, 150, 0
Vertex (1, 2):	250, 200, 0
Vertex (1, 3):	250, 250, 0
Vertex (2, 0):	300, 100, 0
Vertex (2, 1):	300, 150, -10

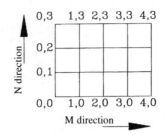

Figure L19.1.

Vertex (2, 2):	300, 200, 0
Vertex (2, 3):	300, 250, −20
Vertex (3, 0):	350, 100, 0
Vertex (3, 1):	350, 150, 0
Vertex (3, 2):	350, 200, −10
Vertex (3, 3):	350, 250, −30
Vertex (4, 0):	400, 100, 50
Vertex (4, 1):	400, 150, 40
Vertex (4, 2):	400, 200, 10
Vertex (4, 3):	400, 250, −20

3. Set VPOINT to −1, −2, 2. Thus see your created mesh in 3D (Fig. L19.2).

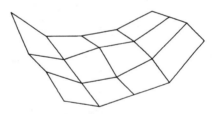

Figure L19.2.

Mesh editing

You may use the PEDIT command to edit 3D meshes, but the options are somewhat different from those for polylines.

Proceed as follows:

1. Select PEDIT. Then PICK your 3D mesh at any point.
2. Select the SMOOTH option. See the smoothed mesh surface (Fig. L19.3).
3. Select the DESMOOTH option. See Fig. L19.2 again.
4. Select the EDIT VERTEX option. Note the 'x' marker which has appeared at vertex (0, 0). RETURN to take the marker to the next vertex (0, 1). Repeat a few more RETURNs, thus taking the marker to successive vertices. Then experiment with the options: PREVIOUS, LEFT, RIGHT, UP and DOWN, noting the differing types of marker movements produced.

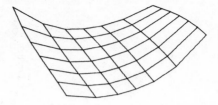

Figure L19.3.

Take the marker to vertex (2, 2). Then select the MOVE option. Now, in response to the `Enter new location:` prompt, enter:

`@0,0,200`   (RETURN)

Thus see the modified mesh (Fig. L19.4a).

Then select EXIT, to come out of the EDIT VERTEX option.
5. Select SMOOTH again, from the PEDIT main options. See Fig. L19.4b.
6. Select EXIT, to come out of the PEDIT command.

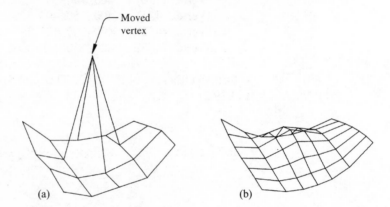

Figure L19.4.   (a) Modified mesh; (b) smoothed mesh.

Associated system variables

We can control the fineness of meshes along directions M and N via the system variables SURFU and SURFV respectively. Also we can vary the shape of a smoothed mesh surface via the SURFTYPE system variable.
  Proceed as follows:

1. Select the SURFU system variable, and enter a value of 12. (The default is 6.)
2. Select the SURFV system variable, and enter a value of 8. (The default is 6.)
3. Select PEDIT. PICK the 3D mesh. Then select the SMOOTH option. See the finer mesh (Fig. L19.5a). EXIT the PEDIT command.
4. The default type of surface on smoothed mesh conforms to a 'cubic B-spline' (corresponding to SURFTYPE setting 6). There are two other types.
    Select the SURFTYPE system variable, and enter a value of 5. This specifies a 'quadratic B-spline' surface.

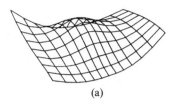

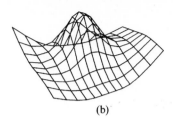

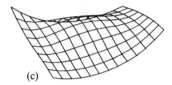

Figure L19.5.   (a) New settings of SURFU and SURFV; (b) quadratic B-spline; (c) Bezier surface.

5. Select PEDIT. PICK 3D mesh. Select the SMOOTH option. See the new mesh surface (Fig. L19.5b). EXIT the PEDIT command.

6. Similarly, reset SURFTYPE to a value of 8 (thus specifying a 'Bezier' surface), and SMOOTH the surface again via the PEDIT command. See the new surface type (Fig. L19.5c).

Holes in meshes

Surface meshes often contain holes of various shapes. This can be achieved using a combination of mesh types forming a border around an open space. However, it is sometimes more suitable to 'cut' a hole out of an existing 3D mesh.

Proceed as follows:

1. Working from WCS, and VPOINT 0, 0, 1, draw the profiles shown in Fig. L19.6a, using LINES and ARCS. (Assume the grid dots shown are 10 units apart, and that the smallest increment is 5 units.)

2. Set the system variables SURFTAB1 and SURFTAB2, both to a value of 10.

3. Select the EDGESURF command. Create a mesh to the outer profile (Fig. L19.6b).

4. Select PEDIT. PICK the mesh created in (3). Select the EDIT VERTEX option. Then, referring to Fig. L19.7a, move vertices a, b, c, d to corners 1, 2, 3, 4 respectively, making use of the END osnap. Now move vertices e, f to midpoints 5, 6 respectively, via the MID osnap. Then, move the remaining vertices shown marked in Fig. L19.7a, to near points on the inner profile, via the NEAR osnap (Fig. L19.7b).

    EXIT the PEDIT command.

5. Select the EXPLODE command, and then PICK the mesh at any point.

6. ERASE all the mesh faces inside the inner profile. (These faces are now considered as separate entities due to the EXPLODE operation.)

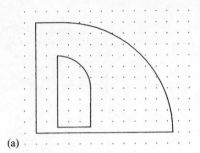

(a)

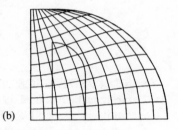

(b)

Figure L19.6.

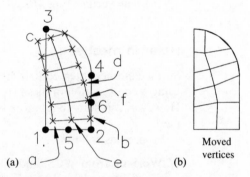

(a)   (b)

Moved vertices

Figure L19.7.

A hole of the required shape has thus now been 'cut out' of the surface mesh (Fig. L19.8a).

7. Get a 3D VPOINT (e.g. −1, −1, 1) to see your mesh and hole in 3D (Fig. L19.8b).

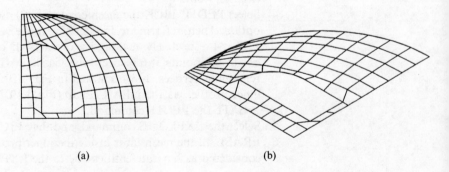

(a)   (b)

Figure L19.8.

Lesson 20

An introduction to 3D solid modelling

AutoCAD 3D solid modelling facilities have been available since Release 11, but until Release 13 could only be accessed via a 'bolt-on' extra package called AME (Advanced Modelling Extension) which had to be purchased separately. Since Release 13, the AME solid modelling capabilities have been brought into the main AutoCAD program so that they are available to all AutoCAD users on the later releases.

Principles of 3D solid modelling

Throughout Lessons 11 and 19, we have been creating our 3D drawings via *surface modelling* techniques. As the name implies, this involves defining 3D shapes via external surfaces. The resulting surface model may thus be thought of as a 'hollow shell' whose interior is not truly defined.

In contrast, a *3D solid model* is defined in terms of the *volumetric shape* which it occupies. Its interior is thus truly defined as a solid mass. This being the case, a solid model has a number of capabilities which would not be available on a surface model. Having known volumetric matter, you can determine mass/volume properties from a solid model (weights, centres of gravity, moments of inertia, etc.). The knowledge of the internal shape also provides facilities such as 3D cutaway sections, and the detection of interference or collision between adjacent 3D shapes.

However, it should be appreciated that surface models can be more versatile than solids where complex definitions of surfaces, hidden line removal and surface renderings are required; are less demanding on computer memory; and in many cases give an efficient approximation of the 3D object being modelled. (For example, a good proportion of the 3D objects we have modelled so far are, in fact, very much akin to hollow shells in reality.)

Thus the two types of 3D modelling system should not be thought of in terms of a hierarchy, but as alternative modelling tools to suit particular applications.

3D solid 'primitives'

Solid *primitives* are simple 3D shapes which may be considered as the basic 'building bricks' from which we will make up our compound 3D solid model. Examples of these primitives available on AutoCAD include: BOX (solid brick); SPHERE; CYLINDER; CONE; WEDGE; and TORUS ('3D doughnut').

We will be using a sample of these primitives in our solid modelling exercises.

Boolean operations

These comprise another essential tool in building up the solid model. Boolean operations are based on algebraic set theory and define the relationship between solid primitives which have become merged.

The three important Boolean operations are illustrated in Fig. L20.1, and may be summarized as follows:

- UNION   This defines the solid matter inside the outer boundaries of the combined shape formed when two primitives have merged.
- SUBTRACT   This defines the solid matter inside the remaining profile of one of the original primitives and the outer boundary of the merged region.
- INTERSECT   This defines the solid matter inside the boundaries of the merged region.

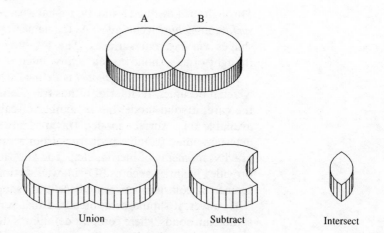

Figure L20.1. Principle of Boolean operations.

Exercise in 3D solid modelling

Proceed as follows:

1. Begin a new drawing on AutoCAD.
2. Working from the WCS, get a 3D viewpoint, e.g. $(-1, -1, 1)$.

3. Select the BOX command. Then, accepting the default `Corner of box:` option, enter:

   `0,0,0`   (RETURN)

   Next, accepting the `Other corner:` option, enter:

   `80,60,20`   (RETURN)

   Thus see the solid box shown in Fig. L20.2a.
4. Change the UCS as shown in Fig. L20.2b.
5. Create a polyline according to the information shown in Fig. L20.3.

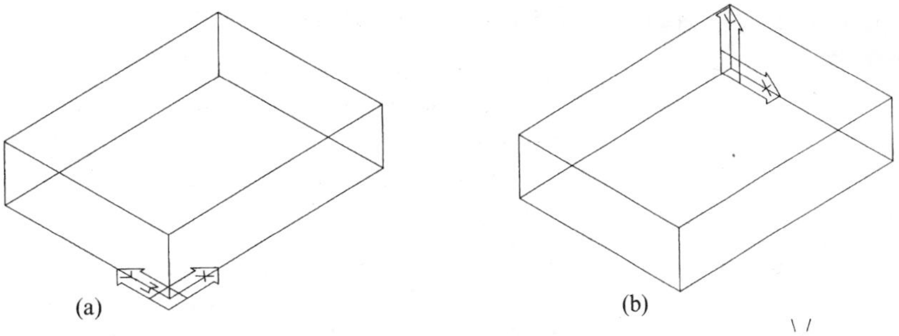

Figure L20.2.   (a) Solid BOX; (b) changed UCS.

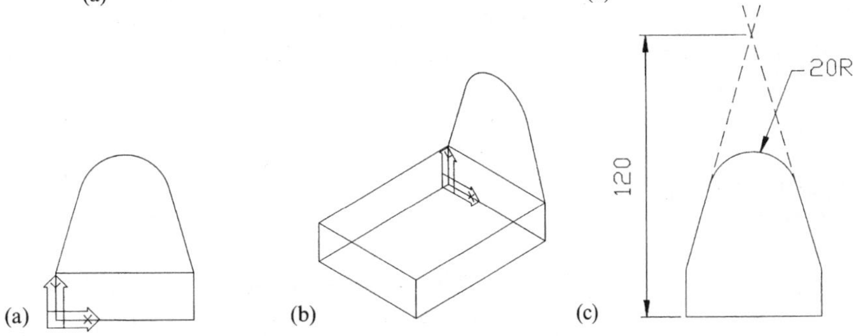

(a)   (b)

Figure L20.3.   (a) Box with polyline; (b) polyline 3D view; (c) polyline details.

(a)   (b)   (c)

6. Select the EXTRUDE command. Select the polyline as the object to extrude, e.g. by PICKing it. RETURN, to complete the selection set. Then, in response to the `Height of extrusion:` prompt, enter a value of 20. Next, enter a value of 0 for the `Extrusion taper angle:`.

   This completes the EXTRUDE command, and your display should be as Fig. L20.4, showing the polyline extruded to a solid shape.
7. Select the UNION command. Then select the solid box and the extruded polyline in turn, e.g. by PICKing them. RETURN to complete the selection set.

   This completes the UNION command. The resulting composite shape should appear as shown in Fig. L20.5.
8. Select the CYLINDER command. Then, in response to the `Center point:` prompt, use the CEN osnap and PICK the rightmost (i.e. the original) polyline fillet radius. Next enter a radius value of 15, followed by a height value of 40.

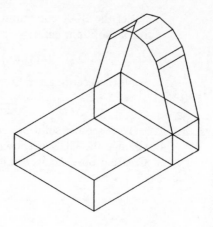

Figure L20.4.   Extruded polyline.

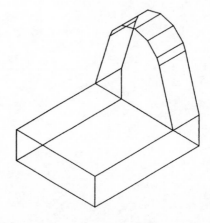

Figure L20.5.   UNION operation.

This completes the CYLINDER command, and a solid cylinder should be shown as in Fig. L20.6.

9. Now perform another UNION operation, selecting the composite solid and the new cylinder. This creates a new composite solid, as in Fig. L20.7.

10. Change the UCS back to the World Coordinate System.

11. Create another CYLINDER of:

Centre point:	10, 30, 10
Radius:	20
Height:	30

See the new cylinder, as in Fig. L20.8.

12. Select the SUBTRACT command. Then, in response to the Source objects: prompt, select the composite solid. Then RETURN. Next, in response to the Objects to subtract: prompt, select the new cylinder. Then RETURN.

This completes the SUBTRACT command, and your new composite solid should appear as in Fig. L20.9.

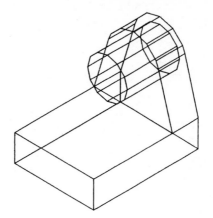

Figure L20.6.   Solid
CYLINDER.

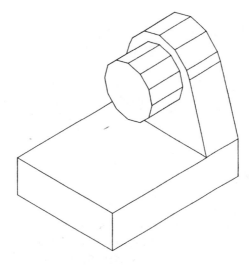

Figure L20.7.   UNION
operation.

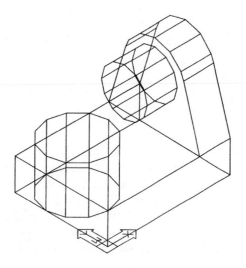

Figure L20.8.   Solid
CYLINDER.

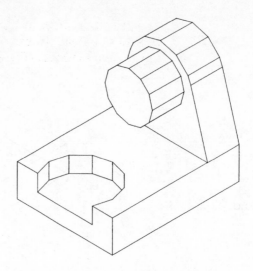

Figure L20.9.   SUBTRACT
operation.

Note: If we had actioned an **INTERSECT** command, instead of
SUBTRACT, we would have achieved a display as in Fig. L20.10.
Such an operation would be useful for, say, determining the mass of
material removed in a spot-face machining operation. Bear this in mind
for future exercises, but, for now, continue.

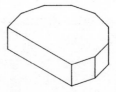

Figure L20.10.
INTERSECTION operation.

13. Now use **CYLINDER** and **SUBTRACT**, to make a 10 radius hole
    concentric to the previous cylinder, as shown in Fig. L20.11.

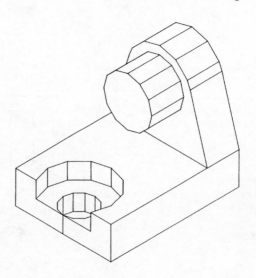

Figure L20.11.   SUBTRACT
operation.

14. Complete the exercise by opening the last hole up into a slot, making a 20 × 10 slot along the base, and making a 10 radius hole through the top 15 radius cylinder (Fig. L20.12).

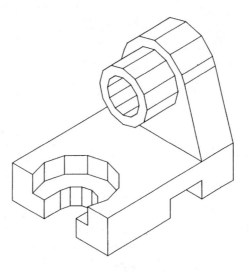

Figure L20.12.
Completed 3D solid
model.

Further exercise in 3D modelling

Using the techniques described in the previous exercise, produce a 3D solid model of the component shown in Figs L20.13 and L20.14. Obtain sizes from the grid points shown in Fig. L20.13. (Take all grid spacings as 10 units, with smallest size increment of 5 units.)

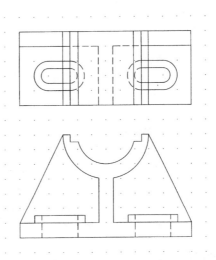

Figure L20.13.

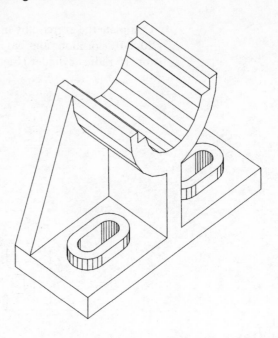

Figure L20.14.

Summary

Consider the work done in Lesson 20 as a 'taster' exercise in the use of solid primitives and Boolean operations. It will serve as a starting point for more advanced solid modelling facilities on AutoCAD, including:

- Solid sectioning
- Conversion of 3D solids to surface meshes for hidden line removal and rendering purposes
- Determining interference values of 'clashed' solids
- Specifying materials and analysing mass properties

Part D

Summary 3D exercise: Helicopter

This part of the book contains a single exercise which serves as a summary of the principles and techniques outlined in previous work. In progressing to the 3D construction of a helicopter, it involves all the 3D modelling skills, and the encompassing draughting techniques, developed in the foregoing lessons.

Create the 3D surface model of the helicopter according to the information and guidance contained in the diagrams supplied in the following pages (Figs D1 to D27 inclusive).

Figure D1.

Conclusion: Full circle

Once the helicopter is constructed, insert it as a block into the house/garden drawing we created in Lesson 16. The approximate position and orientation of the helicopter relative to the house and garden items are shown in Figs D28 and D29.

We may thus complete the evolutionary cycle of our AutoCAD process by obtaining similar perspective displays to those shown in Figs D30 to D33. These include a view of the garden from inside the helicopter and, finally, a view up to the helicopter from our first drawn item—the humble (Mark I) watering-can.

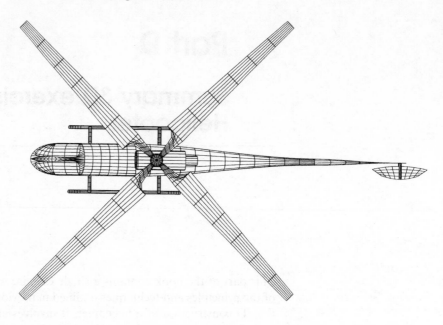

Figure D2.

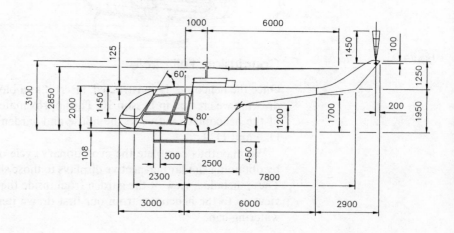

Figure D3.

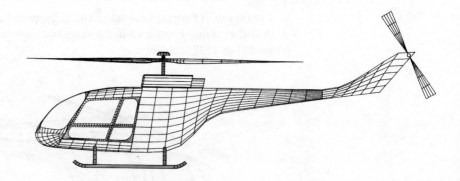

Figure D4,

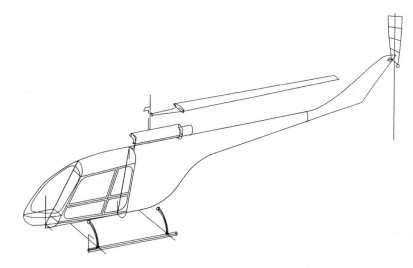

Figure D5.   Constructions
(3D viewpoint).

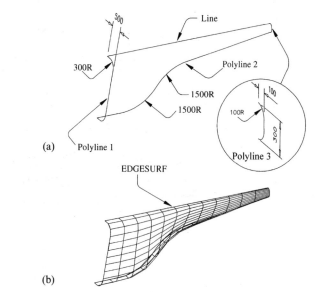

Figure D6.

(a)

(b)

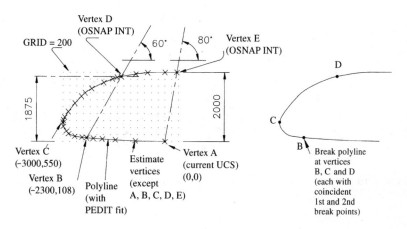

Figure D7.

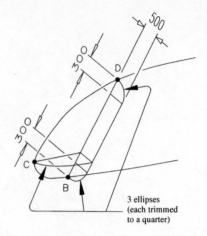

Figure D8.

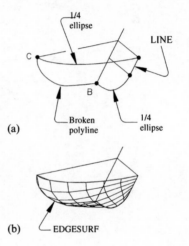

Figure D9.

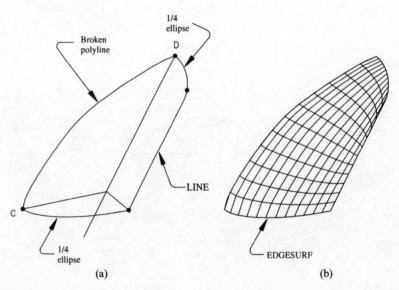

Figure D10.

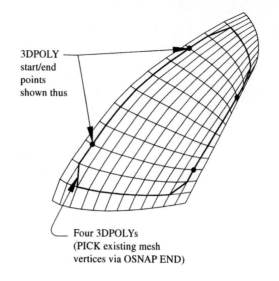

3DPOLY
start/end
points
shown thus

Four 3DPOLYs
(PICK existing mesh
vertices via OSNAP END)

Figure D11.

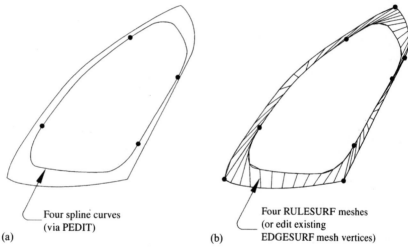

(a)

(b)

Four spline curves
(via PEDIT)

Four RULESURF meshes
(or edit existing
EDGESURF mesh vertices)

Figure D12.

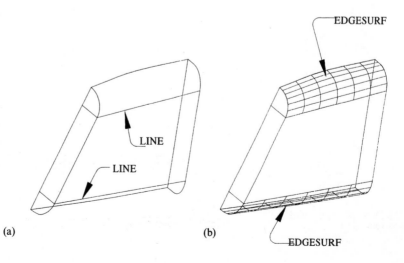

EDGESURF

LINE

LINE

EDGESURF

(a)

(b)

Figure D13.

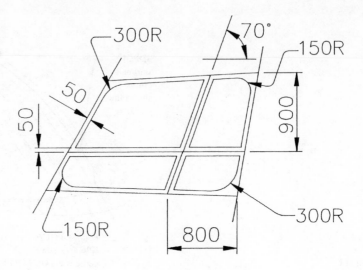

Figure D14.

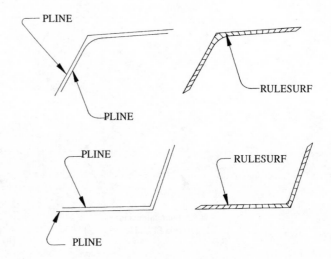

Figure D15.

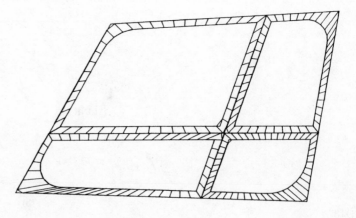

Figure D16.   Completed
RULESURFs.

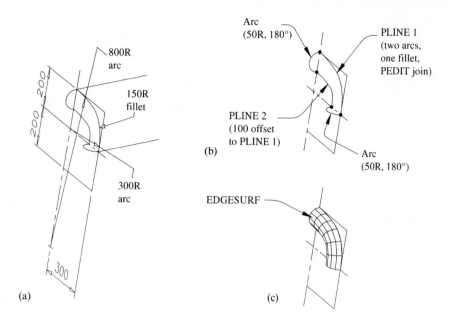

800R
arc

150R
fillet

200
200

300R
arc

300

(a)

Arc
(50R, 180°)

PLINE 1
(two arcs,
one fillet,
PEDIT join)

PLINE 2
(100 offset
to PLINE 1)

(b)

Arc
(50R, 180°)

EDGESURF

(c)

Figure D17.

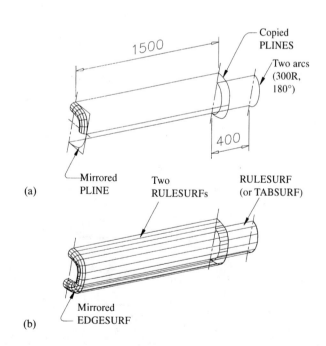

1500

Copied
PLINES

Two arcs
(300R,
180°)

400

Mirrored
PLINE

(a)

Two
RULESURFs

RULESURF
(or TABSURF)

Mirrored
EDGESURF

(b)

Figure D18.

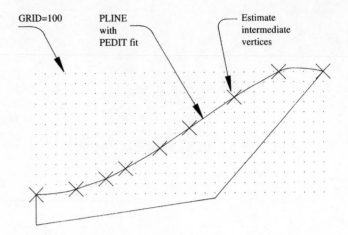

Figure D19.

GRID=100

PLINE with PEDIT fit

Estimate intermediate vertices

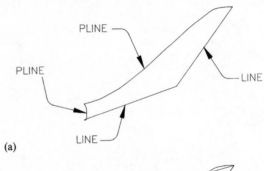

PLINE

PLINE

PLINE

LINE

LINE

(a)

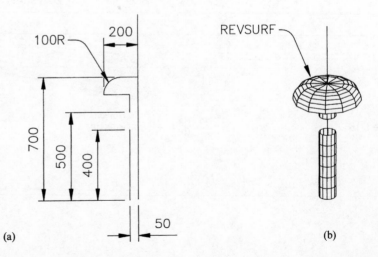

(b)

EDGESURF

Figure D20.

REVSURF

100R

200

700

500

400

50

Figure D21.   (a)   (b)

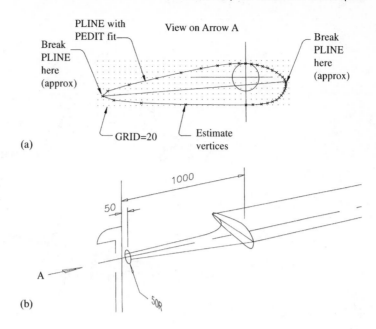

View on Arrow A

PLINE with
PEDIT fit

Break
PLINE
here
(approx)

Break
PLINE
here
(approx)

GRID=20

Estimate
vertices

(a)

1000

50

A

50R

(b)

Figure D22.

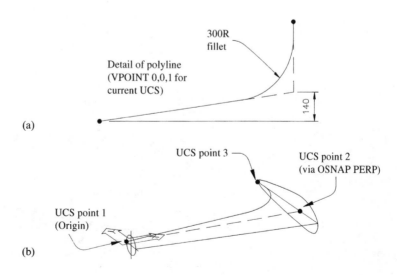

300R
fillet

Detail of polyline
(VPOINT 0,0,1 for
current UCS)

140

(a)

UCS point 3

UCS point 2
(via OSNAP PERP)

UCS point 1
(Origin)

Figure D23.

(b)

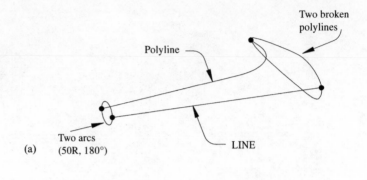

Two broken
polylines

Polyline

Two arcs
(50R, 180°)

(a)

LINE

EDGESURF

EDGESURF

(b)

Figure D24.

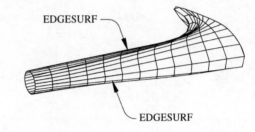

View on Arrow A

LINE 1   LINE 2   LINE 3

300

100

(a)   (b)

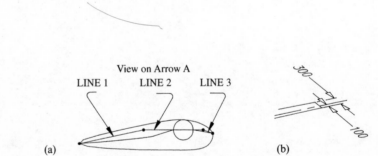

Broken
PLINES

LINE 1

LINE 2

LINE 3

A

(c)

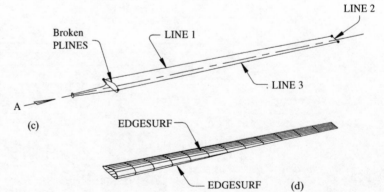

EDGESURF

EDGESURF   (d)

Figure D25.

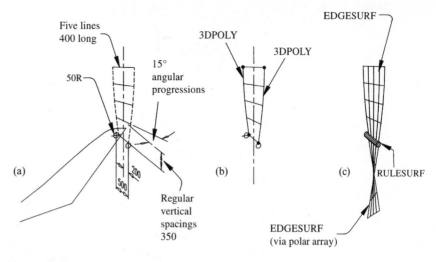

Five lines
400 long

50R

15°
angular
progressions

3DPOLY

3DPOLY

EDGESURF

(a)

(b)

(c)

RULESURF

200

500

Regular
vertical
spacings
350

EDGESURF
(via polar array)

Figure D26.

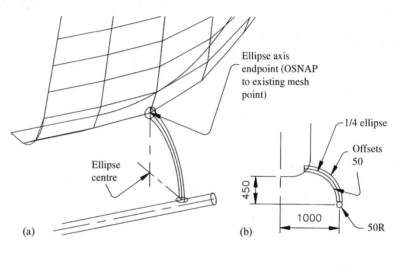

Ellipse axis
endpoint (OSNAP
to existing mesh
point)

Ellipse
centre

1/4 ellipse

Offsets
50

450

1000

50R

(a)

(b)

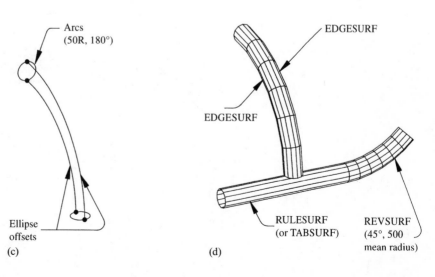

Arcs
(50R, 180°)

EDGESURF

EDGESURF

Ellipse
offsets

RULESURF
(or TABSURF)

REVSURF
(45°, 500
mean radius)

(c)

(d)

Figure D27.

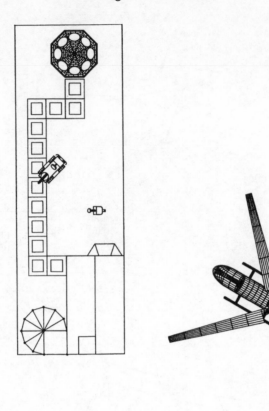

Figure D28.

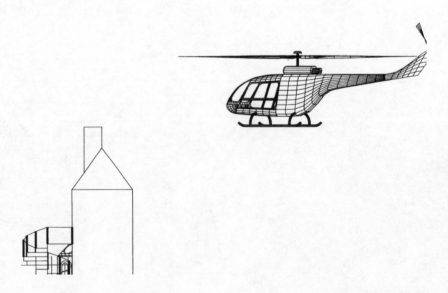

Figure D29.

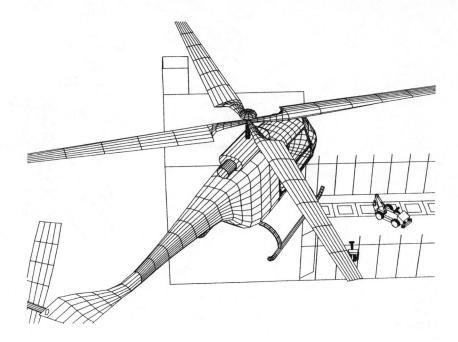

Figure D30.

Figure D31.

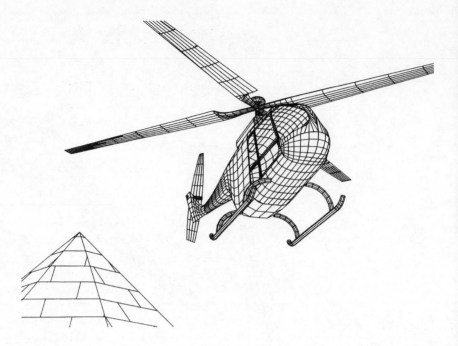

Figure D32.

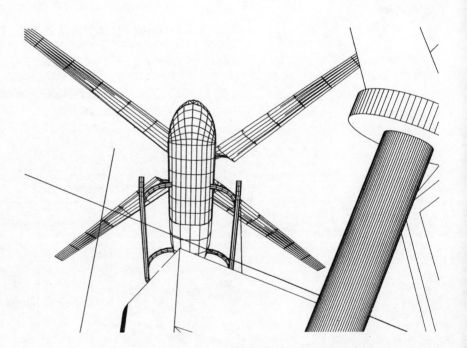

Figure D33.

Appendix A

The AutoCAD program file structure

As stated at the beginning of this book, AutoCAD is a computer software package and, as such, is made up of a collection of programs stored as files. In the MSDOS and Windows operating systems, all files (including AutoCAD drawing files) are given a name of up to eight characters followed by a three-character extension. In AutoCAD, different types of file are classified via their particular three-letter extension. For example, the file ACAD.EXE is the main AutoCAD executable program file, the file ACADUK.MNU is a type of MENU file, and so on.

The most important types of AutoCAD file extension are:

.BAK	Drawing file BACK UP copy
.DWG	AutoCAD DRAWING file
.DRV	Hardware DEVICE DRIVER file
.DXF	DRAWING INTERCHANGE file
.EXE	EXECUTABLE PROGRAM file
.IGS	IGES interchange file
.LIN	LINETYPE library file
.LSP	AutoLISP program file
.LST	Printer plot output file
.MNU	MENU source file
.MNX	COMPILED MENU file
.OVL	Program OVERLAY file
.PAT	HARCH PATTERN library file
.PLT	PLOT output file
.SCR	Command SCRIPT file
.SLD	SLIDE file
.SHP	SHAPE/TEXT FONT file
.SHX	COMPILED SHAPE/TEXT FONT file

Appendix B

Menus, windows, toolbars and dialog boxes

Menus allow you to select AutoCAD commands and options via screen or tablet pointing interaction, as an alternative to typing at the keyboard. It must be emphasized that, when using menus, you are invoking exactly the same commands and options which are available via the keyboard, but are merely taking a different route to access them.

The default configuration of AutoCAD provides a number of different types of menu for alternative selection procedures. These may be classified as:

- Right-hand screen (root) menu
- Top screen menu bar with 'pull-down' menus
- Floating toolbars and palettes (Windows platform only)
- Cursor menus
- Tablet menus
- Button menus

Screen (root) menu

This facility provides the option of a screen menu display down the right-hand side of the graphics screen. This is sometimes referred to as the *root menu* and allows command and option selection by pointing to menu areas at this part of the screen, most appropriately with a pointing device such as a mouse or a digitizing puck. Once activated, the root menu takes the user through a series of hierarchical sub-menus until the complete command and options have been actioned. Some of the menu items are standard AutoCAD commands, while others are 'user-friendly' messages intended to steer the user in the right direction for the successful completion of the command.

For example, if you wished to draw a line, this would be done by pointing to DRAW in the menu display, and then PICKing. A sub-menu is then displayed showing the most-used drawing commands. If you now point to

LINE in this sub-menu, and PICK, a further sub-menu is displayed, showing the LINE options. Fig. App1 illustrates the hierarchical nature of the screen menu and its sub-menus by showing the series of displays provided when actioning the LINE command, followed by a return to the main root menu.

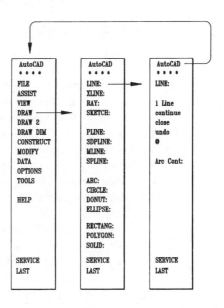

Figure App1.   Screen menu procedure (e.g. LINE command).

Pull-down screen menus

AutoCAD provides a menu bar along the top of the graphics screen, from which sub-menus may be 'pulled down' onto the screen. This is done by PICKing the required menu item (or 'title') from the menu bar with a pointing device.

For example, if you PICK the DRAW title in the top menu bar, your cursor takes the form of an arrow, and a list giving access to the most-used drawing commands is pulled down onto the screen (Fig. App2a). In some cases you may then access the command directly by PICKing your choice from the pulled-down list with the arrow cursor. In other cases the required command is accessed via a cascade of sub-menus (available if an arrow marker is shown rightwards of the appropriate pulled-down item). For example, if you wished to draw an elliptical arc, you could do so by PICKing DRAW from the top menu bar, and taking your pointing device to the arrow marker against ELLIPSE in the pulled-down list. This invokes the sub-menu shown in Fig. App2b, from which you would PICK the option ARC. Fig. App2c shows the selection sequence and invoked cascade of sub-menus required for drawing a DIAMETER dimension via pull-down menu (dimensioning is discussed in Lesson 4).

Further categories of AutoCAD command may be accessed via their own appropriate title in the top menu bar. For example, the title MODIFY can be used to display a pulled-down list giving access to the most-used editing commands, such as ERASE, MOVE, ROTATE (as discussed in Lesson 3). Similarly, the title VIEW can be used to pull down a list giving access to the most-used display commands, such as ZOOM, REDRAW, PAN.

Floating toolbars, palettes and other windows

Toolbars and palettes are available only if you are using the Microsoft Windows or Windows NT versions of AutoCAD. The Windows operating system is discussed in Chapter 2 of Part A. A 'window' in this operating system is a box which may be invoked on the screen at any time during the operation of a program. Among other things, the window may contain text, graphics, pull-down menus or icons (small graphical symbols which may be PICKed with a pointing device, in order to action different commands and options). The window is thus often used as a graphical user interface menu. As such, it is extremely versatile, being movable to anywhere on the screen, and resizable. Other Windows facilities include scroll bars, for repositioning text or graphics inside the window, and the ability to stack a number of different windows in an overlapping cascade fashion so that each title bar remains visible.

Toolbars and palettes are special windows containing icons, each of which represent often-used AutoCAD commands or options. These commands are thus quickly actioned by PICKing the appropriate icons. Being windows, the tool palettes may thus be moved to any new position on the screen by the standard Windows technique of PICKing in the Window Title box, and moving while keeping the PICK button depressed. This procedure is shown in Fig. App3a. You may reshape a tool palette by moving your pointing device to its edge until you see a 'double arrow' symbol appear. If you then move your pointing device while keeping the PICK button depressed, the tool palette will change shape. For example, Fig. App3b shows a square-shaped palette being reshaped to be taller and thinner simultaneously, with the icons being correspondingly rearranged. Later releases of AutoCAD Windows have multiple palettes (including the Standard toolbar and a number of others such as Draw, Modify, Object Properties and Select). When you browse through the icons with your pointing device, explanatory text 'pops up' for each icon, and when you PICK your chosen icon, it may action a *flyout palette* containing further icons which represent options for the chosen command (Fig. App3c).

Figs App3d, App3e and App3f show the standard toolbar, the Draw toolbar and Modify toolbar respectively and define the icons contained within them.

Other windows include the Command/Text Area window (see Part A), the Main Drawing Area window, and the Aerial View window (see Lesson 1), all of which are movable, resizable and have scroll bars for shifting their text or graphics when required. These windows are reshaped in the same manner as toolbars/palettes, but employ separate operations for vertical and horizontal changes (Fig. App4).

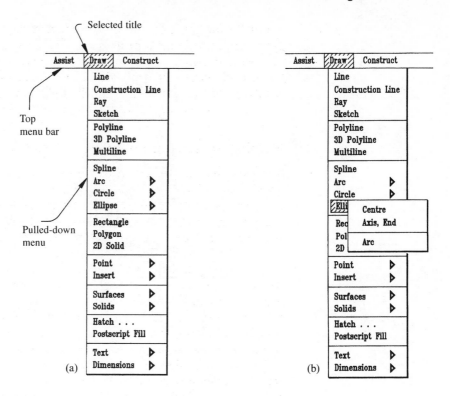

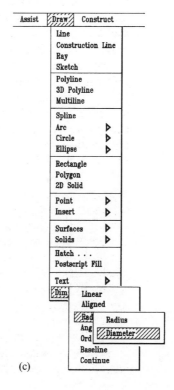

Figure App2.   (a) Pull-down menu (DRAW selected); (b) sub-menu (ELLIPSE selected); (c) cascade of sub-menus (DIM: DIAMETER selected).

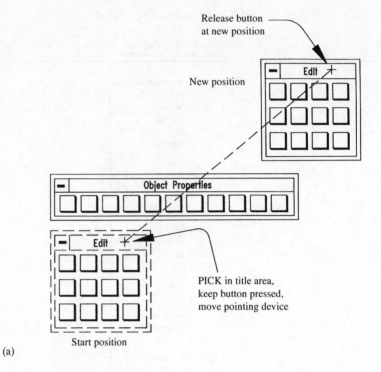

Release button
at new position

New position

PICK in title area,
keep button pressed,
move pointing device

Start position

(a)

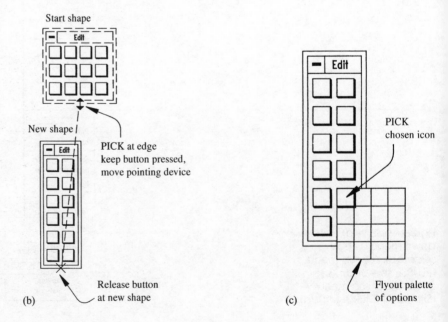

Start shape

New shape

PICK at edge
keep button pressed,
move pointing device

PICK
chosen icon

Figure App3.
(a) Repositioning tool
palettes and other
windows; (b) reshaping
tool palettes; (c) flyout
palettes;

Release button
at new shape

(b)

Flyout palette
of options

(c)

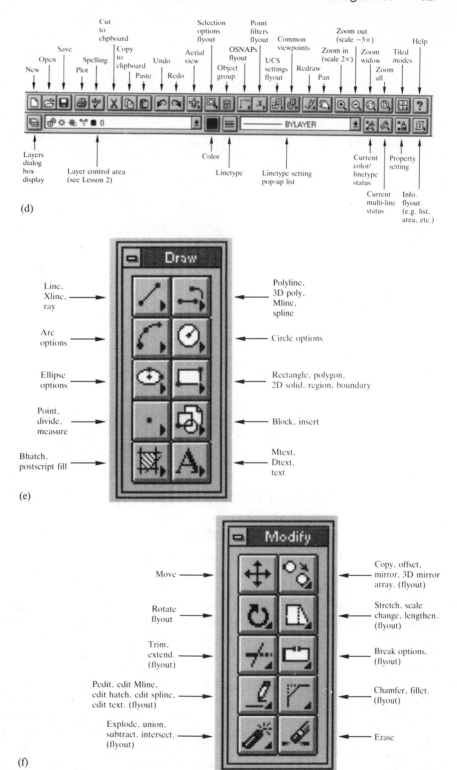

New
Open
Save
Plot
Spelling
Cut to clipboard
Copy to clipboard
Paste
Undo
Redo
Aerial view
Selection options flyout
Object group
OSNAPs flyout
Point filters flyout
UCS settings flyout
Common viewpoints
Redraw
Pan
Zoom in (scale 2×)
Zoom out (scale −5×)
Zoom widow
Zoom all
Tiled modes
Help

Layers dialog box display
Layer control area (see Lesson 2)
Color
Linetype
Linetype setting pop-up list
Current color/ linetype status
Current multi-line status
Property setting
Info. flyout (e.g. list, area, etc.)

BYLAYER

(d)

Draw

Line, Xline, ray
Polyline, 3D poly, Mline, spline

Arc options
Circle options

Ellipse options
Rectangle, polygon, 2D solid, region, boundary

Point, divide, measure
Block, insert

Bhatch, postscript fill
Mtext, Dtext, text

(e)

Modify

Move
Copy, offset, mirror, 3D mirror array. (flyout)

Rotate flyout
Stretch, scale change, lengthen. (flyout)

Trim, extend. (flyout)
Break options. (flyout)

Pedit, edit Mline, edit hatch, edit spline, edit text. (flyout)
Chamfer, fillet. (flyout)

Explode, union, subtract, intersect. (flyout)
Erase

Figure App3.
(d) the Standard toolbar;
(e) the Draw toolbar (all
buttons with flyout
palettes); (f) the Modify
toolbar.

(f)

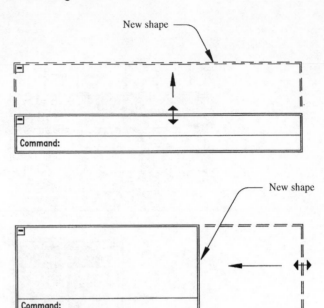

Figure App4.   Reshaping
other windows.

Cursor screen menus

In later releases of AutoCAD, cursor screen menus are available. This facility enables you to display a menu at any chosen position on the graphics screen. In most AutoCAD configurations, the cursor screen menu is invoked by moving your pointing device to the required position on the screen and pressing the third button of your pointing device (or by pressing the second button and SHIFT at the keyboard simultaneously if you have a two-button pointing device). The default cursor menu displays a list of assist facilities, such as OSNAP modes. Fig. App5 shows a typical cursor menu display, invoked in this case while within the LINE command.

Tablet menus

Tablet menus may be used if you are running AutoCAD in conjunction with an electronic digitizing tablet (described in Part A). In this case, your pointing device will be either a puck or an electronic pen, which is connected to, and communicates directly with, the digitizing tablet (or digitizer). In Part A, it was described how the digitizer has a specifically allocated pointing area (or digitizing area) over which the puck or pen may be moved for screen pointing, in a similar manner to the way in which a mouse is moved on any horizontal surface. The remainder of the digitizing tablet is taken up with menu boxes arranged in rows and columns.

Fig. App6 shows AutoCAD's standard tablet menu, which may be attached to a digitizer and operated from the standard AutoCAD menu file once a configuration procedure has been actioned. You will see that some menu squares contain simple diagrams, as well as words, to aid speedy selection. Thus, for example, if you wish to draw a circle, this may be

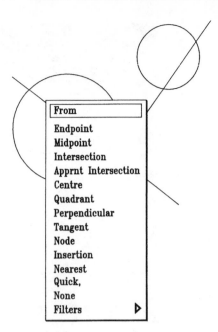

Figure App5. Cursor menu.

achieved by PICKing the CIRCLE menu box (i.e. the box containing the shape of a circle and the word CIRCLE) on the tablet with the puck or pen. This automatically actions the CIRCLE command. Some tablet menus automatically invoke popular combinations of commands-with-options (e.g. ZOOM, option WINDOW). Also, a menu area to the far right of the tablet provides popular numeric inputs, thus bypassing the need to enter these values by keyboard. At the top of the tablet is a menu area left blank for customization purposes. This contains 8 rows and 25 columns, thus providing the facility of 200 extra menu squares containing selections of your own choice. This is particularly useful for compiling standards libraries of component shapes (such as nuts and bolts, standard window frames, electrical symbols, etc.) which could be automatically inserted into a drawing via a single PICK at the appropriate menu square.

To configure your digitizer for use with the AutoCAD standard tablet menu, you should secure this menu (supplied as a plastic template) to your digitizer, and then select the TABLET command, followed by the CONFIGURE (CFG) option. You will thus be taken through a series of screen prompts via which you will be asked to enter the number of menu areas required (four in this case), PICK three corners for each menu area, enter the number of rows and columns in each menu area, and PICK two corners of the allotted screen-pointing area. The appropriate corners are shown on the tablet menu as black dots. The information required for these entries is given in Fig. App7. The tablet menu is then operational, provided the standard menu file ACAD.MNU is currently loaded (which you may check via the MENU command).

Tablet menus generally provide the experienced AutoCAD user with speedier selection procedures than those available with screen menus.

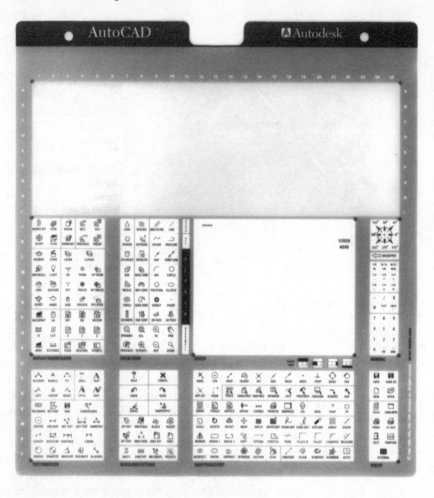

Figure App6.

However, screen menus are easier to learn and avoid the necessity of purchasing a digitizer.

Button menus

All pointing devices (mouse, puck, electronic pen, etc.) have a PICK button. Many pointing devices also have additional selection buttons. (For example, a mouse usually has one or two extra buttons. A puck usually has at least three extra buttons.)

The AutoCAD standard menu file allots common commands for up to nine extra buttons which may exist on a pointing device. This provides fast selection by simply pressing one button per command.

For example, if you have a four-button pointing device, your button menu for the standard menu file is:

1. PICK
2. RETURN

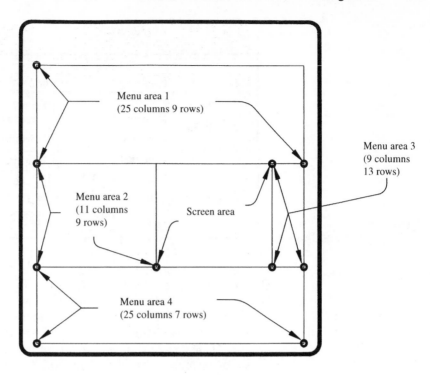

Figure App7.   Tablet
menu areas.

3. Default cursor menu
4. CANCEL (CTRL-C)

Dialog boxes

Some AutoCAD facilities may be invoked by PICKing options from a number of 'pop-up' dialog-box screen displays. Any command that begins with DD will activate a dialog box display, which could thus be accomplished by entering the appropriate command at the keyboard. However, it is more logical to achieve the dialog box display via a menu facility. For example, Fig. App8 shows the Drawing Aids dialog box. This is displayed by selecting the DDRMODES command, which could be actioned via selection from the main right-hand root screen menu, or by toolbar/palette selection in the Windows environment. In addition to the DD commands, some AutoCAD commands, such as OPEN (see Part A) and BHATCH (see Lesson 6), automatically display dialog boxes as part of their own command routine.

Once the dialog box is displayed, the cursor takes the form of an arrow pointer, and you may make selections and enter values by PICKing smaller boxes inside the dialog display. For example, the Drawing Aids dialog box shown in Fig. App8 contains a number of *check boxes* which act as ON/OFF toggles. If a setting is currently ON, a '×' is shown in the check box. If this setting is currently OFF, its checkbox is left blank. Thus you will see that, for example, GRID is shown as currently set to OFF. If you wished

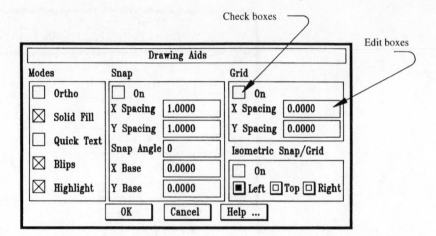

Figure App8. The
Drawing Aids dialog box

GRID to be on, you could achieve this by PICKing the appropriate check box. If, on a later occasion, you wished to switch GRID to OFF again, you would simply PICK this checkbox once more.

Fig. App8 also includes a number of *edit boxes* within the dialog box display. These enable you to make alterations to the values of current settings. For example, you will see that Grid X Spacing is shown with a current setting of 00.00. If, say, you wished to change the value of this setting to 20.00, you could achieve this by taking your arrow pointer to the area of the dialog box beneath the heading Grid, moving into the box rightward of the heading X Spacing, and PICKing. You may then enter the new setting via keyboard input.

Once you are happy with all the settings shown on the dialog box display, you may PICK the OK box at the bottom of the display. This will cause you to exit the dialog box display and return to the drawing screen, with the new settings being confirmed as current. (Alternatively, if you PICK the CANCEL box, the new settings are rejected, and the old ones retained as current.)

Some other dialog boxes contain requestor boxes, which invoke additional sub-dialog boxes. For example, if you wished to make LAYER settings (see Lesson 2) via dialog box, you may do so by selecting the DDLMODES command, or selecting LAYER from either the Data menu or the Object Properties toolbar. If, say, you wished to set the colour of a chosen layer, you would do so by PICKing the Set Color box. This displays the Select Color sub-dialog box, from which you may PICK your required colour from a palette grid.

The *list box* is another common dialog box facility. A list box displays a list of items, from which you may PICK your selection with the arrow pointer. A typical example is the list of files and directories which appear in the Open Drawing dialog box (accessed via the OPEN command). The displayed list may be scrolled up or down by repeatedly PICKing the appropriate scroll bar arrow box, to the right of the list box.

In the Windows and Windows NT versions of AutoCAD, some dialog boxes are also standard forms of windows and may thus be moved to different positions on the screen, as previously explained (page 326).

Appendix C

Standard text fonts and character mappings

txt   The standard AutoCAD text font. This is a very simple font described by a minimum of vectors so it can be drawn very quickly.

monotxt   Monospaced txt font. The characters in this font are the same as those in the standard txt font, except that the space allotted to each character is the same (monospaced). Thus, this font is preferable for construction of lists or tables where the items must line up vertically.

romans   A simplex (single-stroke, sans serif) roman font drawn by means of many short line segments. This font produces smoother-looking characters than those of the txt font.

romand   Similar to the romans font, but defined using double strokes. This font produces thicker, darker characters and is highly recommended for plotting on high-resolution printers such as laser printers.

romanc   A complex (double stroke, with serifs) roman font.

romant   A triplex (triple stroke, with serifs) roman font similar to romanc.

italicc   A complex italic font (double stroke, with serifs).

italict   A triplex italic font (triple stroke, with serifs).

scripts   A simplex script font (single stroke).

scriptc   A complex script font (double stroke).

greeks   A simplex Greek font (single stroke, sans serif).

greekc   A complex Greek font (double stroke, with serifs).

gothice   Gothic English.

gothicg   Gothic German.

gothici   Gothic Italian.

cyrillic   Cyrillic—alphabetical.

cyriltlc   Cyrillic—transliteration.

syastro   Astronomical symbols.

symap   Mapping symbols.

symath   Mathematical symbols.

symeteo   Meteorological symbols.

symusic   Music symbols.

Fast fonts

txt   The quick brown fox jumped over the lazy dog.   ABC123

monotxt   The quick brown fox jumped over the lazy dog.   ABC123

Simplex fonts

romans   The quick brown fox jumped over the lazy dog.   ABC123

scripts   *The quick brown fox jumped over the lazy dog.*   *ABC123*

greeks   Τηε ϑυιχκ βροων φοξ ϑυμπεδ οεερ τηε λαζψ δογ.   ABX123

Duplex font

romand   The quick brown fox jumped over the lazy dog.   ABC123

Triplex fonts

romant   The quick brown fox jumped over the lazy dog.   ABC123

italict   *The quick brown fox jumped over the lazy dog.*   *ABC123*

Complex fonts

romanc   The quick brown fox jumped over the lazy dog.   ABC123

italicc   *The quick brown fox jumped over the lazy dog.*   *ABC123*

scriptc   *The quick brown fox jumped over the lazy dog.*   *ABC123*

greekc   Τηε ϑυιχκ βροων φοξ ϑυμπεδ οεερ τηε λαζψ δογ.   ABX123

cyrillic   Узд рфивк бсоцн еоч йфмпдг охдс узд лащш гож.   АБВ123

cyriltlc   Тхе цуичк брошн фож щумпед овер тхе лазй дог.   АБЧ123

Gothic fonts

gothice   The quick brown fox jumped over the lazy dog.   ABC123

gothicg   The quick brown fox jumped over the lazy dog.   ABC123

gothici   The quick brown fox jumped over the lazy dog.   ABC123

Symbol fonts

syastro	ΩЄU ˋ†→ˋ← ˙ˇ∧ℨ∇ ⊃∼ℒ ††∂ˊUℂ ∼‡Uˇ §ЄU ↓✳☉® ℂ∼∩. ☉♌♎123
symap	◖◌◗
symath	ℂ∞√
symeteo	-123
symusic	

Each of the supplied font includes the standard punctuation characters and numbers, but several provide special alphabets or symbols that you must access by typing particular keys on the keyboard. The following chart shows the character mapping for the non-roman and symbol fonts.

	A	B	C	D	E	F	G	H	I	J	K	L	M	N	O	P	Q	R	S	T	U	V	W	X	Y	Z	[	\	]	^	_	`
cyrillic	А	Б	В	Г	Д	Е	Ж	З	И	Й	К	Л	М	Н	О	П	Р	С	Т	У	Ф	Х	Ц	Ч	Ш	Щ	Ъ	Ы	Ь	Э	Ю	Я
cyriltlc	А	Б	Ч	Д	Е	Ф	Г	Х	И	Щ	К	Л	М	Н	О	П	Ц	Р	С	Т	У	В	Ш	Ж	Й	З	Ь	Ы	Ъ	Ю	Э	Я
greekc	А	В	Χ	Δ	Е	Φ	Γ	Н	Ι	ϑ	К	Λ	М	Н	О	П	Θ	Р	Σ	Τ	Υ	ς	Ω	Ξ	Ψ	Ζ	[	\	]	^	_	`
greeks	А	В	Χ	Δ	Е	Φ	Γ	Н	Ι	ϑ	К	Λ	М	Н	О	П	Θ	Р	Σ	Τ	Υ	ς	Ω	Ξ	Ψ	Ζ	[	\	]	^	_	`
syastro	☉	♀	♈	⊕	♂	♃	♄	♅	♆	♇	☽	☌	✳	☊	☋	♈	♉	♊	♋	☌	♍	♎	♏	☾	♐	=	[	\	]	^	_	`
symap	○	□	△	◇	☆	+	×	∗	●	▪	▲	◀	▼	▶	★	⊢	⊥	✝	✳	♣	♠	♦	○	○	△	[	\	]	^	_	`
symath	ℵ	′	│	‖	±	∓	×	·	÷	=	≠	≡	<	>	≤	≥	≫	∝	∼	√	∪	⊃	∩	∈	→	↑	[	\	]	^	_	`
symeteo	·	·	·	▲	∧	∩	∪	⌣	⌢	⌐	∫	S	∿	∞	R	§	─	╱	│	╲	─	╱	[	\	]	^	_	`
symusic	·	ˎ	♪	○	○	●	#	♮	♭	−	−	×	♩	𝄞	℗	𝄢	·	›	⋯	⌐	^	÷	▽		[	\	]	^	_	`

	a	b	c	d	e	f	g	h	i	j	k	l	m	n	o	p	q	r	s	t	u	v	w	x	y	z	{	|	}	~	<	>
cyrillic	а	б	в	г	д	е	ж	з	и	й	к	л	м	н	о	п	р	с	т	у	ф	х	ц	ч	ш	щ	ъ	ы	ь	э	ю	я
cyriltlc	а	б	ч	д	е	ф	г	х	и	щ	к	л	м	н	о	п	ц	р	с	т	у	в	ш	ж	й	з	ь	ы	ъ	ю	э	я
greekc	α	β	χ	δ	ε	φ	γ	η	ι	∂	κ	λ	μ	ν	ο	π	ϑ	ρ	σ	τ	υ	∈	ω	ξ	ψ	ζ	{	|	}	~	<	>
greeks	α	β	χ	δ	ε	φ	γ	η	ι	∂	κ	λ	μ	ν	ο	π	ϑ	ρ	σ	τ	υ	∈	ω	ξ	ψ	ζ	{	|	}	~	<	>
syastro	✳	′	′	∪	∪	⊃	∈	→	←	↓	∇	ˇ	ˋ	ˋ	ℵ	§	†	‡	ℨ	ℒ	®	☉	{	|	}	~	<	>
symap	♥	♣	♢	♡	˙	·	·	○	○	○	○	◖	◗	‖	⊥	∴	·	♢	♡	◇	♣	♠	♣	{	|	}	~	<	>
symath	←	↓	∂	∇	√	∫	⨍	∞	§	†	‡	∃	∏	Σ	(	)	[	]	{	}	⟨	⟩	√	∫	≈	≅	{	|	}	~	<	>
symeteo	│	╲	╲	─	╱	╲	⌐	⌐	⌣	⌢	(	)	╱	╲	⊣	Ω	α	δ	ϒ	ρ	ρ	φ	·	{	|	}	~	<	>
symusic	·	ˎ	♪	○	○	●	#	♮	♭	−	−	×	♩	𝄞	𝄢	𝄢	☉	♀	♈	⊕	♂	♃	♄	♅	♆	♇	♈	♉	♊	{	|	}	~	<	>

PostScript fonts

cibt City Blueprint. Draftman's fonts, condensed.

cobt Country Blueprint. Draftman's fonts, oblique.

eur EuroRoman. ISO 8859-1 roman characters font (8-bit).

euro EuroRoman-oblique. ISO 8859-1 roman characters font (8-bit).

pan PanRoman. Thin Times Roman style. Includes all the characters for 130 languages, including the standard roman character set. Designed for fast typing of French, German, and Spanish accents (8-bit).

suf	SuperFrench. Thin Times Roman style. Includes all the characters for 130 languages, including the standard roman character set. Designed for transliteration of languages that do not use the standard roman character set into the standard roman character set (8-bit).
rom	Romantic. Times® style, English, plain.
romb	Romantic-bold. Times style, English.
sas	Sans Serif. Helvetica® style, English, plain.
sasb	Sans Serif-bold. Helvetica style, English.
saso	Sans Serif-oblique. Helvetica style, English.
sasbo	Sans Serif-BoldOblique. Helvetica style, English.
te	Technic. Leroy style, plain.
tel	Technic-light. Leroy style.
teb	Technic-bold. Leroy style.

Some fonts, such as sasbo, appear as outlines on screen, but are filled in for printed output.

Examples of the 7-bit fonts are as follows:

cibt	The quick brown fox jumped over the lazy dog.	ABC123
cobt	The quick brown fox jumped over the lazy dog.	ABC123
rom	**The quick brown fox jumped over the lazy dog.**	**ABC123**
romb	**The quick brown fox jumped over the lazy dog.**	**ABC123**
sas	**The quick brown fox jumped over the lazy dog.**	**ABC123**
sasb	The quick brown fox jumped over the lazy dog.	ABC123
saso	*The quick brown fox jumped over the lazy dog.*	*ABC123*
sasbo	*The quick brown fox jumped over the lazy dog.*	*ABC123*
te	THE QUICK BROWN FOX JUMPED OVER THE LAZY DOG.	ABC123
tel	THE QUICK BROWN FOX JUMPED OVER THE LAZY DOG.	ABC123
teb	**THE QUICK BROWN FOX JUMPED OVER THE LAZY DOG.**	**ABC123**

Index

3D display, 60–62
3DFACE command, 224, 238–242
3D point filters, 225, 226–229
3DMESH command, 294–295
3D mesh editing, 295
3DPOLY command, 284
3D solid modelling:
  BOX command, 301
  Boolean operations, 300
  CYLINDER command, 301
  definition and principles, 299
  EXTRUDE command, 301
  INTERSECT command, 304
  mass properties, 306
  primitives, 300
  SUBTRACT command, 302
  UNION command, 301
3D surface modelling, 270, 298

ADI driver, 107
Aerial view (Windows), 104–105
AREA command, 172
ARRAY command (polar option), 76–77,
  134
ARRAY command (rectangular option),
  134
ARC command, 68–70
ATTDEF command, 211
Attributes:
  block insertion, 213
  editing (ATTEDIT command), 214
  defining (ATTDEF command), 211
  defining by dialog box, 212
  definition, 209
  invisible mode, 212
AutoCAD:
  drawing (DWG) file, 7
  drawing screen (traditional), 16
  drawing screen (Windows), 17
  commands, 10
  command options, 10, 16
  definition, 3
  file extensions, 321
  program, 6, 15, 321
Autodesk Ltd, 3

AutoLISP, 5

Batch file, 15
Backup (BAK) file, 7
BASE command, 171
Blip marks, 24, 30
BLIPMODE system variable, 24
BLOCK command, 119–122, 171, 209
Boolean operations (3D solid), 300
Booting-up, 83
BREAK command, 131

CAL (calculator) command, 173–174
CD-ROM, 6, 12
C programming language, 3
CHAMFER command, 129–130, 133
CHANGE command, 132, 222
Character mapping (text fonts), 160,
  335–336
CHPROP command, 132
CIRCLE command, 26, 87–94
Clipboard (Windows), 5, 138–139
Clipping planes, 262–263
COLOR command, 113
Command selection, 19
Command/prompt area, 16, 18
Compatibility, 5
Configuring AutoCAD (CONFIG
  command), 107
Coordinate systems:
  absolute Cartesian, 33, 34
  relative Cartesian, 34, 35, 36
  relative polar, 36, 37
Coordinate display options, 52–55
COPY command, 19, 124
CTRL key operations, 25, 86–87
Cursor (cross-hairs), 25
Cut and paste (Windows), 5, 139

DDINSERT command, 210
DDIM command, 145
DDSELECT command, 137
Device driver, 107
Dialog box, 21, 22, 331–333
Digitizing tablet (digitizer), 10, 13

DIM command, 145
Dimensioning, 144–154
Dimensions:
  angle, 149
  arrow blocks, 150
  associative, 149
  diameter, 147
  editing, 150
  leader, 147
  linear, 146–147
  radius, 147
  toleranced, 148–149
Dimension dialog box, 151–152
Dimension settings, 145–146
Dimension styles, 151–153
Directories, 7
DIST command, 172
DIVIDE command, 168, 170
DOUGHNUT command, 185
Dragging command, 26
Draw toolbar (Windows), 19, 324, 327
Drawing files, 7
DTEXT command, 155
DVIEW command (non-perspective
     techniques), 251–256
DVIEW command (perspective
     techniques), 259–269
DXF files, 5
Dynamic Data Exchange (DDE), 5

EDGESURF command, 274–275
ELLIPSE command, 164–166, 193
Elliptical arcs, 166–167
END command, 80
Entities, 28
ERASE command, 28
EXPLODE command, 117, 120, 138, 167,
     174, 210, 214, 297
EXTEND command, 129

Fit curve, 202–205
FILL command, 188
FILLET command, 56–60, 130, 133
Flood hatch, 178
Floppy disk, 6, 12
Flyout palettes, 18, 324, 326

Graphical user interface (GUI), 8
GRID command, 20, 50
Grid (rotated), 118
GRIPS editing, 136
GROUP command, 138

Hard copy, 12
Hard disk, 6, 12
Hardware, 6, 11
Hatching:
  associative, 181
  boundary (BHATCH command),
       178–181
  editing (HATCHEDIT command), 182
  HATCH command, 174

  internal point, 182
  patterns, 176–178
  styles, 176–178
  User Defined, 174
HELP command, 172
HIDE command, 77, 220
Highlighted objects, 28

Icon (coordinate system), 17, 231–232
Icons (Windows), 8, 9, 324
ID command, 172
Inquiry commands, 172
INSERT command, 120, 121, 122, 209
Invisible edges (3DFACE), 238, 239–242
Isometric drawing, 192–195
ISOPLANE command, 194

JOIN option (in PEDIT), 197

Keyboard, 11

LAYER command, 108–111, 270
Layer control by dialog box, 111–112
Layer control by toolbar, 112
Layer filters, 113
LIMITS command, 46
LINE command, 25, 83–86, 225
LINETYPE command, 113
LIST command, 172
LTSCALE command, 113

Mathematical co-processor, 11
Main group Window, 15
MEASURE command, 171
Menus:
  button, 330
  command guide, 19
  cursor, 328
  pull-down, 15, 18, 323–325
  root, 17, 322, 323
  screen, 10
  tablet, 10, 328–330
Mesh surfaces, 270
Microsoft Excel, 5
Microsoft Windows, 5, 8, 324
Microsoft Windows NT, 8, 324
Microsoft Word, 5, 139
MINSERT command, 211
MIRROR command, 131
MIRRTEXT system variable, 159
MSDOS operating system, 6, 8, 15
Modify toolbar (Windows), 19, 324, 327
Mouse, 8, 12
MOVE command, 124
MTEXT command, 162
MVIEW command, 249

NEW command, 21
NOUN/VERB selection, 137
Numeric input (keyboard), 32
NURBS curve, 206

Object snapping (OSNAP), 39–46, 114–117
OFFSET command, 128
OOPS command, 28, 30
OPEN command, 22
Operating system, 8, 15
ORTHO mode, 87, 168, 170, 194
OSNAP options:
  APINT, 116
  END, 40, 115
  CEN, 43, 116
  INT, 40, 115
  MID, 116, 122
  NODE, 116
  NONE, 115
  TAN, 44, 91–93, 115, 116
OSNAP target sight, 40

PAN command, 99
Paper space mode, 249
Parallel communication, 11
PDMODE system variable, 114, 170
PDSIZE system variable, 114
PEDIT (polyline edit command), 196–208,
  284, 295–296
Perspective display techniques, 257–269
PICKSTYLE system variable, 138
Pickbox, 28, 114
PLAN command, 221
PLOT command, 140–142
Plot file, 142
Plotter, 11, 12, 140
POINT command, 113–114
Point filters, 20, 168–170, 225, 226–229
POLYGON command, 167–168
POLYLINE (PLINE) command, 117,
  185–187
Polyline vertex editing, 197–202
Primitives (3D solid), 299
Printer, 11, 140
Program Manager (Windows), 15
Prototype drawing, 107–108
Puck, 10
PURGE command, 174

QSAVE command, 80
QTEXT command, 159

Random Access Memory (RAM), 11
Raster device, 13
RAY command, 104–106
REDO command, 100
REDRAW command, 28, 30
REGEN command, 101, 114, 159, 188,
  204
Regeneration (drawing), 101
RENAME command, 174
REVSURF command, 275–277
RENDER, 281
ROTATE command, 126
Rough drawing techniques, 25
Rubber banding, 25
RULESURF command, 272

SAVE command, 62
SAVEAS command, 80
SCALE command, 126
Scroll bar, 18
Selection options:
  Crossing (C), 23, 127
  Cpolygon (CP), 124
  Fence (F), 124
  Object pointing, 28, 13
  Last (L), 123
  Previous (P), 123, 125
  Remove (R), 124
  Window (W), 31, 48, 123, 126
  Wpolygon (WP), 124
Selection sets filtering, 124
Series communication, 11
Settings, 24, 50, 52, 83
SETVAR command, 114
SKETCH command, 188
SKPOLY system variable, 188
SNAP command, 20, 50
Snap (Rotate option), 118
SOLID command (2D), 184
SPLFRAME system variable, 204, 205,
  242–243, 278, 285–286
Spline curve, 202, 204, 205
SPLINESEGS system variable, 205
SPLINETYPE system variable, 205,
  285–286
Standards libraries, 121
Standard toolbar (Windows), 20, 324, 327
Starting up, 83
STATUS command, 172
STATUS (dimensions), 145
Status line, 17
STRETCH command, 127
STYLE command, 157–159, 160–162
SURFTAB1 system variable, 280
SURFTAB2 system variable, 280
SURFTYPE system variable, 295
SURFU system variable, 295
SURFV system variable, 295
System variables, 114

TABLET command, 329
TABSURF command, 273
TEXT command, 66, 150, 155
Text:
  display and justification options, 156
  editing, 159
  Edit Mtext dialog box, 162–163
  font type, 157, 335–337
  height, 157
  obliquing angle, 157
  postscript fonts, 336–337
  special characters, 156
  styles, 157–159, 160–162
  symbol fonts (character mapping), 160,
    335–336
  width factor, 157
THICKNESS system variable, 51, 219
TILEMODE system variable, 249

Toolbars and palettes, 10, 18, 324, 326–328
TRACE command, 185
Transparent routines, 173
TRIM command, 127–128, 135

U command, 100
UNDO command, 94–95, 100
UNITS command, 144
UCSICON system variable, 52, 235
UCS (User Coordinate System) command, 63–65, 68, 71–76, 118, 219, 222, 231–234
UCSFOLLOW system variable, 233
UNIX operating system, 12

VIEW command, 101, 102
VIEWPORTS (VPORTS) command, 77–79, 247–248
Visual Display Unit (VDU), 11
VPOINT command, 60, 64, 219–222

WBLOCK command, 215
WIDTH option (in PEDIT), 197
Windows, 324, 328
Word for Windows, 5, 139
World Coordinate System (WCS), 60, 119, 231
WORLDVIEW system variable, 52, 235

XLINE command, 104–106
XYZ coordinates, 224
XYZ lines, 224, 225–227

ZOOM command, 20, 47
Zoom options:
    All (A), 47
    Dynamic, 102–103
    Extents, 102
    Previous (P), 48, 67
    Scale (X), 101
    Window (W), 48